Between Fear and Hope

Between Fear and Hope

*Globalization and Race in
the United States*

Andrew L. Barlow

ROWMAN & LITTLEFIELD PUBLISHERS, INC.
Lanham • Boulder • New York • Oxford

To the people who stand up for justice, who, by so doing, give us all hope.

ROWMAN & LITTLEFIELD PUBLISHERS, INC.

Published in the United States of America
by Rowman & Littlefield Publishers, Inc.
A Member of the Rowman & Littlefield Publishing Group
4501 Forbes Boulevard, Suite 200, Lanham, Maryland 20706
www.rowmanlittlefield.com

PO Box 317, Oxford OX2 9RU, United Kingdom

British Library Cataloguing in Publication Information Available

Library of Congress Cataloging-in-Publication Data

Barlow, Andrew L., 1948–
   Between fear and hope : globalization and race in the United States /
Andrew L. Barlow
       p. cm.
Includes bibliographical references and index.
   ISBN 0-7425-1618-0 (cloth : alk. paper) — ISBN 0-7425-1619-9 (pbk. :
alk. paper)
   1. United States—Race relations—Political aspects. 2. United States—Race
relations—Economic apsects. 3. Racism—Political aspects—United
States. 4. Racism—Economic aspects—United States. 5. Globalization—Political
aspects—United States. 6. Globalization—Social aspects—United States.
7. Globalization—Economic aspects—United States. 8. United States—Social
conditions—1945–   I. Title
   E184.A1.B247 2003
   305.8'00973—dc21
                                                                    2002154989

Printed in the United States of America

♾ ™ The paper used in this publication meets the minimum requirements of
American National Standard for Information Sciences—Permanence of Paper for
Printed Library Materials, ANSI/NISO Z39.48-1992.

Contents

~

Acknowledgments

The ideas contained in this volume are ultimately mine, but they are also ideas shared among many different groupings of people, some of whom I have had the distinct privilege and pleasure of knowing, many of whom I only know through the indirect medium of the written word and visual images. Here, I want to acknowledge the people who directly supported me, goaded me on, and inspired me in the long labor that this book entailed.

First and foremost, my deepest thanks to my wife, Marty Jessup, and my son, Jesse Barlow, for consistently reminding me about the important things in life: love, respect, and mutuality. Your love is the root of the hope I continue to find in this troubled world. To my parents, Lou and Gertrude Barlow, who lived through most of the last century and are still producing music and art in this century. Being rooted in our family's history of activism has allowed me to stay the course and to believe firmly that people can make their history, not just live it out.

Thanks also to my comrades Leni Marin, Elaine Elinson, Rene Ceria Cruz, Mila de Guzman, Robert Allen, Anamaria Loya, Eva Patterson, and Oren Sellstrom for your steadfast activism, your broad vision of the past, the present, and the future, and your obstinate optimism about humanity. Your leadership has enabled me to reach higher.

Special thanks to Fenno Ogutu, my friend and colleague at Diablo Valley College (DVC). Your African view of globalization has kept me focused on the important issues. Thanks also to my DVC colleagues Nancy Malone, Obed Vazquez, Lisa Smiley-Ratchford, Diane Scott-Summers, President

Mark Edelstein, Paul Guess, the late Virgil Woolbright, and Marge Lasky for your friendship and support.

The Berkeley Sociology Department has a long tradition of support for public intellectual activism. Members of the department have welcomed me, a visiting professor, into their midst for sixteen years. My gratitude to Troy Duster, Peter Evans, Michael Burawoy, Ann Swidler, and Margaret Weir for your collegiality. Thanks also to Percy Hintzen, Carlos Muñoz Jr., the late Barbara Christian, Stephen Small, Leon Wofsy, Tamara Kay, Russell Jeung, Ron Choy, and the Center for the Study of American Cultures for your support over the years.

My deep thanks to my students at DVC and Berkeley, who have given me invaluable feedback about the ideas in this book. Your search for a just world inspires me even in the darkest times. I am indebted to the following students for their able work as research assistants: Byron Zamboanga, June Kim, Jennifer Beahrs, and David Harris. Thanks also to Bridget Julien for her thoughtful comments on my manuscript. I am indebted to Dean Birkenkamp, my editor, for believing in this book.

Introduction

Globalization is a new stage in history of which we are just becoming aware. Driven by a scientific and technical revolution that began in the 1970s, globalization is rapidly transforming important features of human social existence. One of the immediate manifestations of globalization is that it brings the world closer together. Today, we find ourselves in communication with and living and working with people from all over the globe. We are becoming increasingly aware of ourselves in relationship to people everywhere. On a grander scale, a scientific revolution is bringing us new understandings of ourselves in relationship to nature. Humanity's basic scientific knowledge, ranging from the laws of the universe to genetics, has taken a gigantic leap forward in the last twenty years. In ways that were unfathomable a generation ago, we are becoming more aware of the universe and the world around us.

Because globalization supports these new forms of self (and other) awareness, it has opened up a new era in which cooperation and community can now be achieved on a global scale. The growing interconnectedness of humanity can be seen in the UN Conference on the Status of Women, the UN Conference on Racism, the Kyoto Accords on global warming, the founding of the first International Criminal Court, various regional peace processes, and many other efforts to solve global problems cooperatively. Globalization has produced growing numbers of cosmopolitan people who are truly multicultural, who live every day crossing boundaries. The ease with which we can now communicate with people everywhere and our growing ability to travel anywhere on the globe is uplifting. In these ways, and others explored in this

1

book, globalization offers humanity a hopeful future of connectedness, in which the eradication of ignorance and fear, so closely bound up with racism, can be envisioned.

But along with hope, globalization is also creating fear. The social form that is ushering in the global era is capitalism. For reasons to be discussed in this book, the development of global markets has created enormous social crises. These crises are manifest in growing inequality (globally and locally) and the decreasing capacity of nation-states to maintain social order. A growing number of people are being excluded outright from the global economy, and the middle classes of even the most developed nations, including the United States, are experiencing growing insecurity and pressures toward downward mobility. The advent of new technologies has also brought with them a host of problems. We now face unprecedented ecological crises, the growing threat of weapons of mass destruction, and the spread of contagious diseases.

The paradox of globalization is that we now have the opportunity to see ourselves in a global context, but many of us do not like what we see. Rather than sharing in a global celebration of progress, the people of the world are becoming, in the words of UN Secretary-General Kofi Annan, aware of our shared insecurity. Rather than seeing global interdependence as uplifting humanity, too many people see globalization as dragging everyone down. In short, market globalization is creating interdependence, but one in which, too often, what we share is the pain and dislocation of inequality and social crisis. A challenging question to humanity today is this: What will we do with our insecurities and fears? Unfortunately, the wealthiest people of the world are showing a disturbing willingness to deny their connection with the rest of the world by defending their privileged positions, including their racial and national privileges. In the United States, most whites are turning their backs on the last thirty years' efforts to eliminate discrimination and to create a nonracial society. At a time when globalization is making people more geographically mobile than ever before, anti-immigrant movements are gaining headway.

The U.S. response to the September 11, 2001, terrorist attacks has been one of fear. The attackers were simply "evil," the United States, the place of the "good" people. No critical examination of world inequality and social crisis came from the Bush administration or from most of the media. Instead, President George W. Bush promised to create an impregnable Fortress America, in which Americans could reaffirm their belief that "it can't happen here, the greatest society in world history." The effort to wall off America from the rest of the world need not have happened. In that awful moment of truth, another possibility presented itself: Understanding terrorism as a global problem rooted in a deep social crisis affecting billions of fellow humans could have led to a new appreciation of global interdependence. Out of this crisis could come a new sense of connectedness to the rest of the world, and even a new understanding about the effects of globalization within the United States. As Deepak Chopra wrote just days after the attacks, "None of us will feel safe behind the shield of military might and stockpiled arsenals. There can be no safety until the root cause is faced. It is imperative that we pray and offer solace and help to each other. In this moment of deep sorrow for the wounding of our collective soul, the only healing we can accomplish as individuals is to make sure that our every thought, word and deed nurtures humanity."[1]

This ability to face fear with love, to embrace humanity everywhere in the world at the moment when it seems most frightening, requires a vision of the present era that gives us the hope that turning outward to the world might offer us a greater security, prosperity, and humanity than turning inward behind walls of national and racial privilege. This book seeks to contribute to our ability to face up to a sometimes terrifying world by objectifying both the sources of crisis and the sources of possibilities that are present in the global era.

The response to globalization in the United States, we shall see, is being thoroughly racialized. Those marginalized from the global economy in the United States are disproportionately people of color, and whites experiencing the disruptive effects of globalization often use racism as a way to buffer themselves from downward mobility. The analysis of globalization's impact on the United States, then, must explain the dynamics of race in American society. This is a difficult challenge, as societal racism today is quite different from that of even a generation ago. The system of racism that I will call structured racism arose in the 1950s as a part of the new, middle-class social order. This system has as one of its main features the ability to privilege whites without overt legal or cultural claims of racial superiority. Before I can begin my analysis of globalization and its impact on race, it is necessary to step back to both a theoretical and historical examination of the development of this new system of racism. This will be the subject matter of chapters 1 and 2.

As we shall see in chapter 3, globalization is undermining the stability of the mass middle-class society, creating ever-greater inequality, and pressuring political elites to reduce the scope of government regulation of business and entitlement programs for the middle class and the poor. This destabilization is the context for the intensification of racism in the United States, driven by middle-class fear and political elites' limited capacity to address the crisis in any other way. The various projects to mobilize racial privileges will be described in chapters 4 and 5.

Globalization, however, is not only creating more fertile grounds for racism; it is also creating some potential new possibilities for opposing racism and for advancing demands for a new type of globalization based on the recognition of social responsibility. As we shall see in chapter 6, globalization is creating new possibilities for a prodemocracy movement and for the development of transnational movements for human rights and labor solidarity. In particular, globalization is creating conditions that may lead to a revitalization of the civil rights movement, to be discussed in chapter 7. Each of these possibilities, it shall be argued, depends on recognizing the growing importance of ethnic communities to social movements responding to the crisis of globalization.

This book is premised on the belief that globalization has the potential to improve the lives of people everywhere. But this potential will not become reality unless people make it so. Globalization compels us to heed the words of Martin Luther King Jr., "We are caught in an inescapable network of mutuality, tied in a single garment of destiny. Whatever affects one directly, affects all indirectly."[2] In the face of social disruptions and crises produced by globalization, we must find the faith in humanity that will enable us to cooperate with people around the world to regulate and direct globalization in socially responsible directions. Even though at present globalization is creating social crisis, it is important to also recognize that it is creating the conditions for people to demand the development of a socially responsible form of globalization. In this book, I look to the people currently left out of the "new world order," the people labeled "ethnic," as the ones most likely to lead the effort to develop socially responsible globalization. Again, King said it so well, "Oppressed people cannot remain oppressed forever. The yearning for freedom eventually manifests itself."[3]

This book is a search for hope in new and largely unchartered territory. The challenge of the subject matter of this book is that it requires us to be willing to face profound global problems in the spirit of seeking solutions to them, with a belief in humanity's potential for inclusiveness and progress. My sincere wish is that I succeed in conveying to the reader a sense of hope in this time of fear.

Notes

1. Deepak Chopra, "The Deeper Wound," *New York Times*, 19 September 2001 (advertisement).

2. Martin Luther King Jr., "Letter from Birmingham Jail," in *Why We Can't Wait* (New York: Mentor, 1964), 77.

3. King, "Letter from Birmingham Jail," 87.

PART ONE

THE BACKDROP

Rediscovering Race in the Global Era

This chapter provides a theoretical framework for understanding race and ethnicity, and delineates the methodology that will be used in this book to study globalization's impact on race relations in the United States. The perspective to be taken in this book is that globalization is creating a new type of social crisis in the United States by increasing inequality and restricting the capacity of the nation-state to regulate markets. As the social order is destabilized, claims of racial privilege are becoming increasingly attractive to many whites seeking to buffer themselves from the crisis. On the other hand, globalization is also creating conditions supportive of efforts to undermine racism. This book, then, examines the ways that globalization creates conditions that intensify both racism and antiracist opportunities.

As we begin our inquiry into the impact of globalization on race relations in the United States, however, we must immediately face up to an important problem: The contested meanings of race, one of the main concepts to be used in this book. The lack of conceptual clarity about race is a major problem for intellectuals, antiracist activists, and the general public. This problem was painfully evident in the Proposition 209 campaign in California in the mid-1990s. Proposition 209 was a 1996 ballot initiative that amended the California constitution to ban governmental affirmative action programs. In the course of that campaign (1994–1996), opponents of the ballot initiative were forced to explain to voters that Proposition 209, entitled the California Civil Rights Initiative, was actually a deceptive effort to destroy civil rights. Proposition 209's opponents had to defend affirmative action—a set of irreplaceable tools to undo discrimination—against charges that it is governmental racial discrimination. Reality was turned on its head: racism was depicted as civil rights, while remedies to racism were depicted as racist. People entirely hostile to efforts to eradicate racism posed as civil rights activists. People who had devoted their entire working lives to the cause of racial justice collectively felt like Alice in a hellish Wonderland in California at the end of the twentieth century. Ultimately, Proposition 209 passed because its advocates were successful in promoting the myth that societal racism no longer exists in California.

As we shall see in chapter 2, the conviction held by many whites (and a small number of people of color) that societal racism is dead was made possible by the development of a qualitatively new system of racism in the 1950s, one that enables white people to maintain racial privileges without explicitly claiming racial superiority. The project of maintaining what Eduardo Bonilla-Silva terms "color-blind racism" involves conceptualizing American society and race relations in a way that liquidates societal racism and places the blame for continuing racial inequality on people of color, and labels government efforts to directly address racial issues as racist.[1] If we are to argue that societal racism still exists—indeed, is being exacerbated in the context of globalization—then we will have to reclaim the concepts of race, racism, and ethnicity from those who would deny the reality of race.

As we set about the task of rediscovering race and racism today, there are three major challenges that need to be met. The first challenge is to develop a theory of race that acknowledges that race is not an inherent, immutable feature of humanity, but a type of social relationship. While acknowledging that race is a social construct, such a theory must also account for the endurance of racism for hundreds of years and the reasons for its persistence and power in American society today, as well as its mutability in new conditions.[2]

The second challenge is to conceptualize a racial system to be termed "structured racism" as the basis for "color-blind" racist ideology. As we shall see in this chapter and in chapter 2, intellectuals' failure to explore until very recently structured racism as a specific form of racism has had serious consequences, especially the inability to refute the widespread acceptance of the "end of racism" thesis.[3]

The third challenge is to conceptualize the ways in which the motivation and capacity of people to struggle for and against racial privileges are altered by the new dynamics of globalization. Saskia Sassen aptly refers to globalized relationships as a "grid" superimposed on top of preexisting social relationships.[4] New global realities, ranging from a web of transnational corporations, to the cosmopolitan lifestyles of global elites, to the ebb and flow of poor immigrant workers across national borders, are coming into being. But these global relationships are primarily taking form in national societies with their own distinct histories. In the United States, the 400-year legacy of highly organized, state-sponsored systems of racism have great significance for the ways in which the "grid" of globalized relationships come into being. The ability to situate the assault on people of color in a global context is especially vital for people trying to grapple with the social crisis associated with globalization.

Making explicit a theory of race and society, and the relationship between race and globalization, will enable us to take up the study of the impact of globalization on race relations in the United States in parts II and III of this book. As well, by clarifying the concept of race, we will be able to reclaim the realities of race from those who would lead us to believe that societal racism no longer exists.

Modernity and the "End of Racism" Thesis

The main proposition setting the terms of the American debate about race today is the claim that societal racism is dead. This proposition is rooted in a specific concept of modern society. "Modernity" refers to a culture and a social structure based on rational, scientific, and meritocratic values.[5] Because of its alleged rational orientation, modern society is claimed to be ruled by a knowledge-based elite of professionals and managers. Ascriptive statuses such as class origins and race and gender supposedly recede in importance in deciding who will receive high wages, power, and prestige.[6] From this perspective, modernization is thought to be a global process, ineluctably spreading its values and social structure around the world due to its greater efficiency and resulting prosperity.[7] Old, "ethnic" cultures, based on tradition and religion, are seen as backward, impeding the spread of modern values and social arrangements. To modernists, the United States is the first and preeminent "new nation," a society formed without a history of caste, a society founded on the principles of democracy, free markets, equal opportunity, and individual merit.[8] Consequently, the United States serves as the model of modernity for the rest of the world to emulate.

Racism, from the modernization perspective, has always been out of keeping with American values. Arthur M. Schlesinger Jr. puts it this way, "The curse of racism was the great failure of the American experiment, the glaring contradiction of American ideals and the still crippling disease of American life."[9] For modernists, "the curse of racism" lies outside the core values of the United States. Modernists emphasize the meritocratic values that they believe provide the motivation for a wide variety of ethnic groups, most notably millions of European immigrants, to successfully assimilate into the great American cauldron.[10] Modernists argue that the cohesion of American society—the antidote to what they see as divisive ethnicity—is found in the meritocratic openness of American society to all.[11]

The historians Stephan Thernstrom and Abigail Thernstrom argue that the forces of modernization were overcoming racial inequality in the United States well before the civil rights movement arose.[12] They assert that when African Americans moved into the "modern" cities during the 1920s to the 1950s, a dramatic improvement ensued in their social status relative to whites. Thernstrom and Thernstrom believe that the civil rights movement of the early 1960s simply completed the process of eliminating racial barriers that were already falling under the pressures of modernity. Referring to the 1940s and 1950s, they write, "The importance of these two decades must be underscored, because it is too often assumed that the significant advances blacks have made in modern times occurred in the 1960s and after, and that they were the result of civil rights protest and federal legislation provoked by that protest. This common view . . . is wrong both about the timing of change and the causes of the change."[13]

To the extent that racial inequalities between whites and people of color persist, modernists typically emphasize ethnic communities' alleged lack of appropriate values. Continuing racial segregation and inequality is claimed to be the result of demoralization, a social pathology often described as a "culture of poverty," rooted in "broken"—that is, single women headed—families.[14] Shelby Steele, for example, writes, "[Ronald Reagan's] emphasis on traditional American values—individual initiative, self-sufficiency, strong families—offered what I think is the most enduring solution to the demoralization and poverty that continue to widen the gap between blacks and whites in America."[15]

While the main efforts to deny the existence of societal racism emphasize people of color's lack of "modern" values, another intellectual current has always lurked at the fringes of the debate: the idea that racial inequality is caused by unalterable genetic differences.[16] This view naturalizes racial inequality as an inalterable fact resulting from the genetic differentiation of human beings into a number of separate subgroups, each with its own specific genetic similarities.[17] The recent completion of the human genome project has rendered illegitimate the fundamental premise of the racial geneticists, that humanity is divided into different genetic pools that correspond to U.S. racial categories. But the effort to naturalize racial inequalities will not be deterred by science alone.[18] One can gauge the extent to which racism is becoming intensified by the reemergence of genetic racism.[19] Furthermore, a new form of genetic racism is now possible, one that seeks not merely to justify racism on a genetic basis, but to use genetic engineering to create racial inequality.[20]

One of the major problems with the "end of racism" thesis is that its advocates typically advance the assumptions of modernization theory without explicitly saying so. Consequently, claims such as the idea that schools and employers would judge candidates by "merit" if it were not for affirmative action are unexamined.[21] Modernists depict American society as besieged by immigrants with backward ideas, again without any examination of the assumptions about the United States' alleged modernity. The resuscitation of modernization theory allows conservatives to render societal racism invisible. "Race" is depicted as a way to group "antimodern" people. Those who insist on acknowledging race as essential to combat racism are depicted as clinging to backward, and racist, ideas. Even efforts to keep data about racial differences in health care or access to government services are depicted as racist.[22] The analysis of globalization provided in this book suggests that the influence of the "end of racism" thesis is growing precisely because it provides a justification for the increasing assertion of white privileges today. The depiction of the United States as the leader of global modernity is used to attack not only non-Western states and people, but also affirmative action and English as a Second Language programs, and to advocate for restrictions on immigration. The depiction of communities of color as mired in pathological values and behavior is enabled by the tacit assertion that the United States is the land of rationality and individual freedom. This book offers a very different view of the United States and the process of globalization, and of race, from that of modernization theory. Throughout this book, we shall see that globalization today is not a rational process, but one that entails the spread of market relationships that have profoundly disequalizing and destabilizing effects on societies everywhere, including the United States. It is also suggested in this book that the "end of racism" thesis is actually a component of the modern system of racism, that is, the ideological justification for "color-blind racism" today. I now turn to the tasks involved in conceptualizing societal racism and the ways in which globalization is affecting race relations in the United States today.

Rediscovering Race (I): The Particularity of Race

For over two and a half centuries, after laws like the Virginia Slave Code of 1705 first defined those eligible for slavery as "black" and those who were free as "white," a clear, publicly acknowledged "color line" was maintained in North America both by law and private practice. Unlike previous distinctions between people (early English colonists, for example, categorized people as English and African, or Christian and heathen), race distinguishes people on the basis of physical features.[23] The use of crude physical features (such as skin color, eye shape, and hair texture) as social markers meant that people from very different societies were lumped together as "black" or "white" (or, later, "Oriental," "Indian," or "Hispanic") for the purpose of treating them unequally. The racialization of African peoples, in this example, meant that those who were categorized "black" could be enslaved because of their physical features, and their status was inheritable by their children. Furthermore, all people defined as nonblack, meaning white, by their physical features were privileged: they were guaranteed they would not be enslaved.

The example of the racialization of slavery in North America reveals much about the social process of racialization in general. "Race" is a social construct entailing the practice of categorizing people on the basis of physical characteristics, assigning privileges to those categorized as "white" while denying opportunities to those categorized as "colored."[24] It is this social practice of privileging and oppressing people that gives significance to the physical features termed "racial." There is no inherent social significance to skin color, eye shape, or hair type.[25] Skin color becomes important when it designates who can be a slave and who is free, eye shape becomes important when it is used to distinguish citizens from the people ineligible for citizenship, and so on. Physical features are made socially significant (i.e., "racial") because of the social practices of privileging and subjugation associated with them. This is the core motive for the "social construction" of race.[26]

The process of racialization is fundamentally a material relationship. Racial privilege refers to people's capacity to make unequal claims to scarce social resources—for example, freedom, citizenship, jobs, political power, housing, education, and prestige—because of their racial designation. The always-present flip side of racial privilege is racial subjugation (or oppression): the denial of equal access to scarce social resources on the basis of racial designation. Without the social practice of privilege and subjugation, race has no salience, and would soon be dropped from use. In this fundamental sense, racism and race are completely bound together. At its root, the social construction of race exists because of racist practices, in a relationship that pits human beings against each other in the struggle for and against privileged access to scarce social resources.[27]

The fundamental relationship of race is a social conflict: white versus nonwhite. Whiteness denotes the status of racial privilege, and all of the nonwhite categories entail statuses formed in the context of the denial of opportunity. Whiteness is thus a relative concept, one that can only be defined by the state of oppression reserved for those designated as nonwhite. In a racialized society, to be categorized as white places one in a position to be treated in privileged ways, both large and small. Some of these privileges may be guaranteed by law, others by informal institutional policies, and still others may be conferred through "microlevel" ceremonies, such as seating practices in restaurants or informal treatment by the police, health professionals, or teachers.[28]

❦ Whiteness is in some ways conceptually separable from white people. The physical features that define an individual as white do not automatically denote a white individual's orientation toward racial privileges. From abolitionists such as John Brown to civil rights movement martyrs Viola Liuzzo, Andrew Goodwin, and Michael Schwerner, millions of white people have actively opposed white privileges. Indeed, white people can morally and politically oppose white privileges as much as anyone else. The fact that some white people oppose racial privileges does not mean that they do not receive such privileges, however. Whether one likes it or not, racial privileging and subordination in many ways operate independently of individuals' wills. Even the most staunchly antiracist whites, then, may receive the privileges of relative sanctity from police harassment and better treatment by real estate agents, helping professionals, potential employers, and so on precisely because these privileges are conferred without the consent of the recipient.

Subordinate racial statuses are also generally imposed without the consent of the people being subjugated. No one chooses to be put in a situation where he or she is treated like a criminal because he or she is black.[29] No one elects to be asked, as are many Asian Americans and Latinos: Where did you come from?[30] No one asks to be thought of as exotic or savage because he or she is Native American.[31] Yet, throughout American history, people have lost their individuality in a multiplicity of ways, as well as their claims to freedom, to citizenship, to jobs, and even to their lives, because they were categorized as "Negroes," "Orientals," "Hispanics," or "Indians."[32]

Rediscovering Race (II): Race and Society

The categorization of people on the basis of physical features for the purpose of treating them unequally is conceptually distinct from other social relationships they experience, such as class, gender, nationality, or sexuality. One of the classic errors of social theory before the mid-1980s was the tendency to see race as a manifestation of something else, such as ethnicity, nationality, or class.[33] However, once the particularity of race relations—that is, white privilege and nonwhite subordination—is grasped, it is still necessary to explain the relationship of race to individuals and society as a whole.

➤ Race is a particular type of relationship, one produced by a conflict (privilege/oppression) over scarce resources in which physical characteristics are social markers. But race relations do not exist in a vacuum. They arise in societies in which other forms of conflictual relationships are always present. For example, class, in the Marxist tradition, is also conceived as a conflictual relationship based on the exploitation of labor by the owners of the means of production. But class and race are different kinds of relationships, and people can and often do find themselves enmeshed in conflicted statuses. Thus, a white worker has contradictory interests on the basis of his or her race and class locations: as a worker, he or she has an interest in uniting with other workers who are being exploited by capitalists. This class interest encourages workers to seek multiracial and multinational unity. On the other hand, as a person with white privileges, a white worker also has a real material interest in preserving his or her privileged access to jobs, political power, citizenship, social services, education, housing, and so on.[34] This racial interest can motivate white workers to deny equality to workers of color. A black worker (indeed, any worker of color) has much less conflict between his or her race and class interests. Multiracial working-class unity will certainly benefit the large majority of African Americans, who are disproportionately compressed into the working class by racism. Similarly, whatever advances the interests of the black community will also give blacks a greater capacity to compel white workers to form multiracial working-class coalitions.[35]

At the level at which people experience everyday life, people cannot be reduced to their race or class interests. In this example, an individual is not just "white" or a "worker." He or she is both. Indeed, people constantly experience potentially contradictory interests from their location in other statuses, such as gender, nationality, and sexual orientation. People are simultaneously experiencing many social conflicts, often in very contradictory ways. How these contradictory statuses are handled is not an abstract question but a fact of history. People do not generally act according to abstract principles (e.g., workers unite!), but according to their perceived interests. To use the previous example, whether or not a white worker pursues the defense of his or her racial or class interests will be determined by his or her belief in the actual likelihood of benefits from one or the other strategy. Of course, individuals form their perceptions of their interests, and subsequent "identity" (or "identities") in a larger context, in which government policies, corporate power, labor unions, and other social movements can all alter the likelihood of an individual choosing to mobilize his or her racial interests.

Another difficult theoretical problem concerning the role of race in society concerns the likelihood that economic and political elites and white nonelites will turn to racism to maintain or enhance their positions. There are two distinct motivations for white people to demand racial privileges.

#Dual-markets   ·Freemarkets

First, racism and national oppression can be and often are used by capitalists and white workers to maintain "dual markets" to buffer whites from a section of the labor force that receives lower wages and less or no benefits.[36] Similarly, dual markets can buffer white businesses from minority businesses competing with them for capital and more lucrative consumers. Second, racism and national oppression can be and often are deployed by political elites to create a sense of allegiance from nonelites on a racial and/or national basis by defining racial or national minorities ("others") as the source of threats to the social order.[37]

The theoretical problem concerning these motives is that economic and political elites do not always support specific forms of racism and national oppression. An examination of U.S. history reveals that in specific conditions, and in specific ways, capitalists and/or political elites have, for limited periods of time, played antiracist roles. The end of slavery, for example, was in a significant part possible because industrial capitalists saw the system of unfree labor and unfree capital as an obstacle to the expansion of "free" markets.[38] The success of the civil rights movement was at least in significant part possible because of national political elites' own reasons for temporarily supporting the black insurgent movement's agenda (see chapter 7). On the other hand, capitalists have often used racism as a tool to maintain a cheap and exploitable labor force. Political elites have often turned to racism and nationalism to bolster national unity and to maintain social stability. Similarly, white workers have, at times, been willing to surrender their potential racial privileges in favor of multiracial, multinational working-class unity, such as during the Congress of Industrial Organization organizing drives of the 1930s. At most times, however, this has not been the case (see chapter 6).

Understanding race relations in society requires much more than conceptualizing the variable relationships between race and class interests. People experience a large array of privileged and oppressed statuses, not only on the basis of race and class, but also on the basis of nationality (citizens versus illegal aliens), gender (men versus women), and sexuality (heterosexuals versus gay, lesbian, bisexual, and transgendered people). The vast majority of people are thus simultaneously oppressed and privileged on different dimensions of social life.[39] Thus, African Americans may claim national privileges and refuse to enter into an antiracist alliance with Latinos.[40] Mexican American women may in some ways feel they have more in common with women from other Latin American or African nations than with Mexican American men.[41] Gay and lesbian people of color may feel estranged from both their own communities and white gays and lesbians.[42]

" White habitus "

Understanding race relations in society thus requires both a sense of the complexity of people's lived social relations and a sense of the power of racism. The sobering reality of American history, unfortunately, reveals an unsettling truth: Racism and national chauvinism have over and over again proven to deliver to those privileged by them (i.e., white American citizens) material resources sufficient to overwhelm other forms of social solidarity. American working-class movements have typically been disunited by racism; so has the women's movement, the gay and lesbian movement, the environmental movement, and so on.[43]

Structured Racism in the Mass Society

One of the most striking features of racism in the United States today is that whites can defend racial privileges without the use of explicit racist ideology. Bonilla-Silva describes the remarkable contradiction between white beliefs about race and the reality of white privileges as follows:

> In the United States, most whites proclaim to be color-blind and express their wish to live in a society where race does not matter at all. Yet whites tend to navigate every day a "white habitus" and seem to be rather "color-conscious" in terms of their choice of significant others (close friends and romantic partners). When confronted with these apparent contradictions between what they believe and what they do, whites argue that "it's economics, not race," "the evidence is not clear," "it's just the way things are," or "it's natural for people to gravitate toward likeness."[44]

Color consciousness extends far beyond the choice of close friends or lovers. The white "habitus" Bonilla-Silva invokes refers to social arrangements that make it possible for a white person to live his or her life in a virtually all-white environment, moving seamlessly from a highly racialized suburban community to a racialized school or workplace to racialized friendship and family networks. It is this social arrangement that is the most significant feature of the racial system of the United States today.

The "white habitus" was the creation of mass institutions in the mid-twentieth century. The development of large corporations with complex administrative structures, the founding of mass public institutions of higher education, and the creation of large-scale government agencies meant that people had to interact with and through impersonal bureaucracies for their jobs, goods, and services. The signature of these large-scale bureaucracies is that they treat each individual in a standardized, impersonal way, as part of an undifferentiated "mass" of workers, customers, or citizens.[45] This development was widely acknowledged in the seminal social criticisms of the 1950s, such as David Reisman's *The Lonely Crowd*.[46]

The mass society reached its apex in the new suburbs, where the children and grandchildren of European immigrants eschewed the old ethnic neighborhoods and its informal street life in favor of private housing in suburban tract communities.[47] The new suburbanites not only changed where they lived, but they also changed how they related to social institutions. Gone were the small stores of the urban community; now suburbanites shopped in malls designed for mass marketing. Gone, in these settings, were the close networks of neighbors; in their place were formal organizations, like parent-teacher associations and neighborhood organizations to protect property values and improve services. In place of urban political machines and labor unions, suburbanites entrusted schools to ensure the upward mobility of their children. Blue-collar work began to have less allure, especially for those who were upwardly mobile. The new workplaces of the suburbanites were increasingly likely to be large corporate or governmental bureaucratic organizations, where workers did white-collar technical, administrative, and managerial jobs. The new arrangements of work, school, and community were institutionalized to an extent that had never before existed. Instant communities emerged: developers built hundreds of homes at a time, mass marketers built malls, and local governments built schools at a frantic pace. The new suburbanites lived and worked in social settings to a great extent created by corporations and government bodies. A new, thoroughly bourgeois pattern of life was emerging on the outskirts of America's cities, organized through mass institutions.[48]

As we shall see in chapter 2, the new suburbs were created by and for whites only, thus enhancing the value of suburbs as sites of racial privileges. Suburbanization involved more than segregated housing: all of the intersecting arrangements and cultures of the mass institutions had a racial character. Mass institutions of public higher education were developed in this segregated context and took on white notions of curriculum, evaluation of students, and the hiring of faculty. Corporations expanded their managerial, professional, administrative, and technical workforces in the same era; and the assumption that only whites are capable of white-collar work was widely accepted.

An important area for historical investigation is to uncover the ways that informal racial standards and values became formalized as normal bases of evaluation in large-scale organizations.[49] Virtually all of the mass institutions of the era—corporate, educational, residential, and cultural—were developed in conditions of complete racial segregation. Even when their segregation later came under challenge in the 1960s, many large bureaucracies, such as many police and fire departments, consciously developed standards intended to keep out people of color (and women of all races). Consequently, the new institutional arrangements structured white privileges into their "normal" operations.

Even more than privileging whites in specific institutions, the new arrangements enabled the structuring of white privileges into the day-to-day patterns of interaction of the mass society as a whole. Once white suburbs were in place, systems of education—including the new public colleges and universities—were built in racially segregated environments. The fact that the educational curriculum was Anglocentric and that the staffs of the new colleges were likely to be almost all white was depicted by academics as meritocratic and nonracial. The fact that white-collar jobs that were reserved for whites became increasingly linked to educational credentials transformed the racial "good ol' boy" networks into the hiring of the "qualified." The racial privileges of the mass society all reinforced one another: only whites could live in suburbs, and thus only whites had access to the new college and university campuses built in the suburbs or the suburbs' well-funded public schools. Whites therefore had the credentials to get access to white-collar jobs. The accumulation of racial privileges eventually meant that whites were much likelier to be able to afford the housing prices in the suburbs. The cycle of privilege was thus structured not only into institutions, but also into the fabric of the mass society as a whole.

Whites' capacity to deny the existence of racism, while continuing to benefit from racial privileges, was (and is) contingent on the development of structured racism. Once the patterns of racial privilege were built into the "normal" day-to-day operation of interlocking mass institutions, the defense of racism no longer required open claims of white superiority. It became increasingly feasible for whites to defend racial privileges by upholding standards of individual merit, community control, and other allegedly "race-neutral" claims. The process of structuring racial privileges into mass institutions took many years. While the first efforts to link suburbs, universities, and white-collar jobs appeared in the 1940s, as late as the 1970s it was still possible for noncollege graduates (e.g., skilled blue-collar workers) to make as much money as college graduates. Furthermore, as the new system of racism arose in the 1950s and 1960s, the civil rights movement contested the new institutional arrangements. In 1966, the discovery of "institutional racism" enabled civil rights activists to expose and challenge the discriminatory practices built into and justified as "normal" by specific institutions.[50]

The concept of "institutional discrimination" proved useful to uncover and challenge specific discriminatory practices in schools, workplaces, government, banks, and real estate (see chapters 4 and 5). But the concept to some extent missed the forest for the trees: racial structures were not only institutionalized, but had also created an entire way of life (Bonilla-Silva's "white habitus"). A new form of racialized social relations had come into being. Before the 1950s, whites could only privilege themselves relative to people of color by active state intervention and explicit racist ideology. Without such active mechanisms, the potential for multiracial integration was much greater than popularly acknowledged, especially as African Americans, Chinese, and Mexicans moved into the manufacturing cities in the mid to late nineteenth century.[51] The creation of mass suburbs for whites set in place the beginning of a true white habitus, in which whites could and did live their lives without interacting with people of color (except the home service workers). This white habitus was further reinforced by white colleges and workplaces. The concept of structured racism, then, is more useful than institutional racism in two regards: first, the unit of analysis is not a particular institution, but societywide patterns of privilege and subordination. Second, it emphasizes the distinct way that privileging works, as patterns of behavior, not primarily as racist ideology or state policies.

Ethnicity, Race, and Racism

Ethnicity is conceptually distinct from race, but is, in some important ways, bound up with it. The social construction of ethnicity, like race, begins with acts of power: The process by which groups are marginalized as "different" and unequal in their access to social resources from the "mainstream" society.[52] The act of defining a people as "different" also defines other people as nonethnic, or "normal" and privileged. Racism, of course, can make people ethnic; people can also be marginalized from society on the basis of their real or alleged ties to another nation (national minority) or, in societies with established religions, on the basis of religion (religious minority).[53] The labeling of people as ethnic is often a crucial component of political elites' efforts to cohere national unity among the nonethnic.[54] As will be discussed in chapter 4, for example, making people "ethnic" and blaming them for social problems may be of particular use to elites as a way of maintaining order among "mainstream" citizens as nation-states lose their capacity to deliver social services and protect people from corporate misdeeds.[55] The history of having been "ethnic" is a common experience in the Unites States. Most immigrants to the United States, including Europeans, have experienced discrimination on the basis of their nationality, and a third of Americans are labeled as racial minorities.

ty is thus produced in the context of domination and discrimina-
values and institutions that give an ethnic group its coherence,
however, are constructed by the subjugated group, not by those who oppress
them. Irish American and Jewish American ethnicities were produced by
those who shared similar experiences of national or religious origin, immigration, and oppression in the United States. In this sense, ethnic groups are
defined by their self-organization around a set of institutions (churches, syn-
agogues, mosques, business associations, labor organizations, and so on), and
their informal social networks of kinship and community, as well as a common set of values expressing their history, experiences, and desires. Ethnic
formations often take form in the context of racial oppression. In this sense,
people's relationship to race is not simply imposed. People of color often consciously utilize their racial location as a resource to resist racial oppression.[56]
This active engagement with race as a site of resistance to racism can be seen
in the fact that people of color are much more likely than whites to be conscious of race because they need to be to confront and oppose racial privileging. People of color are likely to utilize racial commonalities as a way of
developing ethnic communities, in large part to resist racial subjugation. In
this way, race can be mobilized against racism.

Racial ethnicity produces many nonracist and antiracist social uses of
race.[57] The common experience of racial oppression can provide an otherwise diverse grouping of national minorities with a common interest around
which they can develop unity, the practice Yen Le Espiritu terms "panethnicity."[58] Thus, the racial meanings inherent in the ideas of Black Power, the
American Indian Movement, Asian Indians, or Chicanismo all have antiracist connotations. In rare instances, people of color can use race as a way
of developing privileged access to scarce resources—for example, through political favoritism—although such racial privileges are almost always limited
by the absence of significant institutional power behind such arrangements.[59]

The interplay between ethnicity and race can be quite complex. For example, an ethnic group may experience subjugation as a national or religious
minority and simultaneously receive racial privileges as white people. Karen
Brodkin, Matthew Frye Jacobson, and others have observed that European
national minorities were at times depicted as nonwhite by Anglo-Americans
in the late nineteenth century.[60] But the question of whether or not Jews,
Italians, or other eastern and southern European immigrants were white can
be answered by looking at the objective privileges reserved only for whites at
that time. These privileges included citizenship, voting rights, and access to
industrial jobs. European immigrants were thus always white because they received these privileges. But their racial privileges were at times offset by

withering discrimination on the basis of nationality and religion. The clash between racial and national interests may affect people of color as well. While people lumped together in a nonwhite category may have important areas of shared interest, there may be important areas of divergence of interests. Thus, West Indians are likely to be defined as black in the United States, but they are not ethnically African American.[61] Divergent class and gender interests can also be sources of important ethnic divisions.[62]

In sum, Michael Omi and Howard Winant are correct when they observe that racial "projects" entail the uses of race for nonracial and antiracist purposes as well as for racial oppression.[63] But some caution about eclecticism concerning the concept of race must be noted. The fundamental conditions for the existence of race and ethnicity are claims of racial and national privileges and the consequent marginalization and oppression of people of color and other national minorities. Without societal racism, race as the basis for ethnicity would quickly lose its salience. As James H. Cone puts it, the problem of race is, fundamentally, the problem of white privilege.[64]

Connecting Globalization
and Racism: Methodological Issues

One of the chief problems for the study of the relationship between globalization and race is to ascertain the appropriate methodology for the inquiry. One point of reference is global in scope. As Charles Mills, Winant, and Bonilla-Silva show, capitalism has always been global in its reach, and racism has always been an essential condition for capital accumulation and expansion.[65] Globalization, in its present phase, is producing remarkable contradictions. It is simultaneously creating new, transnational social relations that bring people around the world closer together, while creating massive inequality within and between nations, destabilizing existing social orders, dislodging hundreds of millions of people from their home countries, and reducing the capacity of nation-states to regulate society. Because of globalization's contradictory character, it is necessary to investigate both the ways in which it creates conditions that increase the probability of people mobilizing racial and national privileges, as well as the ways in which globalization creates conditions that increase the chances for people to forge a more just social order.

The contemporary period of globalization creates conditions that are intensifying racism in all of the most developed countries (MDCs), and between the MDCs and the less developed countries (LDCs). Rapidly increasing economic and social inequality within and between nations, accompanied by nation-states' greatly reduced capacity to regulate capital or redistribute resources, is disrupting old social orders and often fostering a climate of fear. At the same time, the growing flow of people into Europe and the United States from the LDCs is challenging and reconstituting ideas of citizenship and social membership. These conditions appear everywhere in the developed world, and, in response, growing numbers of people are claiming white privilege as a way of buffering themselves from the threats of downward mobility. In these ways, it is possible to identify specific dynamics of racism that are appearing everywhere in the developed world in response to globalization's social dislocations.

But racism cannot be analyzed solely at a global level; racial projects primarily develop within nations in specific ways having to do with the political economy of each historic national formation.[66] Colonialism and slavery, for example, produced different forms of white supremacy in Europe than in the Americas, mainly because racism was largely *external* to Europe (i.e., the racial "others" were colonial subjects in some other country) while it was *internal* to the development of many American nation-states, and especially the United States, whose "peculiar institution" of slavery and westward expansion gave race an ever-expanding role in the development of social order.[67] Variations in the ways that race is woven into the social fabric together with class, nationality, gender, and sexuality mean that the particular modes of racial stratification and modes of resistance to racism vary greatly from place to place, and time to time. It is for this reason, for example, that an individual can be white in one society and black in another, mestizo in one society and Hispanic in another, and so on.[68] Variations can be local as well as national. In the United States, racial categories like mulatto or those of the octoroon system have come and gone in specific regions at specific times for specific reasons.

The methodological problem in the study of globalization and race is this: How does the analysis of race on a global level articulate with the analysis of race on a national and even a local level? The study of the relationship between globalization and racism must, I believe, start with recognition of global trends in racism, but must primarily focus on the ways in which the specific national histories of race and current racial structures intersect with the new dynamics of globalization. Globalization is creating common conditions stimulating racism throughout Europe and the United States, but these trends materialize in different national settings in quite different ways. Among the variables that affect the impact of globalization on national racial projects and structures are:

1. *The role of the nation-state in society.* States have different capacities to address the social impacts of globalization. Highly developed social democracies, for example, have a greater range of nonracial options for addressing the social problems attendant with globalization than do the neoliberal democracies like the United States and Britain. Conversely, political elites are more likely to racialize social problems if they lack other means to address them.

2. *The history of racialization of society.* The presence of the structural and cultural legacies of previous racial systems increases the likelihood of projects to racialize the impacts of globalization on national societies. Societies without long histories of internal racism may racialize the social problems of the global era, but these new forms of racism are a departure from previous social arrangements (usually to keep people of color out altogether). Societies with a long history of internal racism, and especially the United States, are more likely to racialize the responses to globalization.

3. *The demography of society.* Societies with small numbers of recent immigrants identified as "people of color" will likely racialize their response to globalization less thoroughly than will societies with large numbers of people of color with long claims to membership in that society. Thus, the black ghettoes of England and the banlieus of France are multiracial, multinational communities in which people of color are typically the numerical minority.[69]

4. *The political capacity of people to resist racism.* The racialization of society comes not only from racist projects claiming white privileges, but also from antiracist projects that use race as a basis for mobilization against racial privileges (e.g., the Black Power movement). Societies vary considerably in people of color's capacities to resist racism. In part, this variation is due to demographic considerations, and in part it is a result of the historical development of the political capacities by different minority communities. Thus, while African Americans experience some of the worst forms of racism, they also have developed a powerful capacity to resist racism and make antiracist claims. Africans and Caribbean immigrants in Europe, however, usually are small in number and lack positioning within the political system of the European countries.

In sum, globalization creates a context that produces tendencies toward racism in many different national societies, but the form and content of the racist and antiracist responses to globalization will vary considerably from nation to nation.

The strategy I have chosen for this book is to examine in detail the impact of globalization on one society: the United States. The value of this approach is that it allows for an in-depth investigation of the ways that the specific history, economy, politics, and cultures of one society produce tendencies toward racism and antiracism in the context of globalization. This type of exploration is essential, it seems to me, before we undertake comparative analyses, because it informs us of what it is we must compare.

The focus on the study of a single nation is also based on the observation that even in the global era—perhaps, especially in it—nation-states are the basis for the organization of "society," both for creating the international framework for global interactions and for establishing the basis for national social stability in the global era. As well, by studying one nation, we can examine the specific ways that globalization is undermining old hegemonic concepts of society (in the United States, the middle-class order) and creating possibilities for new ways to understand what "society" is. The United States is not just a nation, of course; it is the global superpower that, by virtue of its military might and large economy, currently has the initiative of creating new legal, administrative, and military infrastructures for the global realities. To understand how the United States addresses racism in the global era is of vital concern to people everywhere in the world today.

Finally, local social formations are also of great importance for understanding race in the global era. Vivian Schelling suggests that "new local-global formations" result from marginalized peoples' location in and resistance to the inequalities and social crises of globalization at a local level.[70] The affirmation of local identities and the creation of "new ethnicities" are achieved by movements arising from marginal communities seeking to empower themselves in the face of the destructive consequences of investments by transnational corporations, the International Monetary Fund and the World Bank, and, often, their own national governments.[71] The intensification of ethnic community solidarity tells us something important about globalization itself: It is currently unable to fulfill most people's needs. Consequently, those who experience its profound dislocations, and especially those left out of the global market system entirely, are left with little choice but to construct new conceptions of social order—economically and politically, as well as culturally. The reassertion of local ethnicities, then, can be seen as a key manifestation of the failure of globalization in its current form to integrate people into either national societies or a "new world order." The very fact of ethnicity bears witness to the marginal relationship much of the world has to the global economy; it also stands as testimony to the decreasing capacity of nation-states to create stable and inclusive social orders. The resurgence of local communities also signifies people's capacities for innovation and their determination to find hope in the face of their oppression.

Conclusion

It is small wonder that Americans are confused about the meanings of race today. We are just beginning to come to grips with the dynamics of structured racism, a system that arose a half century ago. And, on top of that, we now have to explain the impact of globalization on American society, an impact that both intensifies racist and nationalist reactions as well as revitalizes antiracist movements. The failure of intellectuals to maintain a clear analysis of racism, including the liberal retreat from the subject, has had disastrous consequences, enabling the "end of racism" ideology, and racism itself, to gain ground.

Understanding the impact of globalization on race relations in the United States is clearly a difficult task. We are still in the early stages of the development of globalization, and so we only dimly perceive its impact on the present, let alone the future. Americans are experiencing globalization as both the dawning of a hopeful new stage in world history and a time of great fear. Unfortunately, most Americans are viewing the world today through the lens of fear. Out of fear, many Americans cling to a concept of social stability and "normality" from the post–World War II era. This middle-class social order, with its distinctive racial dynamics, is still the basis for the definition of the good life for most Americans. Defending the middle-class social order motivates much of the new racism and nationalism today. Consequently, before we can analyze the impact of globalization on race relations today, we will first have to explore the social history of the middle-class social order.

Notes

1. Eduardo Bonilla-Silva, *White Supremacy and Racism in the Post–Civil Rights Era* (Boulder, Colo.: L. Rienner, 2001).

2. Howard Winant, "The Theoretical Status of the Concept of Race," in *Theories of Race and Racism*, ed. Les Back and John Solomos (London: Routledge, 2000), 181–194.

3. Stephen Steinberg, "The Liberal Retreat from Race," in *Race and Ethnicity in the United States*, ed. Stephen Steinberg (Malden, Mass.: Blackwell, 2000), 37–54.

4. See chapter 3.

5. Max Weber, *Economy and Society*, vol. 1 (Berkeley: University of California Press, 1978), 212–226.

6. Daniel Bell, *The Coming of Post-industrial Society* (New York: Basic, 1973).

7. Talcott Parsons, "Evolutionary Universals in Society," *American Sociological Review* 29 (1964): 339–357; S. N. Eisenstadt, *Modernization: Protest and Change* (Englewood Cliffs, N.J.: Prentice-Hall, 1966).

8. Seymour Martin Lipset, *The First New Nation* (New York: Basic, 1963).

9. Arthur M. Schlesinger Jr., *The Disuniting of America* (New York: Norton, 1992), 14.

10. Robert E. Park, *Race and Culture* (Glencoe, Ill.: Free Press, 1950); Nathan Glazer and Daniel Patrick Moynihan, *Beyond the Melting Pot* (Cambridge: MIT Press, 1970).

11. Thomas Sowell, *Ethnic America* (New York: Basic, 1981).

12. Stephan Thernstrom and Abigail Thernstrom, *America in Black and White* (New York: Simon and Schuster, 1997).

13. Thernstrom and Thernstrom, *America in Black and White*, 70.

14. The usage of this concept has shifted from the original formulation by Oscar Handlin to the present. For a useful review of the history of this term, see Stephen Steinberg, *The Ethnic Myth: Race, Ethnicity and Class in America*, 3rd ed. (Boston: Beacon, 2001).

15. Shelby Steele, *The Content of Our Character* (New York: HarperPerennial, 1991), 9.

16. For a critical review, see R. C. Leowintin, Steven Rose, and Leon J. Kamin, "I.Q.: The Rank Ordering of the World," in *The "Racial" Economy of Science*, ed. Sandra Harding (Bloomington: Indiana University Press, 1993), 142–160. The classic statement of the genetic basis for intelligence is Arthur Jensen, "How Much Can We Boost I.Q. and Scholastic Achievement?" *Harvard Educational Review* 39 (1969): 1–123.

17. For a history of this idea, see Stephen Jay Gould, *The Mismeasure of Man* (New York: Norton, 1981); Linda Vigilant, "Race and Biology," in *Global Convulsions*, ed. Winston A. Van Horne (Albany: SUNY Press, 1997), 49–62.

18. Claude Fischer et al., *Inequality by Design: Cracking the Bell Curve* (Princeton, N.J.: Princeton University Press, 1996).

19. The latest reiteration of genetic racism is Richard J. Herrnstein and Charles Murray, *The Bell Curve* (New York: The Free Press, 1994).

20. Troy Duster, *The Back Door to Eugenics* (New York: Routledge, 1990).

21. Lydia Chávez, *The Color Bind: California's Battle to End Affirmative Action* (Berkeley: University of California Press, 1998), 34.

22. Currently, an effort to ban the monitoring of the impact of government programs on racial groups is under way. The first part of this effort was an executive order issued in 1997 by then California governor Pete Wilson barring state agencies from collecting racial data. I was the lead plaintiff in a lawsuit over that order (*Barlow v. Davis*). A ballot initiative initially entitled the Racial Privacy Initiative is currently being readied by Ward Connerly for the March 2004 election. See chapter 5 for a fuller discussion.

23. Edmund S. Morgan, *American Slavery, American Freedom: The Ordeal of Colonial Virginia* (New York: Norton, 1975).

24. The process of racialization of Native Americans, Asians, and Mexicans is analyzed by Tomás Almaguer, *Racial Fault Lines* (Berkeley: University of California Press, 1994).

25. Vigilant, "Race and Biology."

26. An excellent discussion of the uses and limits of this concept can be found in Winant, "Theoretical Status of the Concept of Race," 181–194.

27. Eduardo Bonilla-Silva, "Rethinking Racism," *American Sociological Review* 62 (1997): 465–479.

28. Michael Omi and Howard Winant, *Racial Formation in the United States* (New York: Routledge, 1986).

29. Nathan McCall, *Makes Me Want to Holler* (New York: Random House, 1994).

30. Lisa Lowe, "Immigration, Citizenship, Racialization: An Asian American Critique," in *Immigrant Acts* (Durham, N.C.: Duke University Press, 1996), 1–36.

31. The process of being made into American Indians is exceptionally well analyzed by M. Annette Jaimes, "American Racism: The Impact on American Indian Identity and Survival," in *Race*, ed. Steven Gregory and Roger Sanjek (New Brunswick, N.J.: Rutgers University Press, 1994), 41–61.

32. W. E. B. Du Bois eloquently speaks to the loss of individuality, "[T]he Negro is a sort of a seventh son, born with a veil, and gifted with second sight in this American world—a world which yields him no true self-consciousness, but only lets him see himself through the revelation of the other world." See W. E. B. Du Bois, *The Souls of Black Folk* (New York: Signet Classics, 1969), 45.

33. For a critique of these theories, see Omi and Winant, *Racial Formation in the United States;* Bonilla-Silva, *White Supremacy.*

34. Raymond S. Franklin, *Shadows of Race and Class* (Minneapolis: University of Minnesota Press, 1991).

35. This is historically demonstrated by Dan Georgakas and Marvin Surkin, *Detroit: I Do Mind Dying* (Boston: South End, 1998).

36. Edna Bonacich, "Inequality in America: The Failure of the American System for People of Color," *Sociological Spectrum* 9 (1989): 77–99.

37. This approach is taken by Almaguer, *Racial Fault Lines.*

38. Eric Williams, *Capitalism and Slavery* (New York: Putnam's, 1980).

39. The methodology for understanding this complex interrelationship has been brilliantly explored by Deborah King, "Multiple Jeopardy, Multiple Consciousness: The Context of a Black Feminist," *Signs: Journal of Women in Culture and Society* 14, no. 1 (Autumn 1988): 42–72.

40. This is precisely what happened in the Los Angeles mayoral election of 2001.

41. Ana Castillo, *The Massacre of the Dreamers* (New York: Penguin, 1994), 23.

42. This contradiction is brilliantly explored by Martin F. Manalansan IV ("Searching for Community: Filipino Gay Men in New York City," *Amerasia Journal* 20, no. 1 [1994]: 59–73) and Marlin Riggs (*Tongues Untied* [San Francisco: Frameline, 1999, video documentary]).

43. Robert L. Allen, *The Reluctant Reformers* (Washington, D.C.: Howard University Press, 1974).

44. Bonilla-Silva, *White Supremacy*, 138–139.

45. The original formulations of this idea are found in the early twentieth-century work of Max Weber, Hans Gerth, and C. Wright Mills, *From Max Weber: Essays in Sociology* (New York: Oxford University Press, 1946), 196–266.

46. David Riesman, *The Lonely Crowd* (New Haven, Conn.: Yale University Press, 1950).

47. It was this phenomenon that led Lewis Mumford to describe the suburbs as "an asylum for the preservation of illusion. . . . Here domesticity could flourish, forgetful of the exploitation on which so much of it was based. Here, individuality could flourish, oblivious of the pervasive regimentation beyond." See Lewis Mumford, *The City in History: Its Origins, Its Transformations, Its Prospects* (New York: Harcourt, Brace and World, 1961), 494.

48. Robert Fishman, *Bourgeois Utopia: The Rise and Fall of Suburbia* (New York: Basic, 1987).

49. Nicholas Lemann, *The Big Test: The Secret History of the American Meritocracy* (New York: Farrar, Strauss and Giroux, 1999).

50. Stokely Carmichael and Charles V. Hamilton, *Black Power: The Politics of Liberation in America* (New York: Random House, 1967).

51. There were also important examples of interracial projects throughout the earlier periods of racism, such as the slave rebellions of the early 1800s and the farming cooperatives established in the South during Reconstruction. On the former, see David R. Roediger, *Wages of Whiteness* (London: Verso, 1991). On the latter, see W. E. B. Du Bois, *Black Reconstruction in America* (New York: Atheneum, 1975).

52. Richard Jenkins, *Rethinking Ethnicity* (London: Sage, 1997), 52.

53. Religion is a much more powerful marker in Europe and the Middle East, where religions have been used for centuries to define citizenship in nations. Efforts to make the United States a Christian nation have waxed and waned. As we shall see in chapter 7, this use of religion is on the rise in the United States today.

54. Étienne Balibar and Immanuel Wallerstein, *Race, Nation, Class: Ambiguous Identities* (London: Verso, 1991).

55. Samir Amin, *Capitalism in the Age of Globalization* (London: Zed, 1997), 61–64.

56. Steve Fenton, *Ethnicity: Racism, Class and Culture* (Lanham, Md.: Rowman & Littlefield, 1999).

57. For a discussion of antiracist racial "projects," see Omi and Winant, *Racial Formation in the United States*, 56.

58. Yen Le Espiritu, *Asian American Panethnicity* (Philadelphia: Temple University Press, 1992).

59. For a discussion of the potential for contract set aside programs ("quotas") to become the basis for a black political machine, see W. Avon Drake and R. D.

Holsworth, *Affirmative Action and the Stalled Quest for Black Progress* (Urbana: University of Illinois Press, 1996).

60. Matthew Frye Jacobson, *Whiteness of a Different Color: European Immigrants and the Alchemy of Race* (Cambridge, Mass.: Harvard University Press, 1998); Karen Brodkin, *How Jews Became White Folks and What That Says about Race in America* (New Brunswick, N.J.: Rutgers University Press, 1998).

61. Percy C. Hintzen, *West Indian in the West: Self-Representations in an Immigrant Community* (New York: New York University Press, 2001).

62. On class, see Manning Marable, *How Capitalism Underdeveloped Black America* (Boston: South End, 1983); on gender, see King, "Multiple Jeopardy, Multiple Consciousness," 42–72.

63. Omi and Winant, *Racial Formation in the United States*, 56.

64. James H. Cone, *Speaking the Truth: Ecumenism, Liberation and Black Theology* (Grand Rapids, Mich.: Eerdmans, 1986).

65. Howard Winant, *The World Is a Ghetto* (New York: Basic, 2001); Charles Mills, *Blackness Visible* (Ithaca, N.Y.: Cornell University Press, 1998); Eduardo Bonilla-Silva, "'This Is a White Country': The Racial Ideology of the Western Nations of the World-System," *Sociological Inquiry* 70, no. 2 (Spring 2000): 188–214.

66. Omi and Winant, *Racial Formation in the United States*, 61.

67. Almaguer, *Racial Fault Lines*.

68. See the excellent collection of articles in Joan Ferrante and Prince Brown Jr., *The Social Construction of Race and Ethnicity in the United States*, 2nd ed. (Upper Saddle River, N.J.: Prentice-Hall, 2001).

69. Stephen Small, *Racialized Barriers: The Black Experience in the United States and England in the 1980s* (London: Routledge, 1996); Loic Wacquant, "Ghetto, Banlieue, Favela: Tools for Rethinking Urban Marginality," in *Os Condenados da Cidade* (Rio de Janeiro: Revan, 2001), 14.

70. Vivian Schelling, "Globalisation, Ethnic Identity and Popular Culture in Latin America," in *Globalisation and the Third World*, ed. Ray Kiely and Phil Marfleet (London: Routledge, 1998), 142–162.

71. Fenton, *Ethnicity*.

CHAPTER TWO

~

The Best and the Whitest: Racism and the Middle-Class Social Order, 1945–1975

The ways in which white privileges are mobilized in the United States in the era of globalization are different from those of past eras, even the recent past. Before we can explore the dynamics of racism (and antiracism) in the era of globalization, however, we must first take a step back to the period immediately preceding this one. That era, one that began in 1945 and ended in 1975, was one in which the middle class became hegemonic in the United States, the basis on which a particular kind of all-sided social order was constructed. One reason we must come to terms with the history of the middle-class social order is that globalization is now undercutting its stability, and it is the defense of this order (i.e., "the good ol' days") that motivates much of the new racism of the global era.

This history is also needed if we are to investigate what Justice Thurgood Marshall so aptly termed "the present effects of past discrimination," a key component of racism in the era of globalization.[1] As I initially discussed in chapter 1, the middle-class social order became the context for a particular kind of racism, despite claims to the contrary. Unlike the racisms of previous epochs, such as the system of state power called Jim Crow racism, white privileges in the 1950s and 1960s became structured into the patterns of interaction in society so deeply that the overt defense of racial privileges became unnecessary. A new type of racism, termed by some "color-blind racism," came into being during this era. The fact that racism was deeply embedded into the middle-class social order in the 1950s and 1960s is important for the study of the dynamics of the defense of racial privileges today, in the global era. As

we will see in the next three chapters, the modes of racial privileging and oppression created in this earlier period provided the groundwork for a more
virulent defense of white privileges in the era of globalization that emerged
in the 1980s and 1990s.

The Rise of the Middle-Class
Social Order, 1945–1975

The idea of the middle class became the defining feature of American society in the 1950s. This historically unique moment when the United States
became a global superpower was pronounced as the onset of an epoch in
which all the world would seek to emulate the U.S. model.[2] Its boosters
crowed that the United States had become the epitome of modern society.
This period of unbridled global domination that began in 1946 started to un-
ravel in the late 1960s and was in disarray by 1975, the year the United
States lost the Vietnam War and the oil crisis (erroneously blamed on the
Organization of Petroleum Exporting Countries) shook the middle class's
confidence. While brief, this thirty-year-long era produced massive and enduring changes within American society.

At the close of World War II, the United States had become more than a
world power, or even the center of an empire. A new term, "superpower," had
to be coined to describe the United States' historically unprecedented geopolitical domination of the world. The United States rose to superpower status
because of the confluence of three factors at the end of World War II: First,
the rest of the industrialized world's economies lay in ruins, while the U.S.
productive capacity was supercharged by the war emergency measures. In
1947, the United States produced nearly one-half of the entire global output
and was responsible for the revival of capitalism in war-ravished Western Europe and Japan. Second, the United States had a monopoly of nuclear
weapons at the end of the war and held a significant nuclear strategic advantage over the Soviet Union until the early 1970s.[3] As a result, the United
States could and did project its military will everywhere on the planet during this period. Third, as a result of its economic and military dominance, the
United States became the center of world economic policy and world diplo-
macy after the war, a fact symbolized by the placement of the UN headquar-
ters in New York City.[4]

Because of the historically anomalous U.S. geopolitical global dominance
in the 1950s and 1960s, American corporations were able to expand their
markets, productivity, and profits at unprecedented rates. The proportion of

U.S. corporations' after-tax profits from overseas investments grew from 10 percent at the beginning of the 1950s to over 20 percent by the early 1970s. Stimulated by foreign profits, U.S. productive capacity in the 1960s grew at a record rate, *tripling* in that decade. This growth was made possible in large part by the capacity of American firms to dominate the other developed nations' markets through the Marshall Plan in Europe and the U.S. military occupation of postwar Japan, as well by the concomitant lack of international competition for U.S. markets.[5]

The rapid expansion of the American economy—the fabled "postwar boom"—gave elites new corporate and governmental tools to create and maintain social order. As Joel Krieger explains, "Growth meant that distributional decisions would be relatively consensual, since diverse constituencies could often be appeased. Class struggle seemed almost anachronistic as trade union elites routinely participated in the formulation of economic policy. Political conflict often seemed reduced to the problem of rational administration."[6] An early effort to develop this new "growth coalition" approach was General Motors' (GM) 1946 offer to the United Auto Workers (UAW) union of a new contract that promised workers increasing wages and benefits as long as GM's profits grew.[7] This contract between the United States' biggest corporation and biggest union, dubbed by the press "The Treaty of Detroit," defused the labor-management conflicts that had beset "Big Auto" and many other industries during the 1930s and early 1940s and were reemerging with a vengeance in 1946. Bolstered by soaring corporate profits, labor peace was achieved with relative ease in many other sectors of the economy as corporations and unions fashioned agreements patterned after the GM-UAW contract. Labor's willingness to enter into these contracts is all the more notable because 1946 was the year in which unions reached their high point in membership as a percentage of the workforce and exercised their muscle in a record number of strikes.

Government was also reshaped during the late 1940s and 1950s by the "growth coalition" strategy of appeasing diverse constituencies. The federal government adopted a host of social programs during the late 1940s and 1950s, fleshing out the skeletal welfare state that had been created by the New Deal policies of the 1930s. The unprecedented wage hikes (including increases in benefits, retirement funds, and social insurance programs), coupled with housing and educational subsidies of the GI Bill, transformed many Americans' understanding of the basic rules of society. In the 1930s and 1940s, social peace amounted to an uneasy truce and, sometimes, open warfare between capitalists and workers. By the late 1940s and early 1950s, the idea that everyone could get a piece of the American dream by cooperating with corporate America had become widely accepted. In 1957, a General Electric executive defended himself against federal antitrust charges by saying, "What's good for General Electric is good for America." In short, the idea of the middle class and cooperation with corporate America as the centerpiece of American society had become hegemonic. During the 1950s, the American dream of home ownership, college education, and disposable incomes to buy luxury items (symbolized by the 1950s' automobiles) became the sine qua non of being American.

This transformation of the social order was not accomplished smoothly. Those who resisted the logic of the middle-class order—especially workers in militant labor unions that did not trust the newfound corporate largesse—found the 1950s to be a time of frightening repression, both by the government through the McCarthy era anticommunist witch-hunts and by corporations, which aggressively sought to dislodge labor unions from their workplaces, especially during and after the recession of 1957.[8] By the mid-1950s, the class consciousness of America was markedly different than it had been even in 1946. Even a casual look at the 1930s and 1940s reveals open and intense conflict between workers and their employers, the phenomenal rise of the Congress of Industrial Unions, and widespread socialist and communist sympathies. During the early 1950s, class lines became blurred. Working-class militancy all but disappeared, driven underground by the carrot of improving wages, benefits and job security, private housing, and higher education, as well as by the stick of McCarthyism. Working-class consciousness was largely marginalized as a foreign ideology alien to American life as the idea of the middle class became hegemonic. Labor union membership began a fifty-year decline from which it has not yet recovered. Poverty—afflicting a quarter of the U.S. population—was forgotten.[9] The continuing system of Jim Crow racism was largely ignored by whites. A new generation of scholars proclaimed America to be the first modern society and declared the end of class conflict. Writing in 1955, the historian Richard Hofstadter opined, "[T]he jobless, distracted and bewildered men of 1933 have in the course of the years found substantial places in society for themselves, have become home owners, suburbanites, and solid citizens."[10]

The emergence of the middle class as the anchor of social stability was more pronounced in the United States than in the other most developed countries. The particularity of the United States among the advanced industrial nations lay in its global domination, coupled with the relative weakness of its labor parties, labor unions, and the welfare state, in conjunction with the relatively strong emphasis on property (home) ownership and individual achievement. By the end of the 1950s, American workers were, in the words of Mike Davis, "prisoners of the American Dream." As we shall see in chapter 7, this new middle-class social arrangement created an important opportunity for the civil rights movement to mount a successful campaign to end legal segregation. But the new middle-class order was not, as the prophets of modernity would have it, hostile to racism per se.[11] Indeed, the new arrangements were qualitatively stamped by the Jim Crow system of legal segregation. The fact that the middle-class order was largely reserved for whites as a matter of law and informal discriminatory practices has great significance for understanding the end of the Jim Crow system in the 1960s. For, as I will now discuss, the development of the new middle-class order in the 1950s made possible the new system of structured racism.

The Erosion of Jim Crow Racism in the 1940s and 1950s

The Jim Crow system was a form of racial segregation based on state power. In that era, the relationships between whites and nonwhites, which privileged the former and oppressed the latter, were secured by the power of the state. While private relations, such as employment, were also racialized informally, the principle guarantors of white privilege in this period were the courts and the police. Michael Omi and Howard Winant insightfully term the Jim Crow system a "racial dictatorship."[12] During the Jim Crow era, the law drew a color line through American society, on one side of which all people of color were disadvantaged relative to all whites, regardless of class, nationality, or color, in both important and petty ways.[13]

The slow death of Jim Crow racism began in the decade in which the system of legal segregation reached its greatest domination of the United States: the 1920s. At the end of World War I, cotton prices tumbled as the British flooded the world cotton market with cheap colonial Indian and Egyptian cotton. In the United States, King Cotton was dethroned. As the demand for U.S. cotton declined, hundreds of thousands of African Americans were expelled from the sharecropping system. The greatest internal migration in America's history began, lasting from the 1920s until the 1960s. At the beginning of the twentieth century, over 80 percent of African Americans lived in the rural South. By the 1960s, some 60 percent of African Americans lived in the urban North.[14] This restructuring of the U.S. economy and the growing urbanization of African Americans undercut the Jim Crow system, which had been predicated on the social arrangement in which African

Americans remained a rural, agricultural labor force in the cotton-growing South after the end of slavery.

The second blow to the Jim Crow system came from the growing domination of the U.S. economy by national corporations. The political and legal system that had been erected in the Jim Crow era was a loose federal system that relegated to each state the right to determine how it would regulate economic and social relations within its respective boundaries. In the decade before World War II, large corporations had begun marketing their products everywhere in the nation and were seeking to create a standardized national legal system to provide national markets with a consistent and stable legal environment. By the late 1930s, a legal movement had begun to incorporate the state laws under the U.S. Constitution to create a single legal system under a relatively centralized national government for the first time.[15] The incorporation cases of the 1930s did not focus on race relations, but they created favorable conditions for the historic legal challenges to racial segregation in the 1950s. The development of a legal infrastructure for national markets thus unintentionally put corporate power on a collision course with the Jim Crow system.

A third factor that set conditions for the destruction of the Jim Crow system arose from the new geopolitical position of the United States at the end of World War II. This new geopolitical dominance made the United States accountable to the world in a new way. As the self-designated "leader of the free world" in the Cold War, the United States was subject to intense criticism for the absence of basic democratic rights for U.S. citizens of color. The racial dictatorship in the United States was especially of concern in the 1950s for newly liberated African and Asian colonies, whose leaders were influenced by the Soviet Union and communist China's promises of equality and independence from imperialism. In order to bolster the United States' international influence, the federal government began to more aggressively challenge legal segregation on the basis of "national security interests." In 1947, Ernest Gross, the legal advisor to the U.S. Department of State, bluntly said, "[T]he United States has been embarrassed in the conduct of foreign relations by acts of discrimination taking place in this country."[16] This opinion found its way into ensuing U.S. government amicus curiae briefs, including in the landmark 1951 school desegregation case *Briggs v. Elliott*.[17]

Despite these growing pressures against white legal power in the United States, the Jim Crow system remained firmly entrenched in southern regional and national politics. In the South, the use of law to deny blacks the right to vote had produced a powerful white political machine, capable of dictating who was to be elected to office and giving elected officials virtually lifetime tenure to their position. The seniority system in Congress ensured

that Jim Crow members of Congress chaired most of the powerful commit-
tees of the legislative branch.[18] The entrenched power of southern politicians
also ensured them domination of both major political parties. The early architecture of the welfare state, created during the mid-1930s, bore the stamp
of Jim Crow racism because of the power of the white South. The New Deal
programs, while expanding the social welfare powers of the federal government, preserved and reinforced patterns of racial segregation. The Wagner
Act, for example, allowed unions to exclude people of color, and, by legaliz-
ing closed shops in segregated industries, made racial integration next to impossible. The National Housing Act of 1934 sought to encourage private
home buying by underwriting bank loans and by establishing the Federal
Housing Administration (FHA). As Jill Quadagno observes, "Until 1949 the
FHA . . . encouraged the use of restrictive covenants banning African Americans from given neighborhoods and refused to insure mortgages in integrated neighborhoods. Thanks to the FHA, no bank would insure loans in
the ghetto, and few African Americans could live outside it."[19] In short, even
though the U.S. political economy was changing, there is no reason to believe that the Jim Crow system was on its deathbed in the 1950s. Indeed, as
the 1950s and 1960s showed, nothing short of the massive insurrection by
the civil rights movement could have swept the Jim Crow system from the
stage of history. Even as southern whites rallied to the defense of the Jim
Crow system against what at first was a small and politically marginal black
protest movement, a new social relationship was beginning to take form in
the North and the West that shook the seemingly impregnable southern
politicians' grip on national power. This arrangement, with its own form of
racism, soon emerged as a powerful force undermining the Jim Crow system.

The rise of the middle-class social order during the 1950s was predicated
on a particular confluence of American geopolitical dominance, a rapidly expanding domestic economy, and the development of a welfare state. This
new arrangement involved a restructuring of class relations, it invoked a new
role for government in American society, and it ushered in a new location for
women in the home. It is not surprising, then, that the 1950s also ushered in
a new era of race relations, in which the mechanisms that supported white
privilege had to be, and were, reinvented.

Suburbanization and the Structuring
of Racial Privilege, 1945–1960

A snapshot of American cities in 1945 reveals the continuing salience of racism
and ethnic solidarity in American life. Social networks still largely revolved

around Little Italys, Jewish shtetls, Irish political machines and churches, and a host of East European communities.[20] Many whites identified themselves not as white or American, but as Italian, Jewish, Polish, Greek, or Irish. Black ghettoes and Mexican barrios were growing, new Chinese immigrants were beginning to reshape Chinatowns, and Native Americans were forming urban Indian communities.

The suburbs of the 1930s were by and large racially segregated, due to federal and local laws and discriminatory practices.[21] Surveying the scene in 1955, Charles Abrams wrote, "[T]housands of racially segregated neighborhoods were built, millions of people re-sorted on the basis of race, color, and class, the differences built in, from coast to coast."[22] The expanding economy and federal subsidies for mortgages created new opportunities for Americans to buy a private home. By the 1960s, the centerpiece of the new middle-class social order lay outside the cities, in massive suburban communities, where the vast majority of the 37 million new housing units were constructed in the decade and half after the end of World War II. Racially segregated welfare state programs, begun in the New Deal era and expanded in the 1950s, subsidized the development of the mass suburbs. The Veterans Administration and the FHA provided subsidized, low-interest mortgages, leading to a doubling of the number of privately owned homes between 1940 and 1960.[23] The FHA program was explicitly biased toward the suburbs and advocated the use of racially restrictive covenants to maintain the "social stability" of the new communities.[24] As a rule, only whites could qualify for loans to live in suburbs. Private developers, led by William Levitt, also practiced open racial discrimination in home sales in the new middle-class communities. Levitt put it bluntly, "I have come to know that if we sell one house to a Negro family, then 90 to 95 percent of our white customers will not buy into the community. . . . We can solve the housing problem or we can try to solve the racial problem, but we cannot combine the two."[25] Levitt's companies maintained their policy of selling only to whites until 1968. People of color who moved into white suburbs were typically greeted with hostility by residents and police alike.[26]

Explicit racial discrimination by developers, realtors, banks, government agencies, and individual home buyers revealed the widespread awareness of the importance of race in the suburbs: These new communities were seen from the beginning as privileged places whose residents were going to do whatever they could to improve the quality of their personal lives at the expense of urban America—that is, people of color. Given the existing racial inequalities created by hundreds of years of discrimination, preserving the suburbs as white communities served to reassure white home buyers that they were indeed escaping the cities into privileged places. Suburbs prior to the 1950s had often been places of class as well as racial privilege. Older suburbs were the prototypical "bedroom communities" for professional and managerial upper-middle-class salaried workers who commuted to offices in central cities. The suburbs developed in the 1950s had a different character: they consisted of mass-built and mass-marketed housing aimed at working-class Americans. In the New Jersey Levittown, for example, new homes were priced from $11,500 to $14,500.[27] In these settings, racial exclusivity was especially vital, for it provided the only assurance that white residents could live a more privileged existence than in the cities, which had a similar class composition to the new suburbs. The new suburban arrangement privileged middle-class whites as well as the rich, as the former could leave the cities and get the benefits of living in communities with a higher standard of living and insulation from the social problems of the poor. Indeed, as the suburbs attracted more jobs in the 1960s and 1970s, the racial privileges of suburban living were extended downward, with more working-class whites moving to these segregated communities to escape from the social costs of life in the increasingly poor and nonwhite cities.[28]

As the tens of millions of descendants of European immigrants left the central cities for the middle-class suburbs during the 1950s and 1960s, their ethnic affiliations were radically transformed and, often, destroyed. Gone were the ethnic neighborhoods, defined by their relationship to another nation, with ethnic ties maintained by a large network of community organizations. Gone were the non-English-language schools, churches, and newspapers. In their place arose a new middle-class culture, based on the private home, the car, and the mall. Many people surrendered their ethnicity entirely, rejecting the cultures of their immigrant parents or grandparents as "old-fashioned" in favor of "modern" living. Even those who held on to some aspects of their ethnicity experienced profound changes. The social life of the suburbs revolves so powerfully around the private worlds of the home and consumption that ethnicity comes to exist only as a vague notion of personal "values" or "identity" instead of the vibrant social life of the ethnic community. Ethnicity is built on a wide array of interconnected social institutions—extended families, religion, labor unions, business associations, social services, and cultural institutions. All these were missing from or radically transformed in the suburban communities.[29] The meaning of community took on more top-down, ritualistic, and organizationally defined and commodified forms, bereft of the possibilities for collective, autonomous action. Suburbanites found their social ties organized by corporations through work and consumption of goods and services (especially at the new malls), and "joined" organizations established by a host of institutions, ranging from parent-teacher associations and religious institutions to Little League to bowling leagues.[30] To the extent that middle-class suburbanites remained ethnically conscious, their relationship to ethnicity was increasingly voluntary and optional, unlike their parents and grandparents, for whom ethnicity had been essential for survival in the face of national and religious discrimination.[31]

The decline of European ethnic communities, either hailed as the triumph of the American dream or decried as a tragedy of modernity, did not by any means signify the declining importance of race for the new suburbanites. To the contrary, the mass suburbs of the 1950s became the sites for the perfection of whiteness and racial segregation. Where the Jim Crow system of segregation relied on law to keep the races separate in geographical areas that were somewhat integrated, the suburbs *structured* racial segregation into spatial arrangements in a more complete way. Legal housing discrimination by government and private developers enabled the suburban developers to guarantee new home buyers—often workers with modest incomes and no assets—the privileges of whiteness. People growing up in suburbs reported that virtually no people of color attended their schools or lived in their neighborhoods. Unlike city residents, many suburbanites could go through their days without ever seeing a person of color, except perhaps a maid or a gardener.[32] Gone were the racial ambiguities of the ethnic Euro-Americans, who might think of themselves as Italian or Jewish rather than as white. In ways that had not existed in urban areas stamped by European ethnicities, whiteness reigned supreme.[33]

Because the suburbs were usually separate entities within large, heterogeneous metropolitan areas, their formation transformed state and local politics. By claiming "local autonomy," residents of suburban communities could utilize their assets to benefit their own communities and to fight for upwardly redistributive policies (and against downwardly redistributive policies) for the expenditure of state and federal funds. All this could be accomplished under the rubric of "local community control" with no reference to the race and class composition of the communities benefiting from these policies. With the completion of the interstate highway system in the 1960s and 1970s, the suburbs developed an even greater degree of social influence as they began to attract jobs and corporate offices. With the shift from bedroom communities to sites of clusters of specialized services for large corporations (termed technopoles), the suburbs became the sites of massive proliferation of medium-priced housing, increasing the white flight from the cities.[34]

The dire consequences of the creation of white suburbs for people of color were soon apparent. The loss of jobs and higher-income residents rapidly sapped the tax base of the cities, setting the stage for the era of "fiscal austerity" that depleted public education, public health, and low-income housing programs in the 1970s.[35] The decline of manufacturing and the expansion of new high-technology industries in the white suburbs and in white regions of the Sunbelt negatively affected people of color's access to the new good paying jobs.[36] Even relatively modern cities like Los Angeles experienced this economic displacement as businesses relocated tens of thousands of jobs to the surrounding suburban counties.[37] Federal urban development policies in the 1960s accelerated this process, as millions of low-income families were displaced from their communities and further ghettoized in public housing projects to make way for the new federal highway system.[38] The racial impact of these policies was so blatant that in black communities the Urban Renewal Program was mockingly called the "Negro Removal Program." As well, the migration of higher-paying jobs from the cities to the suburbs placed people of color at a distinct disadvantage for accumulating wealth.[39] Most importantly, while property values for white home owners skyrocketed, the value of urban properties languished, especially in minority areas.[40]

The exclusion of minorities from the suburbs in the 1950s and their concomitant concentration in the cities thus produced not only greater spatial segregation, but also set the basis for a new politics and economics of racial inequality. With whites and minorities concentrated in different places (typically in different townships, counties, or other political entities), the competition over the distribution of scarce resources—jobs, political power, funding for education, social services, and housing—was now racialized in a new way. In the cities, different ethnic groups contended for power within the same governments. Racial privileges required explicit state sponsorship in the form of Jim Crow laws. In the new arrangement of the suburbs, state-sponsored segregation was no longer necessary to maintain white privilege. White privilege was now structured into the very fabric of American society in a new way: The mobilization of local community power became a powerful platform for the mobilization of racial privileges. The new white communities could now use their political influence and tax base to develop good jobs, schools, and public services, high-end stores, and rising property values without the use of legal racial barriers. The result was the creation of a new and powerful cycle of privilege: Children raised in suburban environments enjoyed significant material and cultural advantages (defined in institutional terms) over children raised in urban cores. In this sense, racial privileging took on an increasingly "private" and "local" character in the 1950s and 1960s, requiring less explicitly racial state action to keep it going.

Mass Educational Credentials
and the Structuring of Racial Privileges

The creation of mass public higher education in the postwar period was another important vehicle both for the development of the middle-class social order and the structuring of race into American society. For most of American history, higher education had been a largely private institution of, for, and by the upper classes. All this changed in the post–World War II era. In 1876, only 1.7 percent of the eighteen- to twenty-four-year-old population was in college; by 1970, the number of college students had grown to 53 percent of that age group. Between 1951 and 1961 alone, the number of students enrolled in institutions of higher education doubled, from 2 million to 4 million.[41] The postwar expansion of higher education set the basis for an even bigger leap in the next generation. The percent of high school graduates enrolling in college grew from 45 in 1960 to 67 percent by 1997.[42]

Appeals for taxpayer support for education were usually based on the claim that schools teach the important technical and scientific knowledge needed to make decisions in a modern, complex society. The function of education, it was argued, was to ensure that those with the most talent learned the skills they would need to gain access to the growing number of white-collar jobs.[43] The concept of "meritocracy"—the selection of the new professional and managerial elite on the basis of competence alone—was born in the 1950s.[44] With this idea, a paradox of democratic openness and elitism was firmly set in place: the new meritocracy was committed to shoving aside the old upper-class elites who had inherited their status along with their stock portfolios, and opening opportunities for entrance into the middle class for the sons and daughters of blue-collar workers. But, on the other hand, the meritocracy was also unabashedly elitist and looked to a future where society would be run by the "best and the brightest."

The transformation of higher education into a gateway to jobs had begun in the late nineteenth century with the restructuring of universities from upper-class finishing schools to research facilities run by professionals.[45] The further expansion of the professions in the New Deal era had set in place the idea that educational credentials were important gateways to a wide range of higher-status jobs. But until the 1940s, the professions that dominated the new universities remained small collections of largely upper-class practitioners.[46] The expansion of university-based professions, stimulated by the growth of the welfare state and corporate management structures, made higher education the gatekeeper not only to powerful and lucrative jobs, but eventually to middle-status managerial and technical positions as well.

Establishing higher education as the gatekeeper to the middle class was not simple, however. While university elites proclaimed this link to be essential, the reality of the relationship between education and occupational status in the 1950s and 1960s belied their claims. The process of making a college degree essential for access to the middle class took a generation to accomplish. As Margaret Weir notes, higher education was not as important for occupational success in the 1950s and 1960s as the leaders of higher education proclaimed. When a union journeyman construction worker still earned more than a college graduate, middle-class incomes were not necessarily earned at jobs that required a college degree.[47] As a result, the demand for college among the first-generation suburbanites remained relatively soft. As late as 1970, only 11 percent of the population aged twenty-five or over had completed four years of college.

Despite these limited returns on a college education, however, many suburban communities became identified with their schools: families in search of good schools began to move to suburbs, and the suburbs increasingly invested in their schools to boost property values. The GI Bill, with its guarantee of free college education to all veterans and their dependents, played an instrumental role in transforming higher education's role in the United States from one of confirming upper-class status on upper-class students to providing mass credentials to a large proportion of the middle class. During the 1940s and 1950s, the institution of higher education was radically transformed, with the sudden appearance of hundreds of state colleges and universities to meet (and create) the new demand. The GI Bill not only transformed American higher education, but it also created a strong case for workers to view educational resources as a way of securing access to higher-status professional and managerial jobs. The message that colleges were the gateways to good jobs was aggressively promoted by federal and state policy makers, suburban developers, teachers' unions, and university elites. Belief in education became central to the ideas of the middle class during this period. The expansion of educational expenditures was nothing short of staggering in the states with the highest concentrations of middle-class communities. In New York, one of the leaders of the public school movement, spending on primary and secondary education alone increased by nearly 400 percent between 1960 and 1972.[48] Similar increases in higher education rapidly expanded the public universities and colleges of the richest states.

The emerging support for public education spending had as much to do with race as with class. By creating all-white suburbs, federal policy and private employer practices made a strong case for educational credentials as well: If whites could fund their own school systems separately from urban schools, then creating a linkage between education and occupation would serve as a powerful guarantee of white privileges. The institutions of mass higher education of the 1940s and 1950s were unabashedly committed to the perpetuation of Anglo values and canons. Early pioneers of urban universities, including public institutions such as the City University of New York and private universities like the University of Chicago, had justified universities as important bastions of "civilization" against the dangers of a growing European ethnic immigrant population.[49] But in the 1950s, the ideology of meritocracy provided a new justification for colleges' offerings: now, it was claimed, education was an objective and neutral process of teaching rational knowledge to the best and the brightest.[50] However, what was termed "objective" was anything but, as history, literature, and the social sciences were largely taught with a complete disregard for the contributions of people of color within the United States and throughout the world. The faculty who taught the masses of middle-class students was overwhelmingly white and male. In short, out of an anxiety for the questionable status of their mass appeal, the public universities tried their hardest to emulate the model of the upper-class, private colleges.

The racial effects of mass higher education were significant. First, the idea that universities reward those who have the greatest academic potential ignored the fact that the large majority of African Americans, Latinos, and Native Americans were completely isolated from higher education in the post–World War II period. In 1940, only 1.6 percent of blacks aged twenty-five to twenty-nine had completed college; by 1960, the number was still abysmally low: 5.4 percent.[51] Latinos were similarly underrepresented in higher education. As George J. Sanchez notes of the 1940s:

[T]he segregation of Chicanos resulted from both residential segregation and the placement of Mexican students in separate facilities because, it was argued, of their language deficiencies. In addition, IQ testing in the 1920s and 1930s contributed to the belief held by educators that most Mexican children were "retarded," thus providing additional evidence to separate them from other students. Even when Chicano youngsters attended the same schools as Anglos, they were often separated into distinct classes for those deemed "slow" or those who could aspire to nothing more than vocational training.[52]

Even the African American college graduates and professionals at that time were not poised to begin the integration of the professions and corporate management. The majority of African American college graduates and professionals in the 1950s had attended institutions then called negro colleges, without which the numbers of nonwhite college graduates in the United States would have been negligible. Surveys of American professions in the postwar period reveal a pattern of virtual racial segregation. For example, while there were several thousand African American lawyers in the 1950s, the elite corporate firms remained virtually all white. As Erwin O. Smigel describes his findings from the late 1950s, "In the year and a half that was spent interviewing, I heard of only three Negroes who had been hired by large law firms. Two of these were women who did not meet the client. Applying the basic standards of the large offices, this is understandable. Few Negroes go to Ivy League preparatory schools or colleges. Few go to the eastern national law schools. So few Negroes are "eligible" for positions in these firms that the issue of employment is rarely raised."[53] As Smigel observes, the racial segregation of the legal profession no longer rested on the direct effects of legal segregation, but resulted from a well-articulated series of institutional barriers that began with education.

People of color faced many other obstacles to professional certification as well. Inherited racial inequalities in income and wealth played a major role in deterring minorities from the expensive educational process (measured in terms of lost wages as well as direct costs). While rates of poverty for African Americans and Latinos declined in the 1950s, the numbers of middle-class minorities remained small. Less than 15 percent of African Americans earned family incomes that were considered middle class in the 1950s. And the black middle class was saddled with many more expenditures than their white counterparts, such as the responsibility of caring for poorer relatives. Without some discretionary income, very few minority families could support their children through the many years of education necessary to achieve professional credentialing.[54]

A second racial effect of the development of mass higher education in the 1950s was that the minority middle classes remained for the most part educationally ghettoized in the 1950s. As Smigel notes about the Wall Street lawyers, access to elite professions required more than attendance in school: As access to higher education increased in the 1950s, a greater emphasis was put on "selectivity," which made the credentials of "good" schools especially important. What made a school "good"? Virtually all of the university builders agreed that a school's success could best be measured by the success of its graduates. But this begs the question as to whether graduates succeeded because of the content of the training they received in school or whether the school succeeded because of the elite character of its students and faculty.[55]

Despite their meritocratic claims, access to such "selective" schools was very much a matter of social ties and "preparatory" training in the "right" elementary and high schools. In this new arrangement, people of color were effectively walled off from the schools and social networks that were the increasingly important springboards to higher education. As well, the minute number of nonwhite faculty at American universities left people of color without mentors and role models. Thus, even though the racial educational gap as measured in years of schooling was beginning to close in the 1950s, a new barrier to minority access to stratified professions was emerging.

Third, the curriculum of higher education presented an important barrier to success for students of color. In the new mass credentialing environment of higher education, the content of the curriculum was claimed to be divorced from any class or race context in which the standards had been taken. Yet the content of the new university curriculum had been more or less consciously constructed on an elitist model. That is, the criteria for "quality education" were adopted by emulating the schools considered to be the "best." That these schools were also the most upper class, and white, was not seen as particularly relevant. But the inherent race and class biases of the new universities were overwhelmingly real, especially to the few minority "outsiders" who managed to stumble through the doors.[56]

The new system of educational credentialing that emerged in the 1950s was a central component of a new form of racial inequality. Unlike the old ethnic "machine" networks that connected European nationalities to specific industrial and governmental jobs (the Irish cop was a real phenomenon in many cities), the new professional networks were race and class specific without being ethnic. This is not to say that the ethnic jobs networks disappeared; they did not. But these networks were increasingly circumscribed in specific sectors, such as police and fire departments, construction and contracting, and some manufacturing and service-sector jobs.[57] The new linkage of educational credentials and professions eliminated many of these ethnic limitations. This can be seen, for example, in the gradual elimination of barriers to Jews in law, medicine, and business during this era.[58] Whereas the ethnic networks had been explicitly exclusive of "outsiders" through informal means, the new gateways and networks that provided access to elite positions were still explicitly exclusive, but through more formalized and structured mechanisms. People of color—including the large majority of middle-class minorities—simply lacked the "qualifications" to get in.

The subjective character of these "objective" screening mechanisms was recognized by middle-class people of color. A black woman manager reports, "There are all kinds of legal mechanisms that people say are objective, while it turns out to be all subjective. It is very discriminatory. . . . The problem with the 'objective' (hiring) process is that . . . people put down their own biases about how a response should be rated. It boils down to people's biases incorporated into an objective process."[59]

The development of meritocratic "qualifications" for jobs institutionalized both social capital and the qualities that Pierre Bourdieu terms "cultural capital."[60] The possession of the "right" social connections and the "right" modes of presentation became the essential preconditions to being "objectively qualified" in the credentialed society. The racial gap in the possession of these resources was due in large part to the ways in which racial discrimination had placed minorities in a context in which social networks and culture were developed, but in a very different setting. To say that people of color were (and are) disadvantaged in relationship to the social and cultural attributes that mark success in the credentialed society is not to say that they lack social networks and culture. But people of color, due to segregation and ethnic solidarity, did develop *different* social and cultural capitals than whites, a fact that became very significant in the struggle to desegregate higher education in the 1980s. In this sense, Melvin L. Oliver and Thomas M. Shapiro's important work on the reasons for and consequences of wealth disparities between whites and nonwhites needs to be extended further. In the new system of mass higher education, people of color became disadvantaged by the "lack" of the "proper" cultural and social network prerequisites for access to tracks leading to elite professions and managerial positions. It was these qualities that became institutionalized for success with the creation of mass higher education.

Conclusion: The Structuring of Race and the Middle-Class Social Order

The termination of the racial dictatorship during the 1960s—that is, the end of Jim Crow segregation—did not signify the end of racism in America. Rather, the new conditions after World War II made the racial dictatorship expendable in much of the United States without undermining the availability of white privileges. The Jim Crow system had taken its form in the specific context of the industrial revolution when the labor market itself was no guarantor of white privileges. "Free market" competition provided capitalists with an incentive to hire whoever would work for the lowest wages, regardless of race. State power, encoded in segregation laws, thus became the basis for the mobilization of white privileges. During the 1950s and 1960s, the restructuring of race relations took a new form in which the Jim Crow racial dictatorship was no longer necessary in order to maintain white privileges. In the emerging middle-class social order of the 1950s, racial privileges were mobilized through an intricate network of place, education, and jobs. The defense of white privilege no longer required the explicit racialization of state power. In the 1950s, it became possible to defend racial privileges by arguing for "local" control of schools or by defending the principle of neutral "merit" and "achievements." In the competition for political power, jobs, and status, whites enjoyed enormous advantages that came from the highly unequal inheritance of wealth from the past and greater access to good schools, housing, and jobs in the present, as well as virtually complete control over the gateways to institutional power, wealth, and prestige. In these ways, whites' continuing privileged access to resources was hidden from view and became simply the natural outcome of the selection of the best and the brightest.

The changing structure of race was mirrored in the changing forms of race consciousness. The consciousness of whiteness in the suburbs was very different than that of most white people during the Jim Crow era. Jim Crow consciousness was white supremacist, in which the assertion of genetic and moral superiority was necessary to bolster an otherwise unclear claim to racial privilege. Between 1950 and 1970, racial consciousness was fundamentally altered, with the percentage of whites who expressed explicit white supremacist views falling considerably.[61] But the decline in white supremacist ideology did not mean the end of racism. The deployment of racial privilege in the suburbs did not require an ideology of supremacy. Indeed, modern whiteness—that is, claims of racial privilege—requires the denial of the importance of race itself.[62] In a world where racial privilege is structured into everyday life, the best defense of racial privilege is to deny that it exists. This way, the recipients of privilege think of their opportunities as the creation of their own efforts and the system that gives them unequal access to these opportunities as fair and meritocratic. Although the dynamics of racial superiority and inferiority always make people of color into the "problem," the disappearance of white supremacy made it seem that only people of color lived in a racialized world, that whites were simply individuals, not occupants of a racial space of power and privilege.[63]

The form of racial privileging described here can be termed "structured racism." The distinction between the Jim Crow system and the system that emerged in the 1950s can be seen by contrasting the modes of mobilization of racial privileges in the two systems. In the Jim Crow era, racial privileges were principally mobilized through top-down state interventions; in the modern era, racial privileges were (and are) qualitatively more "embedded" in the social structure and are mobilized mainly by defending the existing institutionalized patterns of everyday life. The first analysis of racial structures was by Stokely Carmichael and Charles V. Hamilton in 1967, who observed embedded white privileges they referred to as "institutional racism."[64] But the process described here is much more than institutional racism: structural racism describes the multiplicity of ways in which racial privileges are secured through the mobilization of privileges inherited from the past, in combination with the reciprocal effects of institutional patterns of privileging, ultimately secured by the spatial segregation of whites in suburban communities. This social arrangement was only possible because of the special conditions created during the 1950s: the intersection of the postwar boom, the development of the welfare state, and the creation of mass institutions.

The expansion of secure jobs with benefits, backed by government-subsidized housing and education, enabled the mass middle-class social order to come into existence in a racial political and legal context. The arrangements that forged this new social order were still shaped by the continuing power of the Jim Crow system in the 1940s and 1950s. It is hardly surprising that this new arrangement, in the context of hundreds of years of racism, became racialized. The relationship between racial and class privileges supported one of the main features of the middle-class social order: the blurring of class lines. The new suburban arrangement privileged working-class whites as well as the rich, as the former could leave the cities and get the benefits of living in communities with a higher standard of living and insulation from the social problems of the poor. As the suburbs attracted more jobs in the 1960s and 1970s, the racial privileges of suburban living were extended downward, with more working-class whites moving to these segregated communities to escape from the social costs of life in the increasingly poor and nonwhite cities.[65] Similarly, as higher educational credentials became increasingly important for access to good jobs of any kind, the racial content of higher education extended the privilege of greater access to these credentials to lower-status whites, while minorities remained marginal in American universities.

The power that the middle-class social order exerts in the United States today should not be underestimated. As Jennifer L. Hochschild shows, the large majority of Americans continue to identify with the middle class and the aspirations of the American dream.[66] Alternative forms of conceptualization of the United States, such as those associated with militant working-class consciousness, are still relegated to the sidelines of American politics and culture. As we will see in the next three chapters, however, globalization is rapidly undercutting the stability of the middle-class social order in the United States. This crisis manifests itself in a deepening pessimism about the future and fear of the world outside the middle class itself. It also manifests itself in a romantic nostalgia for the "good ol' days," an image brilliantly exploited by Ronald Reagan. In short, most white Americans are meeting the challenges of social change in the era of globalization with defensive and reactionary claims to privileges formed during a historically anomalous moment in world history, one that is gone forever. It is this mind-set that is producing new and fertile conditions for the intensification of racism today. The middle-class crisis, and the use of racism to fend it off, is the subject of the next three chapters.

Notes

1. Justice Thurgood Marshall, dissent from *Bakke v. U.C. Regents* 438 U.S. 482 (1978).

2. Joel Krieger, *Reagan, Thatcher and the Politics of Decline* (New York: Oxford University Press, 1986), 18–19; Mike Davis, *Prisoners of the American Dream* (London: Verso, 1986), 181–201.

3. Howard Zinn, *Post-War America, 1945–1971* (Indianapolis, Ind.: Bobbs-Merrill, 1973).

4. The United States' superpower status today is superficially similar to that of the 1940s and 1960s, but there are significant differences due to the globalization of capital and markets in the 1970s to the present. See chapter 3 for a discussion of the new role of the United States in the global political economy.

5. Barry Bluestone and Bennett Harrison, *The De-industrialization of America* (New York: Basic, 1982), 114.

6. Krieger, *Reagan, Thatcher and the Politics of Decline*, 17.

7. Davis, *Prisoners of the American Dream*.

8. Davis, *Prisoners of the American Dream*, 127–135.

9. Allen J. Matusow, *The Unraveling of America: A History of Liberalism in the 1960s* (New York: Harper and Row, 1984), 10.

10. Richard Hofstadter, "The Pseudo-Conservative Revolt," in *The New American Right*, ed. Daniel Bell (New York: Criterion, 1955), 34.

11. The myth of the meritocratic and open middle class continues to be sowed in the twenty-first century. See Stephan Thernstrom and Abigail Thernstrom, *America in Black and White* (New York: Simon and Schuster, 1997).

12. Michael Omi and Howard Winant, *Racial Formation in the United States* (New York: Routledge, 1986).

13. While legal segregation became national law with the *Plessy v. Ferguson* ruling in 1896, many states had passed segregation statutes decades earlier. The first segregation laws appeared in the North as the industrial revolution took hold in the 1830s. See Derrick Bell, *Race, Racism and American Law*, 3rd ed. (Boston: Little, Brown, 1991), 530–537.

14. Nicholas Lemann, *The Promised Land* (New York: Knopf, 1991).

15. Henry J. Abraham, *Freedom and the Court: Civil Rights and Liberties in the United States*, 3rd ed. (New York: Oxford University Press, 1977).

16. Richard Kluger, *Simple Justice: The History of Brown v. Board of Education and Black America's Struggle for Equality* (New York: Knopf, 1976), 253.

17. The first such case was *Shelly v. Kramer*, 334 U.S. 1 (1948), the U.S. Supreme Court decision that struck down racial covenants, an important devise for maintaining housing segregation. See Kluger, *Simple Justice*, 323.

18. Robert A. Caro, *Lyndon Johnson: Master of the Senate* (New York: Knopf, 2002), especially chapter 3.

19. Jill Quadagno, *The Color of Welfare: How Racism Undermined the War on Poverty* (New York: Oxford University Press, 1994), 23–24.

20. Stephen Steinberg, *The Ethnic Myth: Race, Ethnicity and Class in America*, 3rd ed. (Boston: Beacon, 2001).

21. David L. Kirp, John P. Dwyer, and Larry A. Rosenthal, *Our Town: Race, Housing, and the Soul of Suburbia* (New Brunswick, N.J.: Rutgers University Press, 1995), 22.

22. Charles Abrams, *Forbidden Neighbors: A Study of Prejudice in Housing* (New York: Harper, 1955), cited by Kirp, Dwyer, and Rosenthal, *Our Town*, 26.

23. Kenneth T. Jackson, *Crabgrass Frontier: The Suburbanization of the United States* (New York: Oxford University Press, 1985).

24. Nancy A. Denton and Douglas S. Massey, *American Apartheid: Segregation and the Making of the Underclass* (Cambridge, Mass.: Harvard University Press, 1993), 53–55.

25. Quoted in David Halberstam, *The Fifties* (New York: Villard, 1993), 141.

26. Denton and Massey, *American Apartheid*, 67–74; Reginald Farley, "Black-White Residential Segregation: The Views of Myrdal in the 1940s and Trends of the 1980s," in *An American Dilemma Revisited: Race Relations in a Changing World*, ed. Obie Clayton Jr. (New York: Russell Sage Foundation, 1996), 49.

27. Herbert J. Gans, *The Levittowners: Ways of Life and Politics in a New Suburban Community* (New York: Pantheon, 1967), 6–7.

28. Denton and Massey, *American Apartheid*, 55.

29. Steinberg, *Ethnic Myth*, 44–74.

30. Robert D. Putnam, *Bowling Alone: The Collapse and Revival of American Community* (New York: Simon and Schuster, 2000). Putnam depicts the 1950s as the golden age of voluntary associations. But the reasons for this, and the quality of such "civic involvement," remain murky and contested by numerous critics.

31. Richard D. Alba, *Ethnic Identity: The Transformation of White America* (New Haven, Conn.: Yale University Press, 1990).

32. Wini Breines, *Young, White and Miserable: Growing up Female in the Fifties* (Boston: Beacon, 1992).

33. Matthew Frye Jacobson discusses the declining discrimination against European ethnics and the growing acceptance of their descendants as "white" as beginning with the end of open-door European immigration in 1924. While this is so, the qualitative completion of the process took place in the context of postwar suburbanization. See Matthew Frye Jacobson, *Whiteness of a Different Color: European Immigrants and the Alchemy of Race* (Cambridge, Mass.: Harvard University Press, 1998).

34. This development, however, accelerated the class differentiation of the suburbs, with implications for breaking down the white middle-class homogeneity of the suburbs in the 1990s. See chapter 4.

35. Roger E. Alcaly and David Mermelstein, *The Fiscal Crisis of American Cities: Essays on the Political Economy of Urban America with Special Reference to New York* (New York: Vintage, 1977).

36. Davis, *Prisoners of the American Dream*, 193–195.

37. Melvin L. Oliver, James H. Johnson Jr., and Walter C. Farrell Jr., "Anatomy of a Rebellion: A Political-Economic Analysis," in *Reading Rodney King/Reading Urban Uprising*, ed. Robert Gooding-Williams (New York: Routledge, 1993), 117–141.

38. Robert A. Caro, *The Power Broker: Robert Moses and the Fall of New York* (New York: Vintage, 1975).

39. Melvin L. Oliver and Thomas M. Shapiro, *Black Wealth, White Wealth* (New York: Routledge, 1997).

40. Walter L. Updegrave, "Race and Money," *Money* (December 1989): 155–172.

41. Nicholas Lemann, *The Big Test: The Secret History of the American Meritocracy* (New York: Farrar, Straus and Giroux, 1999), 85.

42. National Center for Educational Statistics, *Digest of Educational Statistics, 1998*, 203, table 183, as cited by Margaret Weir, "The American Middle Class and the Politics of Education," in *Social Contracts under Stress*, ed. Oliver Zunz, Leonard Schoppa, and Nobuhiro Hiwatari (New York: Russell Sage Foundation, 2002), 178–203.

43. Kingsley Davis and Wilbert E. Moore, *Some Principles of Stratification* (Indianapolis, Ind.: Bobbs-Merrill, 1963).

44. Michael Dunlop Young, *The Rise of the Meritocracy* (New Brunswick, N.J.: Transaction, 1994).

45. Magali Sarfatti Larson, *The Rise of Professionalism: A Sociological Analysis* (Berkeley: University of California Press, 1977).

46. Lemann, *Big Test*.

47. Weir, "American Middle Class."

48. Michael Usdan, "Elementary and Secondary Education," in *Governing New York State: The Rockefeller Years*, ed. Robert H. Connery and Gerald Benjamin (New York: Academy of Political Science, 1974), 225, cited in Weir, "American Middle Class."

49. Randall Collins, *The Credential Society* (New York: Academic, 1979), 123.

50. For a critique of law school education's meritocratic claims, see Randall Kennedy, "Training for Hierarchy," in *The Politics of Law*, ed. David Kairys (New York: Pantheon, 1982), 40–61. More generally, see Ivar E. Berg, *Education and Jobs: The Great Training Robbery* (New York: Praeger, 1970).

51. William G. Bowen and Derek Bok, *The Shape of the River: Long-Term Consequences of Considering Race in College and University Admissions* (Princeton, N.J.: Princeton University Press, 1998), 2.

52. George J. Sanchez, *Becoming Mexican American: Ethnicity, Culture, and Identity in Chicano Los Angeles* (New York: Oxford University Press, 1993), 259.

53. Erwin O. Smigel, *The Wall Street Lawyer* (Bloomington: Indiana University Press, 1964), 45.

54. A vivid account of these obstacles and the role of negro colleges as buffers for middle-class African Americans is provided in Juan Williams, *Thurgood Marshall: American Revolutionary* (New York: Times, 1998).

55. Collins, *Credential Society*.

56. Lemann, *Big Test*, 176.

57. Roger Waldinger, *Still the Promised City?: African Americans and New Immigrants in Postindustrial New York* (Cambridge, Mass.: Harvard University Press, 1996).

58. Richard L. Zweigenhaft and G. William Domhoff, *Diversity in the Power Elite* (New Haven, Conn.: Yale University Press, 1998).

59. Lois Benjamin, *The Black Elite* (Chicago: Nelson-Hall, 1991), 73.

60. Pierre Bourdieu, *Language and Symbolic Power* (Cambridge, Mass.: Harvard University Press, 1991).

61. Lawrence Bobo, "Group Conflict, Prejudice, and the Paradox of Contemporary Racial Attitudes," in *Eliminating Racism: Profiles in Controversy*, ed. Phyllis A. Katz and Dalmas A. Taylor (New York: Plenum, 1988), 85–114.

62. Joe R. Feagin and Hernán Vera, *White Racism: The Basics* (New York: Routledge, 1994), 135–161; Eduardo Bonilla-Silva, *White Supremacy and Racism in the Post–Civil Rights Era* (Boulder, Colo.: L. Rienner, 2001).

63. Bonilla-Silva develops a useful typology of the new ideological forms of "colorblind" racism. See Bonilla-Silva, *White Supremacy and Racism*.

64. Stokely Carmichael and Charles V. Hamilton, *Black Power: The Politics of Liberation in America* (New York: Random House, 1967).

65. Raymond S. Franklin, *Shadows of Race and Class* (Minneapolis: University of Minnesota Press, 1991).

66. Jennifer L. Hochschild, *Facing up to the American Dream* (Princeton, N.J.: Princeton University Press, 1995).

PART TWO

GLOBALIZATION AND RACISM

CHAPTER THREE

∾

Market Globalization
and Social Crisis

Racism is not a static relationship, but one that is constantly adapting to, and shaping, its social context. Efforts to mobilize racial (white) privileges arise in the context of specific economic, political, and cultural arrangements that change from time to time. We can ill afford ahistoric generalizations about racism. It is imperative to concretely describe the social factors that inform the motivation and capacities of those who seek to defend or enhance their racial privileges—as well as the social factors that inform the motivation and capacities of those who seek to oppose racial privileges.[1]

As we saw in chapter 2, the reorganization of American society into the middle-class social order in the 1950s and 1960s included the embedding of racial privileges into people's day-to-day patterns of interaction, that is, the structuring of racism. The civil rights movement gradually identified and combated many of these institutionalized forms of racial privileging during the 1960s and 1970s, and to some extent prevented the divide between people of color and whites from getting wider (see chapter 7). But the advent of the new dynamics of globalization in the 1980s began to destabilize the middle-class social order and intensified the deployment of racial and national privileges. Globalization, we shall see, motivates many whites to explore and unleash all of the potential forms of privilege that were built into the middle-class social order in the 1950s. Furthermore, globalization has undercut some of the civil rights movement's traditional means to resist the intensification of racism. In this chapter, I explore the development of a new stage in history and a new set of social dynamics that are associated with the rise of a new form of global

57

capitalism in the 1980s and 1990s. This analysis of market globalization will inform our inquiry into the dynamics of racism and antiracism in the United States today.

Globalization, Technology, and Markets

Global social interactions have always been features of human societies. Trade routes between far-flung corners of the world have existed for thousands of years.[2] The rise of capitalism qualitatively intensified global interactions by organizing them into market relationships. In the *Communist Manifesto*, Karl Marx and Friedrich Engels wrote of mid-nineteenth-century capitalism, "The bourgeoisie has through its exploitation of the world-market given a cosmopolitan character to production and consumption in every country. . . . In place of the old local and national seclusion and self-sufficiency, we have intercourse in every direction, universal interdependency of nations."[3]

In the course of the last 500 years, capitalism has organized most of humanity into the market system, either by enslaving people, transforming them into wage labor, or establishing trade relationships with them. By the twentieth century, there were few regions of the planet that had not been touched and transformed by the expanding network of markets and the exploitation of people that came with them. In this sense, capitalism has always been a global system—a point made by world-systems theorists.[4] The idea that globalization refers to something particular to the late twentieth and twenty-first centuries requires that we distinguish it from the general global character of capitalism.

Malcolm Waters, following Anthony Giddens, explains globalization as "a social process in which the constraints of geography on social and cultural arrangements recede and in which people become increasingly aware that they are receding."[5] Globalization specifically refers to the increasing capacity of people to rapidly (or instantly) interact with one another anywhere on the planet, to share and analyze information gathered globally, and to take a global perspective as a point of reference in their daily affairs. This new capacity has been enabled by the widespread availability of powerful computers, telecommunication devices, and inexpensive transportation. These new technologies have broadly affected human interactions in the past thirty years, as they have developed more applications and come into wider use.

The processes of globalization involve a host of new phenomena. The same goods and services are available virtually everywhere as the distribution of goods and services have become less expensive. Global markets have brought together producers and distributors all over the world. Florists in Minnesota must take into account the situations of tulip growers in Honduras; engineers' incomes in Silicon Valley depend on the demand for computers in China. Globalization has imparted an increasingly cosmopolitan character to all of the world's major cities, where global businesses and workforces from all over the world create and consume new global commodities and culture. Globalization has accelerated the mobility of people, with a new kind of transnational migrant living in two or three societies. Globalization has produced the cultural transformation of virtually every society as the Internet, global movies, and global popular music and fashions exert an influence on local cultures everywhere. These phenomena and many others have led a growing number of observers to postulate that we now live in a new epoch of world history.[6]

One of the most striking features of this new epoch is the aggressive advocacy of free market, laissez-faire policies by the world's leading financial and political institutions. According to neoliberals, the technologies that link together trade, production, investment capital, and labor have finally realized the long-promised efficacy of "free" markets.[7] Manuel Castells explains the economic impact of the new technology, "New information and communication technologies, based on micro-electronics, telecommunications and network-oriented computer software, have provided the infrastructure for this new economy, . . . [allowing] for unprecedented speed and complexity in the management of the economy. Thus, economic transactions and production are able to increase their size dramatically without hampering their connectivity."[8] The new means of communication and information processing provide the infrastructure a new type of versatile and dynamic economy. Policies and programs that enable capital to flow unfettered, to neoliberals, are justified as the best basis for rational decision making about the allocation of capital, goods, and labor in the interests of social utility.[9] Neoliberals, Robert Kuttner observes, claim that "because of the swiftness of innovation and information flows, government could not possibly improve on the inventiveness of entrepreneurship; government could only slow things down. Hence, government needed mainly to get out of the way."[10] From the neoliberal point of view, the creation of free markets requires governments to reduce or end the regulation of national industries, to allow free trade across national borders, and to end or sharply reduce social programs that interfere with private-market activities.[11]

Neoliberal ideology serves as the basis for investment strategies in both the less developed countries (LDCs) and the most developed countries (MDCs) of North America and Europe. The International Monetary Fund's (IMF) and

World Bank's structural adjustment programs have compelled a growing list of nations to conform to neoliberal policies (e.g., cuts in government expenditure, ending of subsidies, devaluation of currency, deregulation of exchange rates, end of price controls, and privatization of state monopolies) as the precondition to receive foreign investments. Between 1980 and 1990, World Bank structural adjustment loans increased from 7 to 187 in sixty countries.[12] Within the most developed regions, cooperative agreements, such as the European Community and the North American Free Trade Agreement (NAFTA), are implementing the neoliberal idea that free markets are the most effective mechanism for making economic decisions in the global era.

The neoliberals are mistaken to fetishize technology or market relations as engines of economic growth, because neither is as powerful as they would have us believe. Instead, powerful social actors always seek to appropriate market relations and new technologies to their interests. The most obvious problem with the ideology of "open markets" is that people, corporations, and governments do not create markets or engage in market behavior on anything like an equal basis. Vast inequalities in "market chances" tend to be enhanced by free markets, for the simple reason that those actors with the most capital have the greatest chances to accumulate even more capital, and governments with the most power have the greatest impact on market outcomes. Nowhere were the neoliberals' ideas of market globalization put into practice more vociferously than in postcommunist Russia, where (mostly American) advocates of "shock therapy" argued that the rapid conversion of state property into private property would lead ineluctably to democracy and prosperity. Similar projections of the salutary effects of free trade on Mexican society were made during the debate over NAFTA in 1994. Yet, the impact of the expansion of markets on both Russia and Mexico has been anything but positive. Both societies have plunged into deep crises (although different types of crises) in reaction to the new global and national market relationships.[13] Even more telling, the flow of capital into the core and away from the periphery in the global era has virtually removed entire regions from market relationships altogether. As Ankie Hoogvelt observes, most of sub-Saharan Africa has been excluded outright from the global markets, with resulting social crises of historic proportions.[14]

The debate over the neoliberal misconceptions of market relationships (and the human tragedies in Russia, Mexico, Indonesia, Brazil, Argentina, sub-Saharan Africa, and so on) raises a profoundly important sociological question: What is the actual relationship of markets to society as a whole? Karl Polanyi poses this question in *The Great Transformation*, a study of the relationship between government policy, social organization, and the rise of market relationships in eighteenth-century England.[15] In this seminal work, Polanyi argues that the commodification of land, labor, and money and the creation of market relations do not determine what happens to a society; rather, it is government policy and the organization of workers and capitalists into historically specific class formations that determine how land, labor, and money are commodified and how markets form. Polanyi's model is useful to assess the societal impact of market globalization today. Rather than looking at the ways in which market globalization is transforming society, Polanyi's model suggests that we look at the multiplicity of ways through which powerful social actors shape and respond to the forces of market globalization.

Like markets, the new technologies supporting globalization do not arise in a neutral social environment. As David F. Noble shows in his history of the industrial revolution, the choice of technologies and their social uses in that era were shaped and constrained by class forces, in which the profit motives of the capitalists typically had the greatest influence.[16] Globalization today is not driven by technology; it is driven by powerful actors situated to create and appropriate new technologies in their interests. Globalization thus principally takes place on terms set by large-scale financial investors: The new technologies have enabled capitalists to create highly mobile, global pools of finance capital that are coordinated through institutions such as the World Bank and the IMF, as well as through private commercial and investment banks. Computers, telecommunications, and cheap transportation have also enabled the decentralization of corporate administrative functions, and the technologies of microminiaturization have enabled the creation of decentralized and mobile production facilities.[17] The most significant impact of these new technological developments has been to give capital greater flexibility and freedom from political and social constraints on capitalists' profit-seeking activities.

Around the world, globalization is often seen as "Americanization." There is some truth to this. The United States is using its historically unique economic and military superpower position to try to hold the political and cultural center of the global economy at a time when global forms for regulating markets are very weak (see chapter 6). As well, globalization is accelerating the concentration of investments and trade *within* the most developed regions (Europe, North America, and Japan) and *away* from the LDCs, a trend Hoogvelt aptly terms the "involution" of capitalism.[18] As the main nexus of global capital, the United States has strengthened its role as the coordinating center for the global economy. But globalization is also creating global relationships and problems that cannot be regulated by one nation, no matter how much the United States claims otherwise. As well, the processes that are termed "global" are not only international, but also operate within *all* nations, including the United States. The image of "the United States" as the chief beneficiary of globalization is thus misleading: While the flow of global capital into the U.S. economy has grown enormously, the main benefits from this expansion have gone to a small portion of the U.S. population. Indeed, the problems of inequality and the curtailment of state power that globalization has produced are affecting people within the United States as well as around the world.

The emergent global capitalist economy is not "American" as much as it is transnational. It is true that American financial institutions and transnational corporations (TNCs) have led the transition to new global investment, marketing, and production arrangements. But in this sense, McDonald's or Hollywood studios are no longer "American" companies seeking to penetrate foreign markets. They are now global TNCs, usually just one component of vast global partnerships, that are just as concerned with business opportunities in China and France as they are in the United States. This shift can easily be seen through the medium of television. The most internationally syndicated television series of the 1980s was *Baywatch*, a thoroughly stereotypical (and racialized) "American" image exported to the world. The most watched show of 2000 around the world was the game show *Who Wants to Be a Millionaire?*—a truly transnational series originally produced in England and then produced simultaneously throughout the world in over a dozen languages. The shift from American export to global television is mirrored in the rise of TNCs in the movie industry, the recording industry, the fashion industry, the automobile industry, retail sales, computer manufacturing and servicing, telemarketing, and many other economic sectors.[19]

The fact that the globalization is shaped and directed by TNCs and Western governments does not deny, however, the profound significance of the transformations currently under way for all of humanity. While economic elites attempt to harness the new technologies to serve their interests, the beginnings of new global social relationships are appearing, relationships that exist separately from—and often in direct confrontation with—global capitalism. Through these global relationships, one of Marx's greatest insights is verified: While ruling classes attempt to shape and constrain technological change in their interests, advances in technology have a strong tendency to escape from their control and to create new social relationships and social problems they never intended or anticipated.[20] In this sense, it is accurate to refer to globalization as a stage in history.[21] The forces now being unleashed (albeit primarily by TNCs and global financial groups today) are transforming human relationships in profound ways from which there will be no turning back.

For now, globalization has given the wielders of capital the ability to exert significantly greater influence on the terms on which social order is negotiated within nations. In particular, globalization has given transnational capitalists greater capacity to dismantle social arrangements that constrain profitability. But global capitalists, while expanding markets, are not capable of—let alone now interested in—creating new social arrangements to meet people's needs. Consequently, globalization has created widespread and growing social crises, some of which threaten the very basis for social stability not only in the LDCs, but also in the MDCs. Moreover, globalization has undermined the capacity of political elites to respond to these crises. It is to a consideration of these dynamics as they affect the United States that I now turn.

Inequality and Market Globalization

Large corporations and banks have been the chief shapers of and beneficiaries of the new global technologies. The principle effects of globalization have been to reshape the division of labor and to increase the mobility of capital. Computers and telecommunications have revolutionized banking, enabling the creation of giant pools of capital from investors all over the earth. These technologies enable investors to quickly move capital to take advantage of new profitable conditions anywhere on the planet and to disinvest from less profitable ones. The creation of global finance capital has produced the biggest wave of conglomeration in history, as corporations frantically merge and form partnerships to create larger and larger pools of liquid investment capital.

The centralization of finance capital has also been accompanied by the decentralization of many corporate functions.[22] The decentralization of administration made possible by computers and telecommunications enables businesses to move their offices to find cheaper labor and lower taxes. Microminiaturization similarly enables manufacturers and service providers to quickly move their production facilities in search of lower wages and taxes. Americans seeking technical support from Microsoft have their questions answered by information technology service providers in the Philippines; consumer services for a host of TNCs are provided by Indian women, mainly in Bangalore. Software developers in India and the Philippines are paid annual salaries of $15,000 to $17,000, as compared to $70,000 to $90,000 for U.S. employees.[23]

One of market globalization's features is that capital is now in a position to compel workers and governments to make concessions by threatening to disinvest if investors do not get what they demand. These demands can be made at many levels. The World Bank and the IMF can use (and have repeatedly used) the threat of withholding capital investments to compel national governments to discard social protections for workers within their nation. Local businesses can threaten local government agencies that they will leave town if they do not get tax concessions, subsidized utilities, deregulation, and so on. Corporations can threaten labor unions that they will leave the United States and relocate offshore where workers are paid a tenth of their U.S. counterparts. The greater bargaining power of capital in relation to both workers and whole societies has dramatically depressed workers' wages and the social wage (health care, education, and benefits) available to workers in every society. Globalization has also produced a new division of labor, with an increasing number of high-paid administrative and technical positions for those managing the global economy, and a vast increase in low-paid service-sector jobs for those providing services for the managerial elites.[24]

As a result of capital's greater leverage, one of the most pronounced effects of market globalization is the rapid growth of income and wealth inequality, both within nations and globally. That is, the rich are getting richer and the poor are getting poorer at a rate never before seen in world history.[25] Large differences in incomes, wealth ownership, life expectancy, infant mortality rates, levels of education, and other indicators have long existed between the most and least developed nations, the product of centuries of colonialism and underdevelopment. Globalization is accelerating these inequalities, as well as the inequality between rich and poor within the LDCs. One of the effects of the growing concentration of capital in the MDCs is the creation of an international division of labor in which the terms of investment and trade are highly exploitative of the LDCs, accelerating the gap between the rich and the poor countries. As a result, the global gap between the richest and poorest people has rapidly widened. In 1800, the ratio of the per capita income of the richest fifth to the poorest fifth of the world's population was two to one. By 1945, the ratio was twenty to one. In 1975, the ratio had risen to forty to one.[26] The assets of the world's 358 richest individuals now exceed the combined incomes of 45 percent of the world's population.[27]

A similar trend toward growing inequality is taking place within the MDCs themselves. The United States, in particular, is experiencing the most rapid growth of income and wealth inequality in the nation's history. Figure 3.1 depicts the growing disparity in American family incomes utilizing the Gini coefficient.[28]

The stability of the inequality between the rich and the poor was maintained both by the expanding middle class and government programs that redistributed wealth downward from 1945 until 1975. Figure 3.1 shows the trend toward greater disparities in incomes that began accelerating in the mid-1970s and has been growing ever since. After thirty years of rising fam-

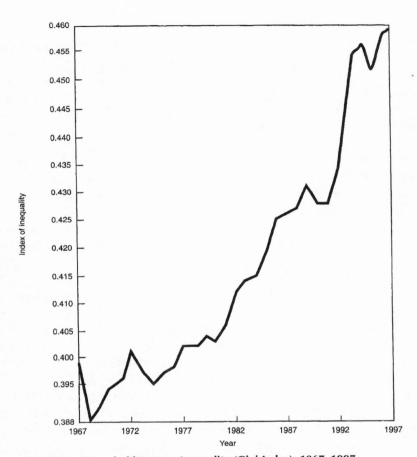

Figure 3.1   Household Income Inequality (Gini Index), 1967–1997

Source: U.S. Bureau of the Census, 1998. Reprinted with permission from Harold R. Kerbo, *Social Stratification and Inequality*, 4th ed., (New York: McGraw-Hill, 2000), 24.

ily incomes and living standards, the wages of the majority of American workers entered a period of real stagnation and even decline in the mid-1970s.[29] Paradoxically, the declining living standards of about two-thirds of the middle class has been accompanied by a rapidly expanding labor market, as corporations lay off full-time employees and recruit frightened and nonunionized workers for part-time or temporary full-time jobs with lower wages and no benefits or job security.[30]

The trend toward greater inequality arose at the moment when the modern phase of market globalization began to appear. By the 1970s, globalized businesses began to eclipse the old American-dominated multinational corporations.[31] The American domination of the post–World War II world came to an end in 1974–1975. The United States and Britain were unable to prevent the Organization of Petroleum Exporting Countries from challenging their historic domination of oil markets, with the resultant tripling of the price of oil. The other event of that year, the U.S. loss of the Vietnam War, signaled the end of the era when the United States could project its will everywhere in the world through military domination. This twin economic and military defeat, coupled with a sharp recession in 1974–1975, transformed American politics, turning elites and the middle class away from the hopeful assumptions of sustained economic growth that had been born in the post–World War II era. From this point on, the "haves" took an increasingly defensive posture, viewing all claims of the "have nots" on social resources with outright hostility and fear.[32]

In this new economy, rising corporate profits have generated enormous wealth for a small fraction of Americans. Indeed, the rich have gotten richer in the last twenty years than in any other period of American history.[33] During the period 1980 to 1995, U.S. corporate revenues increased by 129.5 percent. In 1965, the median Fortune 1,000 chief executive officer's salary was 44 times that of the average factory worker; in 1998, the median wage gap was 326 times.[34] The rich got even richer by investing in the stock market, as tax cuts for the rich in the United States and growing U.S. stock investments from overseas increased the value of stocks fourteenfold between 1980 and 2000.

But as the rich get richer, the poor are getting poorer. The new globalized economy is producing a new kind of poverty. While poverty rates today are comparable to that of the 1950s, there is increasing evidence that poverty in the United States is becoming more intractable. One reason is the rapid disappearance of entry-level jobs from the United States. Entry-level jobs were the back-breaking, low-paid positions at the bottom of industries that required little skill or experience. But, as tens of millions of European immigrants and some African Americans and Mexicans found in the late nineteenth and early to mid-twentieth centuries, these jobs led somewhere else. After working for a period of years on the factory floor, a worker had the potential to move up to a more skilled, higher-paying job. During the 1950s and 1960s, blue-collar workers' children even had a chance to move into managerial and professional jobs. As Gerald D. Suttles shows, the connections between low-skilled, low-paying jobs and better job possibilities made the European American communities of the early twentieth century into "ghettoes of hope."[35] But in the global economy, the vital linkages between low-paying jobs and the middle class have largely been severed. More than 43 million jobs in the United States were eliminated between 1979 and 1995, mostly steady, full-time jobs with benefits in the manufacturing sector.[36] Today, job expansion is most likely to be found in the low-skilled, labor-intensive service sector, where workers have few opportunities to move up because there are virtually no other steps on the job ladder. These jobs—typically low paying, part time, and offering no stability or benefits—have been aptly called "McJobs" after the megacorporation that pioneered the use of computers to control the labor force.[37] A new type of poverty has appeared in the inner cities, in which poor people find themselves cut off from entry-level jobs, stripped of government social services like health care and housing subsidies, and forced to endure horrific conditions in crumbling public schools, all under the mounting presence of police and prisons.[38]

The U.S. economy has become more bifurcated, between jobs that require little skill and education and those that require college or postgraduate degrees. As Margaret Weir shows, the linkage between education and income was greatly strengthened in the 1980s and 1990s, "The 'college premium,' the average amount a college graduate earns over a noncollege educated worker, was 31 percent in 1979. . . . By 1993, the college premium had grown to 53 percent. This difference was driven primarily by the decline of wages of less educated workers."[39] This trend indicates that opportunities to advance out of poverty through entry-level blue-collar work are dwindling; increasingly, the route out of poverty requires a college education and access to professional and managerial positions through formal certification. As a result, access to stable jobs with good pay is much more likely to be favorable to the children of the already educated middle and upper classes.

The other factor making poverty more intractable today is the drastic reduction of government services for low-income Americans. Government assistance for people in poverty was always paltry: In 1993, federal funding for poverty programs amounted to 1 percent of the federal budget, and 3.4 percent of the average state budget.[40] The principle of welfare—that government should provide a safety net to people in crisis—was repudiated with the passage of the Personal Responsibility Act in 1996. The new principle is that government assistance should be tied to ensuring that all able-bodied people must work as a condition for receiving assistance. The new "workfare" programs have already cut half of all welfare recipients off the rolls, as millions of poor people take dead-end, minimum-wage, low-skilled jobs. But, according to a study by the Urban Institute, the elimination of the safety net was expected to push 2.6 million more people into poverty by 2002. The large majority (some estimates are as high as 80 percent) of poor families are in danger of being left in deep and increasingly intractable poverty as they use up their five years of eligibility for federal and state assistance.[41] Drastic reductions of low-income housing subsidies, public health care, and education dollars are further widening the gap between the poor and the middle class.

Globalization is also putting great pressure on the middle class. About a third of this class experienced rising incomes and two-thirds felt the pressure of downward mobility during the 1980s and 1990s.[42] Those receiving higher incomes were mostly employed as professional and technical service providers for finance capital. Some middle-class workers saw a big boost to their fortunes, mostly from stock investments in the 1990s. But millions of middle-class Americans are now scrambling to maintain their standard of living by working more hours at pieced-together part-time jobs. In 1996, the typical married-couple family worked 247 more hours per year than in 1989—an increase of 6 weeks of work per family in just 7 years, and over 15 more weeks since 1979![43] Soaring housing prices in the 1980s and 1990s put the American dream of home ownership out of reach of most young middle-class families, with only a third now able to afford to buy a home.[44] The privatization of social services has added enormous bills to middle-class families' cost of living, while real wages for the median male worker fell 15 percent from 1979 to 1997. As government cuts public funding of education, health care, and retirement, middle-class families have tried to replace public with private services. The costs of private schooling, health insurance, and retirement accounts are draining more of the middle class's income. Desperate to shore up their living standard and unable to resist banks' aggressive marketing, a growing proportion of the middle class is staggering under enormous debt burdens. The default rate on credit cards and mortgages is now at a historic high point, with over a million new bankruptcies declared each year in the late 1990s, increasing 44 percent from 1994 to 1997 alone.[45]

The downward pressures on much of the middle class provide a fertile new ground for the intensification of racism, as whites seek to fend off the growing crisis by mobilizing any and all racial privileges available to them. The growing inequality produced by globalization thus is a new and important contributor to the intensification of racism today.

Globalization and Immigration

The increasing flow of capital around the world has been accompanied by the growing globalization of labor.[46] While the movement of large groups of people from one nation to another is certainly not a new phenomenon, the dislocations and relocations of people produced by market globalization have some distinctive features. Immigration today is taking on far more of a global character, bringing people from all over the world into the urban centers of the global economy. But immigration today also has a strange, counterintuitive character. In past epochs, immigrants left nations that were experiencing economic crises for nations that were experiencing rapid economic growth. In the era of globalization, Saskia Sassen observes, large-scale immigration tends to originate in countries with high levels of capital investment and new job creation, and the immigrants tend to enter nations with high levels of underemployment and declining living standards for many workers.[47] The new immigration is the product not of poverty or overpopulation, but of the process by which global capitalism is reorganizing labor and capital throughout the world.

The new patterns of immigration therefore reflect the pattern of global capital's investments. While many accounts of globalization focus on TNC investments in the developing world, most investments today are concentrated within the MDCs. Most of the foreign direct investment (FDI)—still only 8 percent of the gross world product—is concentrated in the MDCs. About 90 percent of the FDI is found in ten developed economies, and about two-thirds of it is in four countries (the United States, Germany, Japan, and the United Kingdom). As a consequence of this investment pattern, most immigration remains concentrated between nations that are closely linked economically or politically. While immigrants are coming to the United States from all over the world, the most notable feature of the new immigration is the growing numbers of people coming into the United States from within North America, and especially from Mexico. Mexicans today comprise 35 percent of all immigrants to the United States, and are a particularly proletarianized immigrant population, overwhelmingly found in the lowest-paid jobs in manufacturing, the service sector, mining, and agriculture. Some 1.5 million people legally cross the U.S.-Mexican border every day, making this the busiest border in the world.

As globalization has begun to reshape societies, the pace of international migration has accelerated. In the United States, immigrants now comprise over 8 percent of the population, proportionately less than the 14.8 percent of the U.S. population in 1910 born in another nation, but in absolute numbers the highest in U.S. history. The numbers of immigrants have been growing steadily since 1965. Family unification programs have brought millions of immigrants into the United States and Europe in the past thirty years. A large and growing number of temporary business and worker visas are granted by the developed countries each year. Tens of millions have moved overseas to work on the staffs of TNCs. The sheer volume of transborder daily commuting is also increasing, especially in Europe and in North America.[48] While immigrants are still a small fraction of the world labor force, their presence is growing primarily in the MDCs. In many European countries, immigrants comprise nearly 10 percent of the population; in Luxembourg, immigrants are now 34 percent of the population, and in Switzerland, 19 percent.[49] A notable feature of the new immigration is that the destination nations are mostly within the developed world, as are the nations from which people immigrate. Indeed, most of the movement of people today is within Europe and North America.

While in the nineteenth century those who were dislocated were usually poor, the new migration includes large numbers of professionals, scientists, and technicians who are compelled to follow global investment patterns in their areas of specialization. Some developing nations, especially English-speaking ones, are becoming producers of specialists for the developed world: India is producing a large percentage of the United States' computer specialists; the Philippines exports over half of its health professionals, mainly to the United States. India is particularly susceptible to this brain drain, as this giant country produces large numbers of English-speaking scientific and technical workers. Indeed, one-half of all "irreplaceable worker" visas granted by the United States now go to Indians.

Another quality of the new migration is the greater numbers of people who do not permanently leave their nation of birth when they emigrate, but instead develop a new set of relationships both to their nation of origin as well as the nation (or nations) to which they immigrate. Inexpensive transportation and communication is creating a new type of transnational migration: migrants find it much easier to return "home" periodically, to send money to bolster the "home" economy, and to stay in communication with their "home" nation's families and friends. The result is that hundreds of millions of people are today transnational migrants, moving between nations as well as developing a new relationship to the nation to which they immigrate. Indeed, transnational migration is reshaping many national economies. One-third of El Salvador's income arrives by mail from the United States. Transnational migration is increasingly linking families, communities, and whole societies in ongoing, global relationships. The new relationship between people and nations has been aptly termed "place polygamy" by Jürgen Habermas, as more people live between and outside of national societies.[50] Globalization is making the concept of "home" very complex indeed!

The new patterns of immigration reflect the inequalities of market globalization. The transformation of the financial centers of North America, Japan, and Europe into centers of the global economy has created a new and seemingly insatiable demand for immigrant service workers who clean the offices and staff the "back of the house" jobs in the hotels and restaurants that serve the global managers. Immigrants provide domestic labor as nannies, maids, and gardeners, and institutionalized labor as nurses' assistants, medical technicians, and orderlies in hospitals and nursing homes serving the global managers—the people Tom Wolfe sardonically called "masters of the universe." But the new immigrants are also entering high-pay jobs as doctors, nurses, computer engineers, telecommunications specialists, and research scientists, as the increasing centralization of science and technology compels the most highly trained strata to leave their country to advance in their professions.

The relationship between the economics of immigration and the politics of immigration is increasingly conflicted, as the governments of the MDCs seek to regulate the growing presence of immigrants by enacting harsh anti-immigrant policies. These policies, ostensibly meant to both restrict the flow of legal immigrants across borders and to track them within the nation's borders, achieve neither of these stated goals, but are much more successful at achieving two other, covert goals: the creation of a cheap, exploitable labor market and the deflection of middle-class fears from corporate and governmental causes of their problems. As globalization creates a growing demand for cheap labor and for the deflection of the crisis of the middle-class social order, a growing number of people are made "illegal aliens," forced to forge a relationship with the host nation on highly racially and nationally oppressed terms. Immigrants are often caught in the crosscurrents of the present period, in which the realities of the globalization of labor and the capacity of the nation-state to define territory and citizenship on a national basis collide. In this way, as will be discussed in chapter 5, globalization is creating conditions that intensify racism in the United States and in other MDCs.

Globalization and Nation-States

Globalization poses new challenges to the role of the nation-state in society. Capital's greater mobility has given businesses greater bargaining power with governments. Foreign trade and investments are a small but growing proportion of the world's economy. The growth of global production and trade networks has had a major impact on nation-states. A significant number of TNCs have assets larger than the gross domestic products of all but a handful of nations. Foreign exchange trading in the world's financial centers *each day* exceeds the total stock of foreign exchange reserves held by all governments.[51] Organizations like the World Bank and the IMF are able to direct investment capital flows sufficiently to have a real impact on state decision makers, especially in the LDCs. The growing pressure on government to provide businesses with the best climate for profitability of investments has gradually led to a restructuring of nation-states everywhere. As Peter Evans notes, "[A]ny state that engages in policies deemed 'unwise' by private financial traders will be punished as the value of its currency declines and its access to capital shrinks."[52] The IMF also pushes nations receiving loans to accept multilateral agreements on investments, which prevent national governments from regulating the activities of TNCs.[53]

Some observers have predicted that globalization spells the eclipse of the nation-state itself, as the operators of what Robert Reich calls "global webs" shed any allegiance to a single nation and its social needs in favor of the exigencies of global markets and production. The result, at its extreme, can be a process of "destatization," in which nation-states recede in importance and other forms emerge to organize territories. These forms are typically termed "ethnic" by global capitalists and displaced nation-state elites alike. Indeed, in some countries in eastern Europe and Africa particularly, one can see precisely this process of "devolution," in which fragmented territories develop a multitude of new ways to create collective identities. The breakup of Yugoslavia, for example, gave rise to Serbia, Croatia, Kosovo, and Macedonia; within different African nations, clan forms are becoming increasingly important bases of social organization. In Rwanda and Somalia, for example, clan leaders engage in competition for the mantle of "national elites" in order to attract foreign capital to benefit their clan. When President Bill Clinton ordered U.S. Marines to Somalia in 1994 to prevent the collapse of the national government, he discovered, to his dismay, that there was no national government left to save.[54]

But the processes of globalization do not typically lead to the evaporation of state authority. To the contrary, Evans observes, "a look at the nations that have been the most economically successful over the last thirty years suggests that high stateness may even be a competitive advantage in a globalized economy."[55] As we have already seen, globalization has concentrated capital within those regions with the most developed nation-states. Even among LDCs, economies grew fastest in the Pacific Rim nations that had highly developed nation-states. Why is this? Globalization poses two challenges that require strong states to manage. First, global financial, trade, and production relations require a great deal of rule making and organization. The problem for TNCs is that there is at present very little legal or political architecture for the global economy. As a result, the creation of a stable environment for global investments is primarily in the hands of the nation-states of the world's dominant economies. As Waters notes, the scaffolding for the global economy is created by nation-states through the medium of international accords (see chapter 6).[56]

Second, the increasing capacity of global capitalism to make demands on nations to deregulate business and terminate state programs that redistribute wealth and/or power downward requires the creation of new state forms to maintain social order. At this stage of world history, societies are still organized on a "national" basis, and the maintenance of social order—essential to the continuing stability of capitalism itself—requires nation-states to maintain that social order.[57]

This clash between nationally organized societies and the dynamics of globalization is an increasingly important feature of this era, as two worlds (literally) collide. As Sassen puts it, "The global economy materializes in a worldwide grid of strategic places, from export-processing zones to major international business and financial centers. We can think of this global grid as constituting a new economic geography of centrality, one that cuts across national boundaries and across the old North-South divide. It signals the emergence of a parallel political geography of power, a transnational space for the formation of new claims by global capital."[58]

This "parallel" transnational space is today primarily forged by market relationships. But, as Polanyi foreshadows, the new global grid cannot produce social order; indeed, the global market relations undermine preexisting national social orders, both by increasing inequality and by undermining the capacity of nation-states to regulate businesses and create social programs to stabilize societies by redistributing wealth and power downward. National political elites, then, must attempt to fill a crucial space in the clash between global markets and national societies, both to maintain their own power and to stabilize societies in this period of rapid change.

In the MDCs, state builders' response to market pressures has led to the gradual abandonment of the welfare state model. The welfare state was created by economic expansion and supported the "growth coalition" politics discussed in chapter 2. The basic philosophy of the welfare state was that state intervention was necessary to correct market excesses in two specific areas: first, the tendency toward monopoly required state regulation of business activities. Second, the tendency toward increasing inequality required state intervention to redistribute income downward, both to maintain social order and to increase consumer spending.[59] Under the pressures of globalization, however, a new "ideal type" of state is now emerging in virtually all the developed societies, especially in the United States and Great Britain, the nations with historically weak welfare states. The new "type" of state, the private investment state, is based on the following propositions:

1. The deregulation of markets and businesses, in global trade, monopoly practices, environmental pollution, work conditions, and so on, will enhance economic growth.

2. The curtailment of income, corporate, and estate taxes on businesses and wealthy individuals will stimulate new investments and, hence, economic growth.

3. Replacement of redistributive programs aimed at social welfare with government support for personal capital investments (making each individual responsible for his or her personal welfare by saving money to pay for private health care, education, and retirement) thereby will increase productivity.[60]

4. Increasing reliance on the use of repressive force—the military, the police, and prisons—is necessary to maintain social order and to "manage" those without a stake in the global economy.

In the private investment state, the idea that government will guarantee the welfare of all citizens is gone. In this new state system, people get what they pay for. As Jill Quadagno explains, "At the core of this [new state] is the premise that human society consists of a series of market-like relations, that individuals have natural rights to freedom and property, and that the primary role of the state should be to enforce only those rules necessary for reconciling conflicts over individual rights."[61] The state's increasing reliance on police powers and military action follows from this logic. Those who live by accumulating assets must be protected from those who cannot, both within the nation and internationally. Consequently, the only growing sector of public "services" is the criminal justice system in all its forms—criminal law, police, criminal courts, prisons, probation, and so on. Indeed, other public services, especially education and public health, are being drastically impacted by the expansion of the repressive state apparatuses.

The repressive capacity of the state is expanding rapidly through the deployment of new technologies allowing for a much greater degree of control of people within its territories. This can be seen especially in the efforts to regulate immigration and the tracking of noncitizens within a nation. The fact that states can technically monitor and regulate the flow of humanity across and within their borders (a recent development of history, to be sure) opens up enormous new possibilities for anti-immigration policies and the repression of the rapidly growing number of noncitizens.[62]

The private investment welfare state may have become the new model for the organization of government's relationship to American and British society. But, as state builders are all too aware, globalization is creating social crisis, as work gets harder, as the poor get poorer, as the middle class is fractured, and as immigration increases. The maintenance of social order within nations is getting more difficult to manage as the global dynamics assert themselves, and nation-state elites have less resources with which to work. In this way, too, globalization creates conditions supportive of the intensification of racism in the United States.

The Destabilization of the Middle-Class Social Order

Globalization's disequalizing effects and the restructuring of the state have potentially large consequences for the stability of the United States' social order. As we saw in chapter 2, the growth in full-time jobs with benefits and the expansion of the welfare state enabled the creation of a stable middle-class social order in the 1950s. This arrangement was based on five premises:

1. Rapid domestic economic growth fueled by the U.S. geopolitical domination of the world
2. The expanding chances for working American men to get a full-time job with benefits that paid a "family wage"
3. The growing availability of private home ownership
4. Expanding access to a college education
5. Government repression of working-class politics that could challenge this new arrangement

As standards of living rose, as the percentage of Americans owning their own home doubled, as colleges were transformed from elite to mass credentialing institutions, and as McCarthyism drove the organized left underground, most Americans became convinced that "the system" works well for everyone. The "progrowth coalition" political architects of the welfare state even offered those left out of the middle-class arrangement—meaning most people of color—room at the table, at least once they demanded it with insurrections and protests (see chapter 7).

The socially disorganizing effects of market globalization are being felt throughout the world, in both the LDCs and the MDCs. Globalization has already significantly eroded the basis on which the middle-class social order was erected in the United States. Much of the middle class is experiencing a declining standard of living, not so much through falling wages as in the rising cost of housing and the growing number of services (especially education and health care) that people must privately purchase, requiring them to work more hours. Home ownership is already out of reach of a growing number of young families. The proportion of people aged eighteen to twenty-four attending college is falling. Government programs for the middle class—especially education and health care—have declined in quality, further promoting the rush to private schools and medical plans.

Even those of the middle class who are not experiencing downward mobility are feeling what Barbara Ehrenreich terms the "fear of falling." The optimism of the post–World War II boom is now just a nostalgic memory, despite Ronald Reagan's best efforts to keep it alive. The progrowth coalition's assumption that the poor and people of color generally can be promised greater access to jobs, housing, and education with little political cost is no longer politically viable. Since the advent of globalization in the mid-1970s, American politics has increasingly become a war of the "haves" to safeguard their interests from the claims of the "have nots." This defensive mentality is physically embodied in the gated communities of the middle class, the new form of architecture that has emerged during the global era.

The destabilization of the middle-class social order does not mean that most Americans are abandoning the ideology of the middle class, especially the dreams of private home ownership and college graduation. They aren't.[63] But to be middle class today is to experience an anxiety and a defensiveness that is very different from the optimism of the golden age of the middle-class social order from the 1950s to the 1970s. Furthermore, a growing number of people are experiencing an intransigent form of structured poverty, in which thoughts of becoming middle class are becoming distant pipe dreams that are not particularly relevant to the daily struggle for survival.[64] For many Americans, the idea that working hard, owning a home, and going to college secures the good life seems less believable. In short, the idea of the middle class is losing its ability to organize and justify social order in the United States.

This crisis in confidence in the American middle class poses serious challenges to political elites. The maintenance of social stability requires mechanisms for social integration, and the ones that worked so well for the past half century appear to be in serious trouble. Even worse, political elites must confront the potential for political and social destabilization with far fewer resources at their disposal than they had available during the post–World War II boom era. Globalization has created a serious dilemma for both political and economic elites: By pursuing policies that expand global trade, investments, and production, political elites are jeopardizing the social stability that is the sine qua non of profitability for capitalism. How, then, will political elites manage this growing contradiction?

The dominant politics of this era has been to galvanize and appeal to white middle-class voters' fear of falling. From anti-immigrant policies to attacks on civil rights policies such as affirmative action, to a high-profile war on drugs, to the expansion of prisons and the use of the death penalty, to the war on terrorism, politicians have become highly skilled at creating dangerous foes to attack and contain. This mounting list of undesirables—immigrants, "unqualified" people of color, terrorists, drug users, and criminals—serves up an ever-expanding list of immoral "others" to whom the frightened middle class can attach its fear.[65] As criminologists ever since Emile Durkheim have noted, wars on crime create "the good" people and values by sanctioning "the bad."[66] The creation of fear of criminals has done wonders to shore up the ideology of the middle class as the honest, hard-working center of American society. The claim that immigrants are taking away "our" jobs and using "our" social services has also worked to shore up national unity and to provide a convenient explanation of the declining standards of living of much of the middle class. A never-ending war on terrorism, against an enemy that is everywhere, offers undreamed-of possibilities to the political merchants of fear.

In short, as globalization leaves national elites with less capacity to redistribute scarce social resources downward to maintain social order, the politics of maintaining social order become increasingly symbolic and repressive. Antonio Gramsci observes the limits of repression and symbolism for the maintenance of social order that were apparent in prefascist Italy, "If the ruling class has lost its consensus, i.e. is no longer 'leading,' but only 'dominant,' exercising coercive force alone, this means precisely that the great masses have become detached from their traditional ideologies, and no longer believe what they used to previously believe, etc. The crisis consists precisely in the fact that the old is dying and the new cannot be born; in this interregnum a great variety of morbid symptoms appear."[67]

The global era's pressures means that an increasing number of Americans feel left out of the social order (i.e., denied access to stable jobs, home ownership, and college education). More Americans now expect little from the government other than continuing growth of the criminal justice system, as public education, public health, and other social benefits deteriorate. Morbid symptoms, especially racism and fear of foreigners, have appeared. In short, globalization is producing a crisis in the middle-class social order.

As Americans begin to question whether or not they can achieve the goals of the middle class, new political and ideological spaces will open up. On the one hand, political elites and privileged sections of the middle and upper classes, mobilizing and mobilized by fear, seek to defend their wealth, power, and status against the crisis by any means necessary. These means include the intensification of racism and national chauvinism, as well as a willingness to restrict democracy (see chapters 4 and 5). The other form of politics that can be expected to emerge with the destabilization of the middle-class order is one of hope: efforts to make globalization more equitable and just and to recognize humanity's growing interdependence. The movement for global justice will emerge out of a wide variety of social situations, ranging from environmentalists and feminists, to ethnic communities and organized labor. This impulse has already been dramatically manifested at each of the semiannual meetings of the IMF, beginning with the protests in Seattle in 1999, and continuing in Melbourne, Quebec, Prague, and Genoa (see chapters 6 and 7).

In sum, the inequalities and limitations imposed on nation-states by globalization opens up new political spaces to both the left and the right in the search for new bases for social order. There is no a priori reason to predict that one model will automatically achieve hegemony over another. The creation of social order is primarily a historical, not a theoretical process. We live in a period of social and political flux born precisely by the erosion of the middle-class order that was hegemonic in the developed nations throughout the 1950s to the 1980s. As Gramsci said of his time, we now live in an era where the old ways are dying, but the new have not yet been born. In many ways, the most significant feature of the global era is the search for a stable basis for social order in the new conditions imposed by global capital.

Conclusion: Globalization and Racism

The mobilization of racial privilege today takes place in a qualitatively different setting than that of the Jim Crow era or before. As we saw in chapter 2, racial privileges were structured into everyday social life and institutional arrangements during the 1950s and 1960s, particularly through the advent of mass suburbs and mass higher education. An analysis of race today must take into account the new forms and new contexts through which racial privileges can be and often are asserted. In this way, the analysis of the impact of globalization on race relations in the United States must both address the new dynamics of globalization and the structured forms of racial privileging created during the 1950s. The tendency toward inequality and repression in the present era provides a powerful impetus for both racial and ethnic responses to globalization. The disequalizing pressures, the reduction of scope of civic society, the growth of immigration, and concomitant politics of fear described here resonate in specific ways with race relations in the United States. The following two chapters, based on this analysis of globalization, examine race relations in the United States today.

Notes

1. An excellent example of a historical analysis using this methodology is Tomás Almaguer, *Racial Fault Lines* (Berkeley: University of California Press, 1994).

2. Jared Diamond, *Guns, Germs, and Steel* (New York: Norton, 1999).

3. Karl Marx and Friedrich Engels, "Manifesto of the Communist Party," in *Selected Works in One Volume* (New York: International, 1974), 38–39.

4. Christopher Chase-Dunn, *Global Formation: Structures of the World-Economy* (Cambridge, Mass.: Blackwell, 1989).

5. Malcolm Waters, *Globalization* (London: Routledge, 1995), 3.

6. Manuel Castells, *The Rise of the Network Society* (Malden, Mass.: Blackwell, 1996).

7. For a useful overview of the neoliberal free trade arguments and their critiques, see Robert K. Schaeffer, *Understanding Globalization* (Lanham, Md.: Rowman & Littlefield, 1997), 182–216.

8. Manuel Castells, "Information, Technology and Global Capitalism," in *Global Capitalism*, ed. Will Hutton and Anthony Giddens (New York: The New Press, 2000), 52.

9. Charles E. Lindblom, *The Market System* (New Haven, Conn.: Yale University Press, 2001).

10. Robert Kuttner, "The Role of Government in the Global Economy," in *Global Capitalism*, ed. Will Hutton and Anthony Giddens (New York: The New Press, 2000), 151.

11. Bob Milward, "What Is Structural Adjustment?" in *Structural Adjustment Theory, Practice and Impacts*, ed. Giles Mohan et al. (London: Routledge, 2000), 33.

12. Ankie Hoogvelt, *Globalization and the Postcolonial World: The New Political Economy of Development*, 2nd ed. (Baltimore, Md.: Johns Hopkins University Press, 2001), 181.

13. The various kinds of crises wrought by structural adjustment programs are analyzed in Giles Mohan et al., eds., *Structural Adjustment Theory, Practice and Impacts* (London: Routledge, 2000).

14. Hoogvelt, *Globalization and the Postcolonial World*, 173–196.

15. Karl Polanyi, *The Great Transformation* (Boston: Beacon, 1944). For an application of Polanyi's model to analyze the impact of globalization of postcommunist Russia, see Michael Burawoy, "The Great Involution: Russia's Response to the Market" (Sociology Department, University of California at Berkeley, unpublished manuscript, 1999).

16. David F. Noble, *America by Design* (New York: Knopf, 1977).

17. Harry Braverman, *Labor and Monopoly Capital* (New York: Monthly Review, 1975), is the classic and brilliant study of the appropriation of computer technology by corporations to increase the rate of exploitation of labor.

18. Hoogvelt, *Globalization and the Postcolonial World*, 67–93.

19. The ambiguities of "Americanization" are explored by Polly Toynbee, "Who's Afraid of Global Culture?" in *Global Capitalism*, ed. Will Hutton and Anthony Giddens (New York: The New Press, 2000), 191–212.

20. Karl Marx, "Preface to *A Contribution to the Critique of Political Economy*," in *Selected Works in One Volume*, by Karl Marx and Friedrich Engels (New York: International, 1974), 181–185.

21. Michael Hardt and Antonio Negri, *Empire* (Cambridge, Mass.: Harvard University Press, 2000), especially xv.

22. Saskia Sassen, *Globalization and Its Discontents* (New York: The New Press, 1998), xxii.

23. Ted Tan, "Why Asia Can Be a Good Call Center Hub," *Times of London*, 6 August 2002; Geri Gantman "Philippines Offshore Outsourcing: The Next India?" *Business Times of Singapore*, 23 August 2002; Andrew Diederich, "Offshore Shores up IT," *Philippine Daily Inquirer*, 15 April 2002.

24. Sassen, *Globalization and Its Discontents*, 45–49.

25. York W. Bradshaw and Michael Wallace, *Global Inequalities* (Thousand Oaks, Calif.: Pine Forge, 1996).

26. Waters, *Globalization*, 71.

27. Jeff Faux and Larry Mishel, "Inequality and the Global Economy," in *Global Capitalism*, ed. Will Hutton and Anthony Giddens (New York: The New Press, 2000), 93.

28. Harold R. Kerbo, *Social Stratification and Inequality*, 3rd ed. (New York: McGraw-Hill, 1996), 24, figure 2-1.

29. Frank Levy, *Dollars and Dreams: The Changing American Income Distribution* (New York: Norton, 1988), 78–82.

30. Holly Sklar, *Chaos or Community?: Seeking Solutions, Not Scapegoats for Bad Economics* (Boston: South End, 1995); Kevin Phillips, *The Politics of Rich and Poor* (New York: Random House, 1990).

31. Richard Gilpin, *The Political Economy of International Relations* (Princeton, N.J.: Princeton University Press, 1987), 256.

32. Joel Krieger, *Reagan, Thatcher and the Politics of Decline* (New York: Oxford University Press, 1986).

33. Sheldon Danziger and Peter Gottschalk, *America Unequal* (Cambridge, Mass.: Harvard University Press, 1995), 33–66.

34. Jennifer Reingold, Richard A. Melcher, and Gary McWilliams, "Executive Pay," *Business Week*, 20 April 1998, 64–70.

35. Gerald D. Suttles, *The Social Order of the Slum* (Chicago: University of Chicago Press, 1970).

36. Louis Uchitelle and N. R. Kleinfeld, "On the Battlefields of Business, Millions of Casualties," *New York Times*, 3 March 1996, 1, 26.

37. George Ritzer, *The McDonaldization of Society* (Thousand Oaks, Calif.: Pine Forge, 2000).

38. William Julius Wilson, *The Truly Disadvantaged: The Inner City, the Underclass and Public Policy* (Chicago: University of Chicago Press, 1987).

39. Margaret Weir, "The American Middle Class and the Politics of Education," in *Social Contracts under Stress*, ed. Oliver Zunz, Leonard Schoppa, and Nobuhiro Hiwatari (New York: Russell Sage Foundation, 2002), 178–203.

40. Valdas Anelauskas, *Discovering America As It Is* (Atlanta, Ga.: Clarity, 1999), 330.

41. Randy Albeda, "Farewell to Welfare, But Not to Poverty," *Dollars and Sense* (November–December 1996): 16–19; Tracy Kaufman, *Out of Reach: Can America Pay the Rent?* (Washington, D.C.: National Low-Income Housing Coalition, 1996).

42. Mike Davis, *Prisoners of the American Dream* (London: Verso, 1986), looks at the decomposition of the middle class. This trend was first described by Richard Parker, *The Myth of the Middle Class* (New York: Harper and Row, 1972); see also Katherine S. Newman, *Falling from Grace: Downward Mobility in the Age of Affluence* (Berkeley: University of California Press, 1988).

43. Lawrence Mishel, Jared Bernstein, and John Schmitt, *The State of Working America, 1998–1999* (Washington, D.C.: Economic Policy Institute, 1999), cited in Anelauskas, *Discovering America As It Is*, 73.

44. Anelauskas, *Discovering America As It Is*, 212.

45. Peter T. Kilborn, "Mired in Debt and Seeking a Path Out," *New York Times*, 1 April 2001, 1, 16.

46. Nigel Harris, *The New Untouchables: Immigration and the New World Order* (London: Penguin, 1995); Saskia Sassen, *The Mobility of Capital and Labor: A Study in International Investment and Labor Flow* (Cambridge: Cambridge University Press, 1988).

47. Sassen, *Globalization and Its Discontents*, 40–41.

48. Harris, *New Untouchables*, 13–15.

49. Saskia Sassen, *Guests and Aliens* (New York: The New Press, 1999), 161, table 1.

50. Jürgen Habermas, *The Structural Transformation of the Public Sphere: An Inquiry into a Category of Bourgeois Society* (Cambridge: MIT Press, 1989).

51. Vincent Cable, "The Diminished Nation-State: A Study in the Loss of Economic Power," *Daedalus* 124 (Spring 1995): 27, as cited in Peter Evans, "The Eclipse of the State?: Reflections on Stateness in an Era of Globalization," *World Politics* 50 (October 1997): 67.

52. Evans, "Eclipse of the State?"

53. Hoogvelt, *Globalization and the Postcolonial World*, 149.

54. Bradshaw and Wallace, *Global Inequalities*, 75–79.

55. Evans, "Eclipse of the State?" 68.

56. Waters, *Globalization*, chapter 5.

57. Waters, *Globalization*.

58. Sassen, *Globalization and Its Discontents*, xxv.

59. John Kenneth Galbraith, *The Affluent Society*, 4th ed. (Boston: Houghton Mifflin, 1984).

60. Jill Quadagno, "Creating a Capital Investment Welfare State: The New American Exceptionalism," *American Sociological Review* 64, no. 1 (February 1999): 1–11.

61. Quadagno, "Creating a Capital Investment Welfare State," 8.

62. Sassen, *Guests and Aliens*.

63. Jennifer L. Hochschild, *Facing up to the American Dream* (Princeton, N.J.: Princeton University Press, 1995).

64. For an exploration of the survival strategies of people trapped in structural poverty, see Mitchell Duneier, *Sidewalk* (New York: Farrar, Straus and Giroux, 1999); Jay MacLeod, *Ain't No Making It* (Boulder, Colo.: Westview, 1987); Carol B. Stack, *All Our Kin* (New York: Basic, 1997).

65. The expanding targets of the war on drugs are described by Mike Davis, *City of Quartz* (New York: Verso, 1990).

66. Jeffrey H. Reiman, *The Rich Get Richer and the Poor Get Prison* (New York: Macmillan, 1990).

67. Antonio Gramsci, *Selections from the Prison Notebooks* (New York: International, 1971), 275–276.

~

CHAPTER FOUR

It's "Ours": Globalization and the Racialization of Space

One of the defining features of globalization is the shrinking significance of space and time.[1] The technological revolution that produced globalization has in significant ways transformed the world into a global village. People from any part of the earth can be in instantaneous communication with one another via computers, telephones, or television. We now look at websites or send e-mail messages to people without even knowing where they are physically located. Cheap air transportation has made every part of the planet reachable from anywhere within a single day. We live in a time of the greatest mobility of humanity in all of history.[2] In the global era, people are increasingly capable of rapidly or instantaneously interacting with one another across large distances, creating a sense of spacelessness and timelessness in social relationships. Transnational corporations spend billions of dollars advertising the universalistic ramifications of the new technologies, and indeed, the hype has some validity.

The irony of this epoch, however, is that the social crisis of globalization has led to a closing of space, a new premium on the local, not the universal. At the very moment when people can live more timeless and spaceless existences, time and space are becoming increasingly vital to those seeking to defend their interests against the social impacts of globalization. The architectural symbols of the global era are the gated community and the efforts of wealthy communities to enact strict zoning laws preserving "old" (often, in California, old means the 1950s era) styles of architecture. Just at the moment when time and space could become limitless, time and space—the past and the local—are becoming increasingly important to a growing number of Americans.

The purpose of this chapter is to explore the specific ways in which globalization has intensified efforts to mobilize racial and national privileges in the United States through privileged claims to "local" space. As we will see, the new focus on local autonomy and local control has become an increasingly important way for racially and nationally privileged people to fend off the downward pressures of globalization. But the creation of global networks and relationships is also producing new concepts of space—both in cities and nations—that continually undermine these defensive efforts. At the very moment when privileged whites retreat into local space, a new global reality is slowly and inexorably undermining their efforts. In this way, globalization has led to contradictory impulses that racialize space in new, and at times unexpected, ways.

The Creation of Racialized Space in the United States

Racial systems of privilege and oppression have always included notions of space, but they have varied considerably in different eras. In the Virginia colony prior to the racialization of slavery, as Edmund S. Morgan explains, African slaves and English indentured servants lived in the same quarters and were assigned the same work.[3] They also intermarried and rebelled together against the colonial government. The creation of racial chattel slavery in the late seventeenth century was compelled by the colonial rulers' need to socially separate African slaves and English servants. This separation was economic (slavery for blacks and free labor for whites), social (antimiscegenation laws), and legal (the Virginia Slave Codes). But the plantation system itself limited the extent of the spatial separation of the races. One of the most important features of the plantation system was the intimate physical space shared by the people who were enslaved and the slave master. Slave quarters were generally within sight of the masters' home; people who were enslaved regularly interacted with slave masters as servants, laborers, estate managers, wet nurses, and sexual objects or lovers. Black people continually occupied the slave masters' home. While slavery created a powerful color line, the separation of the races was not geographic. The ideology of slavery denied the humanity of people who were enslaved, but contemporary accounts suggest that the relationships between slave masters and slaves were far more complex than this. While geographical separation was limited on plantations, slave masters considered separation essential for freed African Americans. A Virginia slave ordinance, for example, required slaves who were manumitted to leave the state, a tacit recognition that freed blacks staying in the plantation areas would be a threat to slavery.

Geographic separation of Native Americans from whites was necessary to seize native peoples' lands and convert them into both U.S. territory and private property. This separation was encoded into U.S. government policy with the passage of the Indian Removal Act in 1830. For over 200 years prior to that law, European colonists and native peoples often lived in close proximity to one another, in a relationship often described as one of uneasy parity.[4] The creation of geographically isolated "reservations" both recognized the United States' need to seize American Indian land and its inability to get rid of native peoples entirely.[5] The concept of the reservation system evolved gradually, from *Cherokee Nation v. Georgia* in 1820, to the Indian Removal Act of 1830, and to the Termination Act of 1871, as native peoples were placed under the sovereignty of, and, gradually, incorporated into the United States. Native peoples' geographic separation from the United States, ironically, was thus undertaken to incorporate their land—and therefore the people as well—into the United States.[6]

Racial separation in the Jim Crow era was at best incomplete. Some 80 percent of African Americans, technically citizens, remained geographically isolated from the industrial cities in the late nineteenth century, trapped in the southern sharecropping system and stymied by the active efforts of white unions and employers to keep them out of the industrial sectors.[7] But even in the rural South, African Americans and whites generally lived in the same towns and counties. Those people of color who did live in the industrial cities during the Jim Crow era were made separate and unequal by a host of local, state, and federal laws. While segregated, however, the industrial cities, like the southern towns, were as geographic entities multiracial, multiethnic, and multinational from their beginning.

The very existence of segregation laws resulted from the potential for racial integration that lay within industrial capitalism. Without the use of state power to keep the races apart and unequal, the system of free labor and capital on which industrial capitalism was based had the potential to create a nonracial working class in urban America. Employers had an economic interest to hire labor as cheaply as possible. The economic relations of industrial capitalism on their own would have drawn labor into the expanding industrial sectors regardless of race. Preference might have been given to the cheapest labor: that of people of color. The concentration of capital in the industrial cities would have consolidated labor into communities and workplaces on a nonracial basis as well. Only the creation of what Michael Omi and Howard Winant term "the racial dictatorship" of Jim Crow could and did reproduce racism in that era. Only state power and explicit racist ideology remained for whites to claim the privileges of citizenship, political power, and access to industrial jobs. Racial inequality in the industrial capitalist era required Jim Crow laws because no other mechanism to keep people racially separate and unequal existed.

The significance of the creation of mass suburbs in the 1950s (see chapter 2) is starkly highlighted by this history. For the first time, white communities with their own city and county governments were created on a large scale in the United States. For the first time, it became possible for white people to protect their racial privileges by leaving multiracial cities and counties for class and race homogeneous suburbs. As we saw in chapter 2, the white suburbs were made racially homogeneous at their onset because of the existence of the Jim Crow housing laws, which allowed private developers and the federal government to limit access to the suburbs to whites only. In the 1950s and 1960s, however, the full significance of this new arrangement for the mobilization of racial privileges had not yet been realized. For one, people of color who moved to cities had begun to establish toeholds in a number of industries in the 1940s and 1950s, and were benefiting from the post–World War II economic expansion. For another, the civil rights movement challenged racial inequalities and was particularly successful in the late 1960s at integrating public-sector jobs and increasing black political power and access to public education and social services.[8] The civil rights movement also began a legal and political assault on the white suburbs in 1965, demanding that racially integrated low-income housing be required in all communities.[9] Furthermore, in the conditions of the postwar boom, it was possible to provide more jobs and better social services to people of color without taking away anything from whites. At a time when the middle class was expanding, there seemed to be room at the table for everyone.

The conditions that pushed the white suburbs toward an increasingly aggressive assertion of white privileges fully emerged in the mid-1970s. A series of political and economic crises—manifestations of the hidden forces of globalization—propelled white suburbanites to claim their "own" political and geographical space to protect their middle-class status.

Globalization and the Unleashing of the White Suburbs

One of the most important political responses to globalization in the United States has been the shift of political power to the suburbs and the emergence of a movement for local control that politically empowers white suburban-ites. As discussed in chapter 3, the new economic, social, and political dy-namics of globalization have undermined the capacities of the national wel-fare state and the stability of the middle-class social order that came to fruition between the 1940s and 1960s. The promise of "the good life" for the middle class has also been badly shaken by the disequalizing trends accom-panying globalization. In this context, the existence of politically au-tonomous white suburbs has become increasingly important as a way to buffer the "politically relevant" people from social crisis.[10]

Whites have been willing to pay a premium to live in white communities since the mass suburbs appeared in the late 1940s.[11] A generation ago, a large majority of whites—some 84 percent—in the Detroit Area Survey of 1976 said they were unwilling to live in a community that is more than half nonwhite. This was in sharp contrast to the almost two-thirds of blacks who were willing to live in a community that is half nonblack.[12] The "racial premium" of white-ness produced then, and still produces, white flight when people of color start to move into white areas. Whites sell their homes at below market prices (to real estate speculators who make enormous profits by selling houses at huge markups to people of color) in order to move into a white area. Why is the whiteness of a community worth so much to so many people? The answer is de-ceptively simple: Most whites understand that white communities have better schools, better social services, lower crime rates, and better access to jobs. The very terms "good neighborhood" and "bad neighborhood" have been thor-oughly racialized in the United States.[13] This belief is rooted in more than racial prejudice; it is also about people's calculations about how to advance their personal interests by claiming geographically defined racial privileges.

When the mass suburbs were forming in the 1940s and 1950s, the fact that whites were privileged was openly encoded in the Jim Crow legal system. At a time when law and legally protected private discrimination mandated that whites have political power and access to jobs and education on an unequal basis, living in a white community guaranteed racial privileges. In the form-ative days of the suburbs, when most of the new blue-collar suburbanites were often close in economic conditions to many people of color, whiteness con-ferred crucial privileges. First, making the suburbs white conferred to their residents the privilege of living in a relatively class-homogeneous environ-ment, which made it to possible to drastically cut property and sales taxes at the same time that they were being raised to fund expanding programs for the poor in the cities. Second, restricting the suburbs to whites conferred the racial privilege of receiving better schools and social services because the lo-cal tax dollars raised were used for one specific class project: the conferral of middle-class status. Third, all-white communities supported white referral employment networks. Judging from the "racial premium" whites are still willing to pay to live in a largely white community, the belief in the benefits of whiteness persists into the present. The most remarkable feature of the new mechanisms that privilege suburban whites, however, is that they now protect these racial privileges with little or no overt racism. All that was needed to make the defense of white privileges disappear from view was to sever the connections of the suburbs and the cities.

The movement for suburban local autonomy became more aggressive as soon as the civil rights movement began to challenge the racial segregation of the suburbs in the 1960s. Martin Luther King Jr. was shocked at the ferocious response to the Southern Christian Leadership Conference's 1965 campaign to compel suburban Skokie, Illinois, to desegregate its housing. In fact, whites' vicious reaction to a protest march there led King to a new strategic understanding of the movement for freedom and equality, "[M]any of [our] white allies have quietly disappeared," he warned in 1967. "The paths of Negro-white unity that had been converging crossed at Selma, and like a giant X began to diverge."[14]

But in the late 1960s, even as Richard Nixon successfully mobilized suburbanites into his Silent Majority coalition, people of color could still make effective claims on middle-class resources. Cities continued to be the centers of jobs, housing, and shopping, and communities of color could and did politically mobilize to demand a fair share of the resources, attracting billions of dollars to social programs in urban areas during the 1960s. The linkage between schooling and jobs was still formative, and colleges (with their racial biases) were not yet fully functioning as gateways to the middle class. Both blue-collar and public-sector white-collar jobs provided people of color with access to middle-class incomes. With the postwar economic expansion still under way, white suburbanites had relatively little anxiety about their futures. And so, even though whites largely abandoned the civil rights movement after 1965, a full white backlash against people of color had not yet developed. Even though some suburban whites deserted the Democratic Party and voted for Richard Nixon in 1968 and 1972, Nixon relied for his political base more on the formerly Jim Crow Sunbelt—Texas, Florida, and Georgia—then he did on the northern suburbanites. Indeed, Nixon himself embodied the vacillating racial politics of that era: While he attempted to symbolically appeal to a white backlash, Nixon quietly gave in to important civil rights initiatives. In 1971, for example, Nixon supported the creation of racial set aside programs ("quotas") for affirmative action in the construction industry, and in 1974 he ordered suburbs to submit plans detailing how they would provide low-income housing in their communities.[15] As well, state and federal courts issued historic rulings making suburbs accountable for desegregation efforts. In 1973, a Michigan federal district court ruled that suburban whites had to take responsibility for desegregating Detroit school districts through cross-district busing, and in that year, the U.S. Supreme Court came close to outlawing all patterns of segregation in public education.[16] In the most suburban state of the era, the New Jersey Supreme Court in 1975 required suburbs to accept their "fair share" of low-income housing.[17]

While racial antipathy toward the cities had defined suburbs from their origins, the revolt of the suburbs began in earnest in 1975. The interaction of double-digit inflation, a sharp recession, real oil and gas shortages, and the American defeat in Vietnam announced the beginning of a new era. As the full impact of globalization appeared, local and some national politicians began to appeal to suburbanites to defend their "own" communities, depicting urban areas as the places of nonwhites who were a real threat to white suburbanites' living standards and security. Meanwhile, the flight of whites from the cities accelerated during this period. But even more significantly, so did the flight of capital, as new technologies enabled companies to decentralize operations and move important components of their businesses outside the urban cores.

The revolt of the suburbs was recognized and encouraged by a milestone U.S. Supreme Court decision in 1975: *Milliken v. Bradley*.[18] In this case, the Court reversed a lower court that had ordered cross-district busing with suburban schools to remedy proven racial discrimination by the Detroit public school district. The lower court had two major reasons for its decision: the Detroit schools, by then with an 80 percent black student body, could not desegregate on their own; and second, whites had moved to the suburbs mainly to avoid sending their children to the Detroit schools, and were thus complicit in the inner-city school segregation. The Supreme Court reversed this ruling on procedural grounds, holding that suburban communities could not be forced to bear the burden of desegregating urban schools without proof of intentional discrimination by each school system. Touted by advocates of local community control such as former suburban Detroit congressman and new President Gerald Ford, *Milliken* became a political line in the sand. Scholars, including Owen Fiss and Gary Orfield, have credited *Milliken* with stopping much of the momentum toward school desegregation that had started with *Brown v. Board of Education* in 1954. Even more, *Milliken* put suburbs on notice that they could develop local school systems with little fear that they would have to pay a "social tax" for people of color's limited opportunities. Suburbs were now free to go their own way.

By the end of the 1970s, efforts at local control had become part of the twin conservative drives to "get the government off the backs of the people" and to slow down the growth of the suburbs. Suburban middle-class whites joined forces with large corporations throughout the United States in the late 1970s and early 1980s to cut property taxes (which, not surprisingly, largely benefited corporations). These cuts, spearheaded by the passage of Proposition 13 in California in 1979, set the basis for drastic reductions in government spending on education, public health, and social services. These cuts both confirmed and accelerated the racial gap between cities and suburbs. While urban areas with low property values suffered the consequences, many suburban communities passed local bond issues to supplement local school budgets.

Suburban communities also resisted the placement of low-income housing in their areas. In their superb history of this campaign of white resistance in New Jersey, David L. Kirp, John P. Dwyer, and Larry A. Rosenthal chronicle the political campaigns of the 1980s and 1990s that successfully gutted the New Jersey Supreme Court's 1975 *Mount Laurel* decision requiring suburbs to build their "fair share" of low-income housing. In 1981, suburbanites elected Thomas Kean, an antigrowth governor who in his 1984 State of the State Address denounced the *Mount Laurel* decision as an "undesirable intrusion on the home rule principle," and later added that it was "communistic."[19] Suburbs mounted a strong counteroffensive against the *Mount Laurel* decision. "One defendant, the village of Harding," Kirp, Dwyer, and Rosenthal note, "passed a $600,000 bond issue to fund its defense, thus raising the astonishing amount of more than $2,000 for every man, woman, and child."[20] In the absence of dried-up federal and state funding for low-income housing in suburbs, the strongest advocates of building low-income housing were big developers who, by building twenty units of low-income housing, could get permits to build hundreds of market-priced units.[21] By the 1980s, opponents to desegregating the suburbs no longer needed to use racial rhetoric; the issue had become protecting the suburbs from "rapid development." The fact that suburbanites were protecting their racial privileges had been made invisible by ignoring the racial history of the suburbs.

The consequences of the suburban campaign for "local control" can be found in the continuing patterns of racial segregation throughout the United States. Douglas S. Massey and Nancy A. Denton have surveyed the extent of segregation of blacks and whites in the thirty metropolitan areas with the largest black populations using 1980 census data. They found that one-third of blacks in America live in conditions they term "hypersegregation." That is, they "live within large, contiguous settlements of densely inhabited neighborhoods that are packed tightly around the urban core. In plain terms, they live in ghettoes."[22] Furthermore, Massey and Denton report that the decentralization of black housing, even in suburbs, has not increased the residential integration of blacks and whites. "Often, black 'suburbanization' only involves the expansion of an urban ghetto across a city line and does not reflect a larger process of racial integration."[23] All in all, Massey and Denton find that blacks are over- or underrepresented in an average of 80 percent of neighborhoods for the thirty metropolitan areas they study. Furthermore, they show that black-white residential segregation patterns remain remarkably persistent, so that in the decade from 1970 to 1980 there was almost no change in the rate of segregation.[24]

Segregated white communities do not remain white solely by the momentum of the past. Racial discrimination in suburban real estate and mortgage lending markets is still responsible for much of the continuing housing segregation.[25] A 1991 study by the Federal Reserve Bank revealed powerful racial disparities in banks' decisions about mortgage lending. Poor whites, for example, were as likely to get loans as upper-class African Americans, and poor Latinos had their mortgage applications rejected 51 percent more frequently than poor whites.[26] The highest disparity in the mortgage rejection rate was found to be between upper-class blacks and upper-class whites, with blacks rejected 280 percent more frequently. Real estate agents also regularly "steer" nonwhites away from white areas. Various studies, including an audit by the U.S. Department of Housing and Urban Development, have found that whites are much likelier to be notified about the availability of a home or a rental unit in a predominately white area than are blacks or Latinos.[27]

Suburbanization has not only sheltered much of the white middle class from the social crisis of globalization. Geographical segregation in this form also confers racial privileges on many white people who are poor. As Massey and Denton show, ghettoization concentrates the black poor (and increasingly Latino, Asian, and Native American poor) in census tracks where the majority of residents are people of color *and* poor. Conversely, suburbanization has *dispersed* the white poor into census tracks where the majority is white and middle class.[28] Put another way, there are very few white ghettoes in the United States. The dispersal effect of whiteness provides access to important resources for poor whites: they can live in suburban communities with tax bases and the political clout to produce "good" schools, they live closer to job opportunities, they are less likely to be subject to police harassment, and they are more likely to receive a wide range of public services. As a result, a comprehensive study of the efforts of welfare recipients to find entry-level jobs reports that those living in suburbs are more successful than those in central cities.[29]

Conversely, exposure to the downward pressures of the global era imposes a harsh racial "tax" on middle-class minorities as well as the poor. The lack of residential mobility traps many middle-class minorities in neighborhoods with poor schools and other government services, further harming their chances for upward mobility. Residential segregation also hampers middle-class blacks from amassing the assets needed for upward (and outward) mobility by depressing the value of homes. A study of the housing markets in three cities reported that between 1984 and 1989 the median price of homes in predominately white areas increased by *triple* the rate of homes in predominately black areas.[30]

The trend toward local autonomy of government in the past twenty years has created a powerful platform for the exacerbation of racial inequality. The main trend in law and policy from 1937 until 1975 had been toward the centralization of decision making by the federal government over state and local governments.[31] The civil rights movement of the 1950s and 1960s had both capitalized on and accelerated this restructuring of the U.S. government. But after 1975, a new localism began to appear in American law and politics.

The shift of jobs to the suburbs, coupled with the decline in socialized public services in cities, has had a severe racial impact on inner-city residents. While middle-class Americans of all races struggle to maintain their standard of living, poor people in cities have encountered the virtual disappearance of the economic ladder out of poverty: the entry-level job. Entry-level jobs are those positions that offer job training and access to other positions higher up the ladder in the same industry. William Julius Wilson described the impact of the removal of jobs from the industrial cities to the suburbs in the late 1970s.[32] He observed that the flight of jobs to the suburbs left poor people in areas of concentrated poverty with little access to jobs or social services. The isolation of ghettoes (and barrios, Chinatowns, and urban Indian communities) has produced a new type of poverty, in which despair too often replaces hope. Wilson has been correctly criticized for his assertion that societal racism is declining, that middle-class minorities have escaped the main effects of racial inequality,[33] and for his depiction of ghettoes as pathological communities incapable of stabilizing themselves in the worsening economic and social conditions.[34] Nevertheless, his pioneering depiction of economic restructuring and its impact on ghettoes remains an important contribution to our understanding of the dynamics of racism in the era of globalization.

In sum, the suburban-urban conflict with all of its powerful racial implications was unleashed by the weakening of centralized government and the downward mobility pressures associated with globalization. Gary Orfield vividly describes the outcomes:

Suburbanization not only redistributes taxable wealth, but also redistributes jobs and educational opportunities in ways that make them virtually inaccessible to minorities confined by residential segregation to parts of the central city. . . . It greatly increases the physical scale of racial separation, particularly for children, since middle class white families with children become rarities in many central cities. It overlays the system of racial separation and inequality with a system of political and legal separation. Thus, the best services, education and access to new jobs are made available to affluent, virtually all-white communities that openly employ a full range of municipal powers to attract desirable jobs from the city, while preventing low- and moderate-income families, or renters of any kind, from moving into the communities. As a consequence, black and Hispanic political aspirations are concentrated very largely on municipal and educational institutions that lack the tax base to maintain existing levels of services, to say nothing of mounting new responses to the critical problems of these expanding minority communities.[35]

In these ways, the defense of local control has become an important form for the defense of white privileges and minority subordination in the United States. One of the most pernicious aspects of this new form of racial politics is that white privileges can now be mobilized without any mention of race. All that must be done to make race invisible is to ignore the racist policies and practices that made the suburbs white to begin with and to fantasize that the "good life" of the suburbs has nothing to do with the devastation of the inner cities over the past two decades.

Trends of Globalization Undermining Localism

Despite the continuing predominance of "vanilla suburbs and chocolate cities," there is some evidence to suggest that a countertrend to this pattern of racial segregation is developing in the United States. An analysis of the census 2000 data by the Center for Regional Policy Studies at the University of California, Los Angeles, shows that whites remain the racially most isolated group, but the percentage of whites living in neighborhoods over 90 percent white has declined by an average of 13.7 percent between 1990 and 2000.[36] This decline suggests two new developments: the growth in the numbers of people of color living in predominately white suburbs and the increasing number of whites living in urban core areas.

These trends reveal the ways in which globalization is undermining as well as fostering the racial project of local autonomy described earlier. As early as the 1960s, some suburban communities decided to adopt a progrowth strategy and aggressively recruited businesses to leave the cities. Businesses were lured by promises of no property or business taxes, offers of subsidized utilities and land, and, best of all, a labor market without unions. Federal policies, such as the Federal Interstate Highway Program, also subsidized the flight of capital from the cities. The introduction of new technologies in the 1970s and 1980s enabled businesses to decentralize their operations, accelerating further their search for cheaper labor and lower taxes in suburbs. But capital flight from the cities had a very different consequence than the flight of privileged white professionals and managers. The shift of jobs outside the old urban cores compelled lower-income workers to move out after them. By the 1980s, the old arrangement of suburbs as bedroom communities whose residents worked in urban downtowns was fast disappearing. The new metropolises that took their place were no longer recognizable as cities or suburbs. The arrangement of concentrated business districts surrounded by successive rings of urban and suburban dwellings gave way to sprawling metropolises with many business areas interspersed among residential areas and strip malls. The archetype American city was no longer New York; it was now Los Angeles, a megametropolis that stretches from San Diego to Santa Barbara, and from the Pacific Ocean to Las Vegas.[37] From the San Francisco Bay Area to the East Coast Corridor, the new metropolitan areas rapidly took shape in the 1980s, fundamentally changing the arrangement of living and working spaces in the United States.

The racial implications of this new spatial reconfiguration are significant. The integration of suburbs into the global metropolises has to some extent led to a growing racial complexity of formerly white areas as people of color who can afford to buy a home have moved out of the cities in pursuit of the jobs that left before them. Those formerly suburban areas that have become sites of new investments and increasingly dense populations are now experiencing a new type of urbanization, complete with high-density rental units, traffic jams, rising crime rates, and overwhelmed public services. The areas that have remained suburbanized in the old sense—and white, to boot—are relatively wealthy communities whose residents can use high property values and zoning laws to maintain islands of privilege within the metropolitan web.

Another trend countering white suburban autonomy has been the return of some of the white upper and upper-middle classes to the former urban cores. Some downtowns—especially those of New York and San Francisco—have become urban mirrors of the white, upper-class suburbs. In these and other cities, white "gentry" are using high property values and zoning laws to drive out anyone who can't afford to purchase a condominium or home. Formerly hard-hit urban areas such as New York's Harlem and San Francisco's Mission District are becoming rapidly gentrified, with a major exodus of working-class people of color and an influx of white home buyers. As the old cores of the global cities become gentrified, a new type of "satellite city" is appearing in the metropolises that function as the dumping place for poor, property-less workers who can no longer find low-income housing anywhere else.

The racial map is further complicated by the rising number of immigrants carving out their own ethnic niches in the global metropolises. As we saw in chapter 3, unlike the previous immigration waves of industrial capitalism, global capitalism is creating the mobility of people of all classes from a much wider array of nations. The preponderant trend in the United States is the influx of poor Latinos and Asians into the service sector. Stuck with low-paying jobs, most of these immigrants cannot afford to purchase private homes, are subject to housing discrimination in white areas, and often wish to remain in ethnic communities to defend their interests. As such, they tend to cluster in areas of the global metropolises with low-income rental units and immigrant social services. Even those national minority ethnics who can afford to purchase homes are often willing to pay a premium to live in a sub-urban ethnic enclave to retain cultural, political, and economic associations that might be of benefit to them.[38] Indeed, immigrants to the United States often form ethnic groups with surprising new innovations, such as the Cambodians in Oakland, California, who have developed a culture that incorporates many African American ethnic notions.[39]

In these ways, globalization has both spawned white suburban resistance and gentrification, and has simultaneously created new regional metropolises that undercut efforts to maintain white privileges through local control. The preponderant trend, however, still favors white middle- and upper-class suburbs, because the new metropolises still lack the sophisticated coalitions that would give them political power. As well, the capacity of propertied whites in suburbs to insulate their communities from the downward pressures of globalization has not diminished, in part because of the growing wealth of these communities—the other side of globalization's impact. Consequently, we can expect the political efforts to localize public service spending, with its profound racial consequences, to continue for the foreseeable future.

Localism on a World Scale: Anti-immigrant Politics and Globalization

Just as suburban localism has profoundly structured race relations and ideas about community, a larger type of localism—nationalism—is a growing and powerful shaper of American responses to globalization. The rise of nationalism and xenophobia in the United States—and much of the rest of the world—is, in a sense, counterintuitive. We live in a time of a global flow of capital and commodities, an era of increasing communication between peoples throughout the world. Many countries, developed and developing, are now sites of global cities, with a new cosmopolitan character that results from the growing diversity of their populations. A drive through any of two dozen American cities reveals the riches of the world. Thai neighborhoods give way to Mexican barrios; Russian areas segue into Syrian communities. Decent Thai, Chinese, Indian, and Mexican food can now be found even in small Midwestern cities. Immigrant communities' growing diversity and size bears witness to one of the most significant features of globalization: We live in a time of the greatest mobility of humanity in world history.[40] The U.S.-Mexican border region, in particular, is home to 12 million people and is expected to double in population by 2020. The San Diego port of entry has 60 million legal crossings into the United States from Mexico each year, and thousands of residents of San Diego cross the border to work in Mexican maquiladora factories each day. The border region itself has been widely recognized as a new type of transnational space. The European Union similarly has begun to blur national boundaries, with a common currency and open labor movement across all of Europe.

It would appear that globalization is making boundaries like the U.S.-Mexican border more irrelevant.[41] But that is clearly far from what is happening. The irony of globalization is that we live in a time of mounting anti-immigrant sentiments and policies in all of the most developed nations. As Nigel Harris points out, anti-immigrant policies in Europe and the United States are of recent origin.[42] Until the twentieth century, most industrializing societies, including the United States, actively encouraged immigration to alleviate persistent labor shortages. Indeed, in the nineteenth century many European states tried to prevent emigration while encouraging immigration.[43] Xenophobia, however, has long been a phenomenon accompanying nation building in Europe and the United States, as national elites used fear of people labeled "foreigners" as a way to cohere political control over growing populations. But states lacked the technical and political means to control their borders effectively.

While Jews served as the main "foreigners" of Christian Europe, Native Americans were the first antipodal "others" of the United States. Tomás Almaguer explores the ways in which the exclusion of native peoples from early California society helped unite disparate European immigrant populations divided by national origin, class, and gender. Depicting indigenous people as unassimilable savages was a powerful way to project the founding of California as the march of Anglo "civilization." Poor and marginalized European immigrants, often termed "white trash" at the time, launched genocidal attacks on California Indians as a way of gaining respectability in the newly white society.[44] By defining native peoples as uncivilized, early white California came to know what civilization was.

Anti-immigrant policies in the United States, which had first focused on controlling non-English Europeans in the immediate postcolonial period, took on an increasingly racial form in the industrial era, beginning with the exclusion of the Chinese from citizenship in the 1850s.[45] But even as particular groups were singled out as the unassimilable "others," industrial capitalism's demand for labor overwhelmed many national barriers. In nineteenth-century Europe, workers could move between most nations without visas or passports. In the United States, those Europeans and Canadians considered white—and Mexicans, some of whom were entitled to citizenship in the United States under the Treaty of Guadalupe-Hidalgo and therefore enjoyed a crucial white privilege for a time—were greeted by Emma Lazarus's poem engraved on the Statue of Liberty, "[B]ring me your tired, your poor, your huddled masses yearning to breathe free." Even those Europeans who were viciously discriminated against for their nationality (e.g., the Irish and the Italians) were granted the powerful racial privileges of citizenship and the right to vote, privileges they used to eventually escape from the ravages of national minority status.[46]

The first general restrictions on immigration in the twentieth century responded to the maturation of capitalism and the political capacity of nation-states.[47] In the United States, as the ratio of capital to labor increased, the demand for new sources of labor declined, and the growing power of organized labor put a greater premium on social stability than on open-door immigration. It is no accident that Henry Ford, the capitalist who believed that social peace could be best achieved by making workers into consumers, was also virulently anti-immigrant. The resulting restriction of European immigration to the United States was foreshadowed by a massive xenophobic campaign, punctuated by the Red Scare of 1919 (a Brown Scare in the Southwest) and the rise of the Eugenics movement. The Ku Klux Klan became a national political force, with a membership of over 9 million in 1924, drawn to the Klan by its anti-Catholic and anti-Semitic campaign against European immigrants and Mexicans as much as by its white supremacist ideology.[48]

Xenophobia was whipped up in the late industrial era for two distinct reasons. First, fear of foreigners was increasingly useful as a political device to cohere national unity (a sense of "us") as the U.S. population became more diverse in national origin and class polarization increased. The internment of Japanese Americans and Japanese nationals of other countries during World

War II, for example, was used to overcome Americans' ambivalence about the war. Second, xenophobia was used to create immigration policies that drove down the cost of labor within the United States. This motive, used against Chinese contract workers in California in the 1850s and Filipino dock and cannery workers in the 1930s, also led to the restriction of Mexican immigration for the first time during the Great Depression.[49] After severely restricting Mexicans' legal access to the United States in 1930, the Immigration and Naturalization Service (INS) conducted Operation Deportation, in which over a million Mexican nationals were rounded up and deported from the United States with no legal rights of appeal. Most of those deported already had jobs, homes, and families in the United States, and, of course, quickly returned to their homes. Operation Deportation's impact was not the exclusion of Mexicans, but the guarantee of their inclusion in the United States as undocumented workers. The new status of "illegal aliens" meant that Mexicans could be compelled to accept low wages and horrendous work conditions, and lacked the legal and political means to do anything about it. In the mid-1950s, a second wave of exclusion—the INS's infamous Operation Wetback—reinforced Mexicans' oppressed status, excluding (and leading to the undocumented repatriation of) over a million people.[50]

The historic uses of anti-immigrant policies and practices are being exacerbated in the global era. As discussed in chapter 3, globalization's impact on the United States has been to undermine the middle-class social order, both by increasing inequality and reshaping the welfare state into a "private accumulation" state. Added to this, globalization has kindled a large wave of immigration to the United States, both due to the growing crisis of the Third World and the growing demand for service workers in the United States. Globalization also requires the reconfiguring of the U.S. relationship with other national economies, particularly those of the Asian nations. The new international division of labor has led to a growing number of high-end positions for immigrants in some sectors of the U.S. economy. The intersection of these factors has drastically increased the potential for both nationalistic and exploitative anti-immigrant policies. First, political elites are searching for ways to shore up national solidarity as the middle class comes under attack; and second, employers are seeking ways to depress wages, both for immigrants and legal citizens. Thus, as globalization undercuts the old, postwar middle-class social order, the political and economic attacks on immigrants and foreigners can be expected to increase, as indeed they have.

Ronald Reagan, who best articulated the ideological assault on the welfare state, well understood the value of anti-immigrant politics to bolster the middle-class order. Warning of a "brown tide sweeping across the Texas border," Reagan strongly backed the Immigration Reform and Control Act (IRCA) of 1986. The IRCA's framers added a new dimension to existing immigration law: provisions to punish employers for hiring illegal aliens. In order to mollify Latino and Asian community advocates who worried that employers would discriminate against all foreign-born workers, the bill also included an amnesty program for undocumented people who had been in the United States continuously for at least five years. Studies of the IRCA's impact suggest the critics were correct to be worried: the flow of undocumented immigrants has grown, and the employer sanction provision has contributed to decreasing wages for both legal and undocumented immigrants. A General Accounting Office report in 1990, for example, found a "serious pattern" of labor market discrimination against legal immigrant workers, much of it attributable to employer sanctions.[51]

The passage of Proposition 187 in California in 1994 expanded the use of anti-immigrant politics to bolster the middle-class social order. California was, at that time, enmeshed in a recession largely caused by cuts in military spending. Governor Pete Wilson was in serious trouble with his suburban white political base and had been almost written off as a viable contender for a second term, but then he endorsed the ballot proposition entitled the Save Our State Initiative. Proposition 187 sought to bar all undocumented people and their children (therefore including many U.S. citizens) from receiving any state services except for emergency health care. Supporters argued that this law was needed to stop a mounting horde of illegal aliens from entering California to get access to its (allegedly) generous education, welfare, and social service programs. These "illegal aliens," 187 supporters alleged, were responsible for the declining quality of life of the middle class, because they were consuming public funds to which they did not contribute and were committing crimes. A founder of STOP-IT, a southern California organization, proclaimed:

> The indomitable American spirit is being awakened. . . . Americans don't like the graffiti in their neighborhoods. They don't like the traffic and overcrowding and the crime. American citizens don't like some of the neighborhoods in Southern California being taken over by illegals. . . . I have a feeling the reason there haven't been any more riots in L.A. is because so many people lined up to buy guns. White American citizens got guns to fight back against the illegal aliens and the criminals.[52]

The facts, that undocumented people provide essential labor, do pay taxes (property, sales, and even income taxes), and receive almost no benefits because they are already barred from most social services, did not have a significant impact on white voters. Proposition 187 won by a landslide. The proposition was immediately stayed and later largely struck down as unconstitutional by a federal court, which reminded Californians that only Congress makes immigration law. But 187's political impact was still felt: Wilson handily won reelection as governor in 1994, and the anti-immigrant movement moved to the center of national Republican politics.

Republicans used California-style anti-immigration politics to win over white middle-class voters to the historic Contract for America in the 1994 midterm election that put Republicans in control of both Houses of Congress. Ever the political opportunist, President Bill Clinton co-opted the Republican strategy and forged bipartisan support for the passage of two new anti-immigration laws. The first was the Illegal Immigration Reform and Responsibility Act of 1996, which restricts federal court review of INS decisions and severely limits immigrants' rights to bring lawsuits. The second was the so-called welfare reform bill, the Personal Responsibility Act of 1996, that made legal noncitizens ineligible for virtually all forms of means-tested public assistance for the first five years after entry into the United States. Half of all the projected savings from so-called welfare reform came from this single provision. In response, of course, hundreds of thousands of panicky permanent residents rushed to become citizens.[53]

The depiction of the border as the frontline defense against drugs entering the United States has justified a massive buildup of Border Patrol personnel and the growing presence of police and military on both sides of the U.S.-Mexican border. In 1993, President Clinton supported the doubling of the number of Border Patrol agents and, in 1995, the use of military surveillance units to detect illegal border crossings. The INS budget nearly tripled in size between 1993 and 1999, to $4.2 billion.[54] The INS initiated three massive efforts to erect barriers (both with patrols and walls) to prevent illegal border crossings in California (Operation Gatekeeper), Arizona (Operation Safeguard), and Texas (Operation Rio Grande). Over 1.5 million people were arrested at these three border regions per year by the late 1990s.

In response to these policies, smuggling illegal immigrants has become a multibillion-dollar industry, with smugglers now organized into large, professional organizations.[55] Vigilante posses of whites roam the border region, urging white people to defend the border with guns.[56] Forced to enter the United States through remote desert routes, some 1,450 migrants died from exposure to extreme heat between 1996 and 2000. More activities associated with entering the United States illegally have been criminally sanctioned. Smuggling a person across the border—such as not reporting an illegal brother or sister—is an "aggravated felony" under the 1996 Immigration Reform Act, as is returning to the United States after being deported. Both crimes carry up to twenty years in prison.[57] Furthermore, immigrants deported for felonies are ineligible to return to the United States for twenty years and are held without bail while the deportation process is under way.[58]

The problem with these increasingly Draconian anti-immigrant measures, like their predecessors, is that they have failed to achieve their stated goals. During the decade of heightening restrictions, immigration to the United States has continued to grow, both legally and illegally. In fact, almost half of all illegal immigrants enter the United States legally on visitor, student, or guest-worker visas and become illegal when their visa expires. While the U.S.-Mexican border is heavily guarded, there is very little internal enforcement of immigration laws, particularly the employer sanctions mandated by the IRCA.[59] Indeed, as Saskia Sassen suggests, immigration pressures have little to do with government policy and more to do with international economic and political relationships.[60] What, then, is the purpose of increasingly harsh anti-immigration measures and enforcement if globalization is increasing the pace and complexity of immigration to the United States?

The answer to this puzzle lies in the politics of the social crisis that globalization is engendering in the United States. In an era of growing inequality and reduced capacity for nation-states to address social problems, attacks on immigrants serve two purposes: they lower the price of their labor, and they enable political elites to mobilize a symbolic form of national unity. Efforts to restrict immigration fail to restrict the flow of people, but they make it easier for employers to discriminate against immigrants (and often nonimmigrant Latinos and Asians), especially undocumented workers, who can easily be fired from a job if they demand more pay or better work conditions. Indeed, undocumented laborers run the real risk of not being paid for the work at all, with no legal recourse against unscrupulous contractors.[61] Restrictions on legal immigration suppress wages and benefits for illegal immigrants and legal immigrants facing employer discrimination because they might be illegals with easily obtained fraudulent documents. While to some extent dual labor markets restrict this downward wage pressure to immigrant workers, the fact that immigrants play a key role in the industrial and service sectors means that their lower wages and benefits exert a downward pressure on many U.S.-born workers as well.

The anti-immigration measures are also important politically to maintain white people's belief in the middle-class social order. This task is becoming more difficult each year, as the downward pressures make the American dream more unattainable to a growing number of Americans and the resources available to nation-states become less available. By placing the blame on immigrants for job losses and cuts in social services, political elites shore up the American middle-class ideology without expending scarce resources on less symbolic problems, such as the deteriorating public educational or public health systems. "The unprecedented expansion of border policing," Peter Andreas concludes, "has ultimately been less about achieving the stated instrumental goal of deterring illegal immigration and more about politically re-crafting the image of the border and symbolically reaffirming the state's territorial authority."[62] For these reasons, the tendency of political elites to find ways to pursue restrictionist, anti-immigrant policies can be expected to intensify, and with them, the racist labeling of immigrants, especially Latinos and Asians, as un-American "others."

Confusing the Global and the Local: The U.S. War on Terrorism

The U.S. response to the September 11, 2001, terrorist attacks on the World Trade Center and the Pentagon tragically provides a graphic example of the uses of nationalism and xenophobia in the global era. The problem of terrorism is itself a product of globalization, as decades of growing inequality and the destruction of nation-states have plunged large swaths of humanity into poverty and statelessness, making them easy pickings for warlords and criminal gangs to organize. Large numbers of hopeless and desperate people in the Middle East and Central Asia, regions devastated by colonialism and by decades of wars instigated by the United States and the former Soviet Union, have turned to leaders who advocate terrorism. These terrorist groups are well organized, well funded, and capable of achieving international political goals unthinkable in other stateless areas (such as parts of Africa or eastern Europe), where people turn their desperation and hopelessness against one another within the same locale.[63]

The attack on the World Trade Center and the Pentagon reveals the ways in which antiglobalization and anti-Americanism are bound together in much of the world. Unable to physically attack the abstract web of global capitalism, the terrorists chose to attack the nation that acts as the surrogate organizer of many of global capitalism's needs in the absence of developed global political and legal mechanisms. In short, the terrorists gave global capitalism a local face by viewing global capitalism and the United States as equivalents. By targeting the United States as the enemy, the terrorists demonstrated that they had no idea that globalization has created social crisis everywhere, including in the United States.

Unfortunately, the Bush administration's response replicated the terrorists' error by depicting the attack as an act of war against the United States and ignoring the impact of globalization on the Middle East. There was another alternative available to the United States: The attack could have been viewed as an international crime against the people of the world, and not an act of war against one nation. After all, almost a third of those killed were nationals of some sixty countries other than the United States, and the terror, as well as the economic and political consequences of the attack, was felt everywhere in the world. Unable to find the responsible parties—allegedly members of one organization of a loose network that sprawls over much of the Middle East, Africa, Central and South Asia, the Pacific, and Europe—the United States again substituted nationalism for a global analysis by attacking the Taliban regime of Afghanistan, removing that weak state from an area that already is virtually stateless. This framework both mistook the victim and the perpetrator, and tried to reduce both to nation-states. By so doing, the United States contributed (once more) to the crisis of the Middle East, furthered by its role in inflaming the Israeli-Palestinian crisis and by adding Iraq and Iran to its list of terrorist nations. As tragically, by putting itself in the position of avenger of "infinite justice" (the original code name for its military response) the United States made itself again the target of anger in the region, the very anger that produces popular support for terrorism in the first place.

The confusion of the global and the national in the war on terrorism has had serious consequences within the United States as well. President George W. Bush proclaimed that the United States had no responsibility for anti-American sentiments and argued that the root of the anti-American terrorism is a culturally depraved (evil) wing of Islamic and Arab cultures that envies American pluralism and individualism. "God," the president told a joint session of Congress, "is not neutral in this battle." The elevation of the United States as an innocent Christian nation under attack by uncivilized Muslim barbarians produced an enormous wave of American chauvinism, complete with crowds chanting "USA" at ball games and American flags being displayed everywhere. People who opined that the activities of global capitalism and the Pentagon might not be in Americans' best interest were assaulted by Attorney General John Ashcroft as traitors who condone terrorism. The externalization of anti-Americanism, and the assignation of "evil" to undefined Middle Eastern cultures, put millions of American Muslims and Arabs (and anyone who "looks" Arab or Middle Eastern) under suspicion. The wave of brutal assaults, murders, and other acts of discrimination against anyone thought to "look Arab" (including Indian Sikhs, Egyptian Christians, and even Latinos) was a chilling reminder of the power of xenophobia in a period of crisis. Panicked Americans now openly advocate anti-immigrant policies that before September 11, 2001, were considered extremist. Proposals for an outright ban on immigration, labeled extremist in the 2000 presidential campaign, are now considered a reasonable position. The practice of racial profiling, which was on the retreat in 2000 and 2001, has been embraced by large numbers of Americans in the wake of the terrorism. A CNN/USA Today/Gallup Poll taken a few days after the attack found that 58 percent of Americans supported intensive security checks for Arab Americans, 49 percent favored special identification cards, and 32 percent supported "special surveillance" of them.[64] The war on terrorism has in these ways furthered the tendency for those in the United States who can to use their privileges (in this case, citizenship and race) to defend against the social crisis of globalization. But, as with other efforts to recoil from global engagement and claim local privileges, this set of policies will certainly engender the very problems they are designed to end.

Conclusion: Contested Spaces, Contested Identities

One of the basic questions that every society must answer is: Who are "we"? The criteria for membership in a society are complex, ranging from formal criteria like legal citizenship, to informal factors like the social ties that one develops by living and working in the society.[65] Globalization has produced a contradictory set of impulses for answering this question for the United States. Globalization is increasing the United States' engagement with the rest of the world and the concomitant inclusion of immigrants into the U.S. economy and society, while heightening anti-immigrant sentiments and newly invigorating efforts to impose U.S. national interests on the entire planet. Globalization is creating new cosmopolitan spaces in the large cities at its core and is also stimulating the intensification of efforts by suburbanites to distance their communities from the cities. Globalization is producing paradoxical conditions that both increase the breaking down of barriers and intensify efforts to create walls between people. In short, globalization is producing a new type of conflict over membership in society.

The most palpable outcome of this conflict has been the increasing use of localism as a way of addressing the new dynamics associated with globalization. This localism is highly racialized, as both its suburban and anti-immigrant forms define "we" as white and "them" as not white. The racialization of localism comes from the essential point of the localist project: To create claims of privileged access to scarce social resources for white, middle- to upper-class people. Both forms of localism deny the essential fact that people on both sides of the "us-them" duality are participating in the same society. Suburban isolationists deny their inherent connection to the cities, while American nationalists deny the essential role of immigrants (legal and illegal) in the U.S. economy, and the growing engagement of the United States with the global economy.

While the racist and nationalist response to globalization can be expected to intensify, we would do well to remember that globalization is also undermining these trends by creating new ties between people. The growing numbers of Latino and Asian immigrants have already altered the political equation of the largest states. New possibilities for multiracial coalitions are appearing in American politics. The global cities are being remade, with new spaces that are not yet easily racialized. New possibilities for transnational politics are also being explored, both under human rights regimes and in grassroots forms of solidarity (see chapter 6). In these ways, we can anticipate more possibilities to contest the fearful, local responses to globalization in the future.

Notes

1. Anthony Giddens, *The Consequences of Modernity* (Cambridge, U.K.: Polity, 1990); David Harvey, *The Condition of Post-Modernity* (London: Blackwell, 1989).

2. Nigel Harris, *The New Untouchables: Immigration and the New World Order* (London: Penguin, 1995).

3. Edmund S. Morgan, *American Slavery, American Freedom: The Ordeal of Colonial Virginia* (New York: Norton, 1975).

4. Vine Deloria Jr., "American Indians," in *Multiculturalism in the United States: A Comparative Guide to Acculturation and Ethnicity*, ed. John D. Buenker and Lorman A. Ratner (New York: Greenwood, 1992), 173.

5. Tomás Almaguer, *Racial Fault Lines* (Berkeley: University of California Press, 1994), 107–150.

6. Much of the struggle of native peoples today is not for land but for sovereignty. See Alvin M. Josephy Jr., Joanne Nagel, and Troy Johnson, *Red Power: The American Indians' Fight for Freedom*, 2nd ed. (Lincoln: University of Nebraska Press, 1999).

7. W. E. B. Du Bois, *The Souls of Black Folk* (New York: Signet Classics, 1969).

8. Jill Quadagno, *The Color of Welfare: How Racism Undermined the War on Poverty* (New York: Oxford University Press, 1994).

9. David L. Kirp, John P. Dwyer, and Larry A. Rosenthal, *Our Town: Race, Housing, and the Soul of Suburbia* (New Brunswick, N.J.: Rutgers University Press, 1995).

10. The term "politically relevant people" is insightfully used by Max Weber to explain elites' political calculations in decision making. See Max Weber, *Economy and Society*, vol. 2 (Berkeley: University of California Press, 1978), 667.

11. Before that time, many European whites remained ethnic by choice, as their membership in an ethnic community gave them important capacities to mobilize resources. The middle-class order provided an alternative for most descendants of European immigrants only after World War II. See chapter 2.

12. Reginald Farley et al., "'Chocolate Cities, Vanilla Suburbs': Will the Trend toward Racially Segregated Communities Continue?" *Social Science Research* 7 (1978): 335.

13. See summary of surveys from the 1980s and early 1990s in Douglas S. Massey and Nancy A. Denton, *American Apartheid: Segregation and the Making of the Underclass* (Cambridge, Mass.: Harvard University Press, 1993), 94–96.

14. Martin Luther King Jr., *Where Do We Go from Here: Chaos or Community?* (Boston: Beacon, 1968), 4.

15. Quadagno, *Color of Welfare*, 113.

16. *Keys v. Denver District 1*, 413 U.S. 189 (1973). For an analysis, see Owen Fiss, "The Uncertain Path of School Desegregation Law," in *Equality and Preferential Treatment*, ed. Marshall Cohen, Thomas Nagel, and Thomas Scanlon (Princeton, N.J.: Princeton University Press, 1977), 155–191.

17. Kirp, Dwyer, and Rosenthal, *Our Town*, 77.

18. *Milliken v. Bradley*, 433 U.S. 267 (1974).

19. Kirp, Dwyer, and Rosenthal, *Our Town*, 219.

20. Kirp, Dwyer, and Rosenthal, *Our Town*, 96.

21. Kirp, Dwyer, and Rosenthal, *Our Town*, 102–104.

22. Massey and Denton, *American Apartheid*, 77, see also 76, table 3.4.

23. Massey and Denton, *American Apartheid*, 70.

24. Massey and Denton, *American Apartheid*, 61–67; a similar finding for the period 1940 to 1980 is reported for Chicago by Gary Orfield, "Ghettoization and Its Alternatives," in *The New Urban Reality*, ed. Paul E. Peterson (Washington, D.C.: Brookings, 1985), 161–193.

25. Massey and Denton, *American Apartheid*, 96–109.

26. Robert C. Smith, *Racism in the Post–Civil Rights Society* (Albany: SUNY Press, 1995), 67, table 4.2.

27. Massey and Denton, *American Apartheid*, 99–101.

28. Massey and Denton, *American Apartheid*, 124, table 5.1.

29. Isabel V. Sawhill et al., eds., *Welfare Reform and Beyond: The Future of the Safety Net* (Washington, D.C.: Brookings Institute, 2002).

30. Walter L. Updegrave, "Race and Money," *Money* (December 1989): 159.

31. See the discussion of the incorporation movement in chapter 3, as well as in Henry J. Abraham, *Freedom and the Court: Civil Rights and Liberties in the United States*, 3rd ed. (New York: Oxford University Press, 1977).

32. William Julius Wilson, *The Declining Significance of Race: Blacks and Changing American Institutions* (Chicago: University of Chicago Press, 1978).

33. Charles V. Willie, *Caste and Class Controversy* (Dix Hills, N.Y.: General Hall, 1979); Roy L. Brooks, *Rethinking the American Race Problem* (Berkeley: University of California Press, 1990).

34. Joan Moore and James Diego Vigil, "Barrios in Transition," in *In the Barrios: Latinos and the Underclass Debate*, ed. Joan Moore and Raquel Pinderhughes (New York: Russell Sage Foundation, 1993), 27–50.

35. Orfield, "Ghettoization and Its Alternatives," 163.

36. Ralph and Goldy Lewis Center for Regional Policy Studies, *Census 2000 Fact Sheet* (Los Angeles: Center for Regional Policy Studies, 2001).

37. Mike Davis, *City of Quartz* (London: Verso, 1990).

38. Mary S. Pardo, *Mexican American Women Activists: Identity and Resistance in Two Los Angeles Communities* (Philadelphia: Temple University Press, 1998), especially 82–104.

39. The fluidity of ethnicity is well explained by Yen Le Espiritu, *Asian American Panethnicity* (Philadelphia: Temple University Press, 1992).

40. Harris, *New Untouchables*.

41. Joseph Nevins, "The Remaking of the California-Mexico Boundary in the Age of NAFTA," in *The Wall around the West: State Borders and Immigration Controls in North America and Europe*, ed. Peter Andreas and Timothy Snyder (Lanham, Md.: Rowman & Littlefield, 2000), 99.

42. Harris, *New Untouchables*.

43. Saskia Sassen, *Guests and Aliens* (New York: The New Press, 1999).

44. Tomás Almaguer, *Racial Fault Lines* (Berkeley: University of California Press, 1994), 117.

45. Stephen Steinberg, *The Ethnic Myth: Race, Ethnicity and Class in America*, 3rd ed. (Boston: Beacon, 2001), 3–11.

46. This distinction between racial privileging and national minority oppression is, unfortunately, blurred in otherwise excellent accounts of the European immigrants in America, such as Matthew Frye Jacobson, *Whiteness of a Different Color: European Immigrants and the Alchemy of Race* (Cambridge, Mass.: Harvard University Press, 1998).

47. Sassen, *Guests and Aliens*, 76–98.

48. Kenneth T. Jackson, *The Ku Klux Klan in the City* (New York: Oxford University Press, 1967).

49. The exclusion of Japanese immigrants by the Gentleman's Agreement in 1905 had a different class dynamic: Japanese were singled out mainly to deny them legal rights to land they had begun to acquire in the late nineteenth century in the Northwest.

50. Gerald P. Lopez, "Undocumented Migration: In Search of Just Immigration Law and Policy," *UCLA Law Review* 28, no. 615 (1981): 623–633.

51. Debra L. DeLaet, *U.S. Immigration Policy in an Age of Rights* (Westport, Conn.: Praeger, 2000), 67.

52. Cited in Ruth Conniff, "The War on Aliens: The Right Calls the Shots," *The Progressive* (October 1993): 22–29.

53. John Fredriksson, "Bridging the Gap between Rights and Responsibilities: Policy Changes Affecting Refugees and Immigrants in the United States since 1996," *Georgetown Immigration Law Journal* 14, no. 3 (Spring 2000): 757–778.

54. Peter Andreas, *Border Games: Policing the U.S.-Mexican Divide* (Ithaca, N.Y.: Cornell University Press, 2000), 89.

55. Andreas, *Border Games*, 95–96.

56. Mike Davis, *Magical Urbanism* (London: Verso, 2000), 43.

57. Bill Ong Hing, "The Immigrant As Criminal: Punishing Dreamers," *Hastings Women's Law Journal* 9, no. 1 (Winter 1998): 79–96.

58. Cecilia M. Espenoza, "Crimes of Violence by Non-citizens and the Immigration Consequences," *Colorado Lawyer* 26, no. 10 (October 1997): 89.

59. Andreas, *Border Games*, 101.

60. Saskia Sassen, *Globalization and Its Discontents* (New York: The New Press, 1998), 49.

61. The Day Laborer Program of San Francisco–based La Raza Centro Legal was established in 1999 for this reason.

62. Andreas, *Border Games*, 95.

63. J. M. Coetzee, *Disgrace* (New York: Viking, 1999).

64. Sam Howe Verhovek, "Americans Give in to Racial Profiling," *New York Times*, 23 September 2001, 1.

65. Sassen, *Guests and Aliens*.

CHAPTER FIVE

~

It's "Mine": Globalization, Racism, and the Erosion of Social Responsibility

One of the great ironies of globalization is that it is producing a retreat from the civic sphere. It would seem reasonable to expect that the advent of new means for binding people together across the globe would greatly expand civic life. After all, the expansion of means of communication, information processing, and transport have raised at least the potential for people to form new social ties across previously closed boundaries. In some ways, the world has indeed become a "global village," in which instantaneous communication and universal cultural expectations have reshaped people's understanding of themselves in a global context.[1]

The principal social response to globalization in the United States has not been to embrace global relationships or understanding, however. Instead, we live in an era in which public-spirited universalism—the concern for the well-being of "the people" as a whole—is a decreasing priority. In its place, a new focus on individual responsibility has arisen. From health care, to poverty, to education, to retirement, Americans are now told that their well-being is up to them, that people must fend for themselves as far as their personal welfare is concerned. In the last chapter, I examined the ways that people are using racial and national privileges to retreat from the global into locally defined spaces. In this chapter, I look at the ways that people use racial privileges to buffer themselves from the social crisis of globalization by renouncing social responsibility and by claiming that individuals are responsible for their own fates.

The "great shift" in public consciousness occurred in the United States during the 1970s.[2] During that decade, Bruce J. Schulman argues, the American middle class lost confidence in expanding prosperity in the face of a series of social traumas. Within a few years—1974 to 1976—the United States lost the war in Vietnam, the oil crisis (erroneously blamed on the Organization for Petroleum Exporting Countries) tripled the price of gasoline, and high inflation rates and a recession crippled the middle class's buying power. These crises reflected changes in the global political economy and the United States' place within it. In the current era of globalization, the large investors and transnational corporations who are the main beneficiaries of the new global technologies have gained significant new bargaining power over political elites (see chapter 3). This has resulted in greater income inequality as well as the retreat from redistributive social programs and regulatory mechanisms that were the hallmark of the type of state found in all of the most developed capitalist nations over the past fifty or so years.

A growing focus on individual and family welfare and a retreat from a concern for the public good has resulted from these trends. The welfare state's pledge to enable all Americans to participate in the middle class—backed by promises of full employment, adequate housing, and access to a good education—has been replaced by a government dedicated to individual asset accumulation. In the new private investment state regime, the government's role is to facilitate individuals' efforts to take care of their own needs and those of their families through market activities. The universal entitlement programs of the welfare state are disparaged as misguided efforts that took away individuals' responsibility for their own well-being.

The retreat from the welfare state has meant the privatization of many benefits and entitlement programs formerly provided by government or corporations. This trend is most pronounced in the United States, which always had the least developed welfare state of any industrialized society. The U.S. welfare state, to some extent, had socialized the costs of health care, housing, and education, and, to a more limited extent, redistributed social resources downward. The political rhetoric of the welfare state era stressed social responsibility and universalistic rights and entitlements. But the social entitlement programs developed from the 1930s until the 1960s bore the stamp of Jim Crow white supremacy and thus largely excluded people of color or treated them unequally.[3] Much of the civil rights movement's efforts in the 1960s and 1970s were aimed at equalizing access to welfare state programs (see chapter 7).

Today, as these social programs are cut back or eliminated outright, Americans are able to get benefits and services they can individually afford to purchase and little else. The decline or elimination of social insurance programs has pressured individuals to purchase their own private health care insurance and fund their own retirement plans. The decline of funding for public education has led to the rapid proliferation of private schools, paid for by private individuals. Corporate benefit packages are a thing of the past for many workers. Work is becoming increasingly "casual," with a growing number of workers hired as "contractors" lacking all legal protections and benefits as employees. Government tax and investment policies, under both Republican and Democratic administrations, have been reshaped to facilitate the growing focus on individual wealth accumulation.

The narrowing vision of social responsibility and the concomitant rise of individualism reveal a profound contradiction of globalization. The appropriation of new technologies for production, communication, and transportation by large corporations and financial institutions has simultaneously brought the world closer together and, by assaulting the middle-class social order, has torn apart what had been understood as civic society in the post–World War II boom era.

Personal Wealth and Race

The retreat from the welfare state and the rise of the private investment state in the global era mean that what had previously been considered social entitlements are now increasingly seen as individuals' personal responsibility to obtain, distributed through the private marketplace. The distribution of what Max Weber calls "market chances"—that is, opportunities to buy or sell in order to gain social resources—is typically thought of as depending on income. That is, the more an individual earns, the more market chances he or she has. While there is considerable and growing income inequality in the United States (see chapter 3), some economists note that incomes have remained stable or increased for most American families during the 1990s and consequently surmise that the middle class is doing just fine.

This assessment does not take into account two crucial factors, however. First is that income stability actually marks a downward trend in the standard of living as most Americans are forced to assume enormous new expenses from the privatization of previously social entitlement programs. As the Clinton administration attempted to explain in its early effort to enact health care reform, the privatization of health care alone is responsible for the declining standard of living of a sizable portion of the American population.[4] The privatization of retirement and education are even greater drains of American families' income.

The second factor missing from this rosy assessment of the middle class is the increasing importance of personal and family wealth to provide people with access to opportunities. Ownership of assets is increasingly vital for success in the privatized society. With the retreat of government and corporations from social benefits, those without assets are exposed to the vagaries of the labor market and life's crises with no safety net to catch them if they fall. Americans are compelled to rely on personal savings accounts, home equity loans, and the sale of other assets to tide them over during crises brought on by the loss of a job, death of a spouse, or long-term illness. Without assets to fall back on, such personal crises can become catastrophic and can even snowball into homelessness. Assets are also necessary to start a new business, to invest in upward mobility opportunities (especially education) for a child, to purchase expensive benefits, such as private health insurance, and to purchase a home. Tax code revisions have greatly reduced capital gains taxes, further increasing the value of, and the inequality of, privately held assets.[5] The exploding value of stocks and bonds—with over 90 percent of privately owned shares held by the top tenth of Americans—was the most important source of the rising standards of living in the 1990s.[6] But the absence of assets literally excluded over half the population from the private wealth expansion of that decade.

The causes and consequences of wealth inequality are distinct from people's income-earning capacity. Income statistics measure the amount of money (or, for the poor, the value of social entitlements) an individual or family earns in a given unit of time, typically one year. The problem with income as a measure of market chances is that people's income-earning capacity can fluctuate wildly in their lifetime. An individual can wait tables after graduating from college and appear poor in income terms, even as he or she is taking the first steps that lead to a $300,000 a year income as a corporate lawyer a decade later. Even more significantly, people's yearly income is rarely the sole or even the main basis for their market chances. Their ownership of assets (or lack thereof) is often crucial to their market chances. Wealth (in this case, personal or family assets) refers to privately owned forms of property that have the potential to increase in value. The main sources of private wealth in the United States are stocks and bonds, real estate, and savings accounts. Wealth ownership is vastly more unequal than income inequality. The reason for this is that wealth inequality tends to get magnified over generations. Those who inherit significant assets are better positioned to take advantage of market chances to increase their wealth than those who do not. For example, those who possessed significant assets—about 10 percent of Americans—were able to enjoy the historic bull market of the 1990s; those who had little or no assets could not. Thus, wealth measures the accumulation of advantages over generations, not just on a year-by-year basis. The absence of wealth thus measures the lack of opportunities over generations.

In one of the most important studies of race in the 1990s, Melvin L. Oliver and Thomas M. Shapiro explore ways in which systematic racial discrimination against black people throughout American history affects racial inequality in wealth ownership today.[7] Blacks' individual median incomes are 62 percent that of whites. But blacks' median individual net worth (which, for most people, means the value of their home and savings account) is only 8 percent that of whites.[8] The huge (twelve to one) median black-white ratio in individual asset ownership dramatically reveals the impact of past discrimination on the present. For the first half of the United States' existence, the vast majority of black people could not own property—indeed, most *were* property. For most of the second half of the nation's history, Jim Crow legal segregation and the sharecropping system put harsh racial barriers in the way of African Americans seeking to accumulate capital. Of course, some African Americans did amass wealth during the slave and Jim Crow eras. But the gigantic gap in median individual asset ownership reveals the ways that racism in the past systematically prevented African Americans as a group from asset ownership as compared with whites.

The differences in asset ownership are not just a function of income inequality: African Americans who earn $50,000 a year own assets worth on average 20 percent of the value of assets owned by whites at the same income level.[9] In this sense, the black middle class is not the equivalent of the white middle class. The lack of assets puts significant roadblocks in the way of most black middle-class families, making it difficult for them to purchase a home, send their children to private schools or elite colleges, or to start a business, let alone to protect themselves from crises like an illness or the loss of a job. The lack of assets also means that the main income-enhancing activity of the last two decades for wealthy Americans—the rising value of stocks and bonds and real estate—largely eluded the black community.[10]

While the median disparity in wealth ownership is somewhat less pronounced for Latinos and Asian Americans than it is for blacks and Native Americans, the impact of inequality in asset ownership is an important and understudied issue for many minority communities. Because of the complexity of immigration and the uneven process of assimilation into U.S. society, major disparities in asset ownership—and thus disparities in the potential for future asset formation—can be found between people of different nationalities and people within a single nationality who all may be categorized within the same racial group. For example, the first wave of Cuban Americans to come to the

United States as refugees from socialist Cuba in the late 1950s were mostly upper-class families who brought with them all of their liquid assets. As well, the U.S. government accorded these immigrants political refugee status, making them eligible for government subsidies, such as Small Business Administration loans. In contrast, refugees from the U.S.-sponsored war in El Salvador in the 1980s were often poor workers who had been displaced from their homes and jobs. These refugees, who often were not even accorded legal immigrant status in the United States because they were denied refugee status, had little or no assets. While both groups are Latino, that is, are racialized in similar ways, the role of assets in their ethnic community building and assimilation into the United States could not be more different. Similarly, the contrast between the life chances of wealthy Taiwanese immigrants and extremely poor Laotian immigrants could not be greater, although both are termed "Asian" in America. The problems of poor immigrants are further compounded by recent policy changes denying access to welfare benefits to legal immigrants. Given the growing number of immigrants from less developed countries entering the United States, the barriers to opportunities because of the lack of capital are increasingly important problems to be studied.

In sum, the enormous expansion in the value and importance of private assets in the 1980s and 1990s had major racial effects, accentuating the highly unequal "market chances" not only in class, but also in racial terms. Middle-class people of color have been significantly less able than middle-class whites to use privately owned assets to buffer themselves from the downward pressures on their living standards created by declining wages and cuts in social services. The shift under way in the United States from public funding of education, health care, and other social services to privately purchased benefits and services accentuates the racial disparity inherited from the past. The dynamics of globalization are thus exacerbating racial inequalities inherited from the past in a way that reverses the equalizing trends of the 1950s–1970s welfare state policies and programs.

Privatization has produced yet another specific effect on African Americans: The reduction in government-run social services and military employment has led to massive displacement of middle-class African Americans, who disproportionately work in public-sector jobs.[11] As Andrew Hacker observes, "Over a third of all black lawyers work for the government, as do almost 30 percent of black scientists. Blacks account for over 20 percent of the nation's armed services, twice their proportion in the civilian economy. They hold almost a fifth of positions in the Postal Service, and have similar ratios in many urban agencies. . . . On the whole, then, the business world has not done much to expand black employment."[12] The widespread cutbacks at every level of government during the 1980s and 1990s have disproportionately fallen on African Americans. Public-sector employment has not been as pervasive for the Latino or Asian American middle classes, as they lacked the political muscle of the civil rights movement that was necessary to gain access to public jobs in the 1970s, when most of the gains in black middle-class employment occurred. The Latino and Asian American middle classes instead largely expanded through the development of small businesses and, especially for some Asians, professional and technical positions. Cutbacks in public employment, then, have largely had a specific and negative impact on the black middle class disproportional to its effect on other racial minorities.

Individual Educational Achievement and Racism

Just as personal wealth is becoming more important as a way to gain access to education, health care, retirement, and so on in the global era, so is personal educational attainment. The link between educational attainment and occupational status is becoming increasingly strong. Those who do not graduate from college are increasingly at a disadvantage in today's economy. The idea that individuals should be rewarded for their own work and talent is being used more frequently to justify the process for selecting people into schools that serve as gateways to desirable jobs. Standardized tests and "neutral" criteria like grade point averages are becoming more important in educational advancement than at any time since the mid-1960s. The administration of George W. Bush, in particular, has aggressively promoted national standardized testing in the name of promoting quality public education. The main argument used to convince California and Washington voters to oppose affirmative action programs in 1996 and 1998, respectively, was the idea that people should be judged by their qualifications and achievements, not their race.

This new focus on individual achievement is part and parcel of the policies of the private accumulation welfare state and the growing middle-class fear that are integral to the era of globalization. The welfare state had to an extent placed the potential for individual success in the context of group or societal rights, responsibilities, and entitlements.[13] The fixation on individual attainment results from the fear of downward mobility gripping much of the middle class. The resulting climate of anxiety promotes individual competition and a predisposition to reject all social entitlements as fetters on individual liberty. While Americans still believe in the value of equal opportunity, a majority of white Americans view efforts to address systematic forms of class, race, and gender inequalities in society as deviations from this ideal.

Indeed, the insistence that people's access to jobs or education is a matter of individual effort renders profound class, race, and gender inequalities in life chances invisible altogether. At the extreme, the undeniable facts of class, race, and gender inequalities in the context of the assumption that everyone has a fair chance can and has served as a breeding ground for biological explanations as a way of thoroughly "naturalizing" inequality.[14]

The new attention to individual achievement raises questions about the ambiguous meanings of "merit." Implicit in the argument that people should be judged by their own achievements is the belief that we know what merit is and how to measure it. The idea that people should be selected for jobs and schools on the basis of merit first surfaced in the 1880s as founders of modern universities first made their case that technical and scientific knowledge makes professionals the leaders of society.[15] By the 1950s, as mass higher education spread downward into (and helped forge) the middle class, the belief that people should be selected by schools or for jobs on the basis of their knowledge became more widely accepted.

Writing in 1958, Michael Young observed a deep contradiction in the principle that power should be wielded by those with knowledge, "the meritocracy" as he termed it.[16] On the one hand, the meritocracy stands in opposition to the rule of society by an inherited elite caste. In this sense, the meritocracy embraces the democratic ideal that every individual has equal opportunity to make it on the basis of his or her own hard work and talent. On the other hand, the defenders of the meritocracy are unabashedly elitist in the sense that they must defend the criteria that are the basis for selection of the "most capable" to schools and jobs. If these standards are not defended, then the best and the brightest will not be selected for the best schools and jobs, and society as a whole will lose as "incompetent" people become the decision makers.[17]

The architects of mass public higher education aggressively promoted the ideology of merit to justify their efforts to make colleges the gateway to the middle class in the 1950s and 1960s (see chapter 2). In the modern world of high technology and science, they argued, individuals must be rewarded for the knowledge they attain, not the wealth or race to which they were born. Society's leaders would be those with the credentials that marked them, in the words of John F. Kennedy, as "the best and the brightest." The linkage between college degrees and jobs became stronger in the 1970s as the unionized, full-time, blue-collar jobs that had provided access to middle-class status began to fall drastically, and the new high-technology jobs supporting transnational corporations began to proliferate. With access to the middle class now running almost exclusively through college, the ideology of selection by individual attainment had the potential to become dominant.

But virtually at the same time, critics of the idea of the meritocracy began to make their case.[18] "Merit," they argued, was not a neutral description of the knowledge needed to become a leader of society; instead, it was an ideology used to justify the rule of society by the wealthy, the white, and the male, hiding their inherited privileges behind claims of technical competence and scientific knowledge. College curricula, in particular, came under the critical scrutiny of students in the Black Power, Chicano, and American Indian movements in the late 1960s. The biases toward white, male, and upper-class experiences and interests were also critiqued in the practices screening people for access to the professions. As ethnic studies programs were established in the 1970s, a movement for multicultural diversity was born, gradually compelling universities and employers to adopt multidimensional selection procedures in which the life experiences of people from underrepresented groups could be plus factors in both student admissions and hiring for academic positions.

The need to critique and recast the official culture of merit in order to create equal opportunity thus became explicitly recognized in higher education. The development of ethnic studies programs, the creation of bridge programs for disadvantaged students, and efforts to make universities truly multicultural in curriculum and student life have all been part of the effort to transform the institutional culture of higher education in ways that can both enrich the curriculum and increase the opportunity for success by students from diverse cultural backgrounds.[19] Efforts to desegregate occupations by race and gender have not resulted in the lowering of standards, but in higher standards for all employees, as women and people of color bring different mixes of skills and knowledge to the job. Disputing academic and job "standards" and the claims of neutrality of the hiring and selection process have always been at the heart of efforts to institute affirmative action programs. Advocates of affirmative action programs have long argued that the hiring (and contracting) processes of most higher-prestige jobs have historically rested heavily on informal "good ol' boy" networks in which inherited social ties, not merit, carried great weight (or determined) who would get the job or slot in a school. As well, the standards used to select candidates for schools and jobs have traditionally discriminated against minorities and women.[20] The rationale for affirmative action programs is to provide remedies for precisely these problems.[21]

The growing anxiety of middle-class whites in the era of globalization has fostered desperate efforts to protect their access to selective credentials and jobs "by any means necessary." The backlash against multiculturalism intensified as the trend toward more restricted opportunities began to threaten the white middle class. A debate over multicultural diversity ensued in the 1980s, dubbed the "culture wars" by the popular media. Conservative writers lambasted the multicultural agenda as an attack on intellectual rigor by soft-minded, subjective advocates of particular group interests.[22] In the 1990s, the idea of multiculturalism was attacked by two important California ballot initiatives: Proposition 209 sought to end public affirmative action programs in 1996, and Proposition 21 sought to end English as a Second Language (ESL) programs in 1998. Both initiatives passed handily, as middle-class suburban whites agreed with the propositions' sponsors that affirmative action programs undermine standards that validly measure individual achievement, and that ESL programs promote values that diverge from those needed to succeed in American society.

The reassertion of so-called race neutral concepts of achievement and selection processes in the late 1990s have already dramatically reinforced racial as well as class privileges. When the University of California (UC) barred the use of race and gender as factors in the student selection process, the admission of African American, Latino, Native American, and Filipino students to the university's most selective campuses plummeted. Between 1997 and 1998, UC Berkeley admissions of African American undergraduates dropped by 51 percent, Latinos by 43 percent, and Native Americans by 39 percent. Between 1998 and 1999, the drop was even more precipitous, with African Americans constituting 3.9 percent of the undergraduate student body, down from nearly 14 percent a scarce four years before. Measured in comparison to their percentage of high school graduates in California, the UC Berkeley entering class in 1998 was the least diverse of any class admitted since 1970.[23] The new "race neutral" admissions process produced these radical results by heavily weighing factors in which minority students were at a serious disadvantage. For example, the University of California gave extra grade points for Advanced Placement courses, which are often not available in poor inner-city schools. Relying on such measures of achievement, UC Berkeley rejected over 700 minority applicants with grade point averages of 4.0 in 1998. For another example, law schools have defended the LSATs as race neutral because they predict students' grades, regardless of race. But, as William C. Kidder shows, grades are also race and gender biased in law schools where white men dominate the faculty and curriculum, and so both the LSATs and grading practices are similarly biased.[24]

Another version of the dogmatic reassertion of "race neutrality" appeared in the U.S. Supreme Court's decisions in the 1990s concerning the Voting Rights Act. The majority in *Shaw v. Reno* (1993) found that race-conscious redistricting is suspect for discrimination and admonished states to be very cautious about tampering with existing district lines. As J. Morgan Kousser and Lani Guinier show, however, *Shaw* and subsequent decisions assume that maintaining the status quo is race neutral, when in fact it is anything but.[25] The problem revealed by this claim of neutrality is the severing of the past from the present. The creation of the belief that the status quo is race neutral manifests a breathtaking willingness to ignore the specific ways that past systems of racial discrimination influence the present.

The new trends toward standardization and race neutrality fly in the face of the evidence that *any* standardization inherently involves the privileging of some culture as "official," and the "official" imprimatur has always been the historical privilege of upper-class white males. The claim that the choice of candidates for schools or jobs is "neutral" if the institution does *not* acknowledge race covers up the many forms of racial advantage that operate in the selection process. The reappearance of these so-called race neutral practices, after thirty years of trying to change them, is not based on some new insights about standards or success in ending the use of informal networking ("good ol' boy" networks/old school ties) in the selection process. Instead, we are witnessing the return to universities' overreliance on old standbys, such as grade point averages, test scores, and the "quality" of the candidate's high school, despite a multitude of studies demonstrating that such standards are not predictive of student success and are highly discriminatory.[26] It is no surprise that the effect of the "new" admissions processes are almost as effective as legal segregation in keeping African Americans, Latinos, and Native Americans out of selective universities. As well, the elimination of affirmative action has enabled employers to return to informal and subjective hiring practices that privilege their friends and families or anyone with whom they "feel comfortable," generally people who look and act like themselves. The dogma of individualism thus cloaks the abandonment of efforts to critically scrutinize the biases inherent in American educational institutions and the workplace concerning the processes of selection themselves.

Individual selection on the basis of standardized achievement criteria is often justified as a level playing field. But this approach cannot give people an equal opportunity to succeed. Inheritance—and barriers to opportunity—takes forms other than wealth. Another asset that can be inherited is social capital—that is, contact with people who can provide access to valuable resources. An individual may inherit from his or her family and community personal ties to mentors and sponsors, who can ease the way to (or even guarantee entrée to) selective schools or jobs. These contacts can be especially valuable at the beginning of careers, when any competitive edge—a summer job working in a prestigious law firm, for example—can make all the difference in the selection of candidates to the "best" schools (where "best" is defined as the greatest chance of access to elite jobs after graduation). The converse is also true: The absence of inherited access to networks of influence can place an individual at a significant disadvantage in gaining access to such resources. Indeed, the lack of mentors and sponsors can and often does leave people feeling completely unable to even imagine how they could successfully enter into, or survive in, let alone compete in such selective settings.[27]

Pierre Bourdieu delineates yet another form of inheritance that is of great significance for increasing (or decreasing) individuals' opportunities for asset formation: cultural capital.[28] Cultural capital refers to the degree to which the culture of a group of people is recognized as officially "valid" in powerful social institutions. Those who are raised in settings where they learn to think and behave according to the culture valorized by official institutions are thus advantaged (in terms of access to wealth, power, and prestige) over those who have to "unlearn" their own culture and then "relearn" another culture in order to succeed. The focus on individual achievement measured by standardized selection procedures thus has the effect of rewarding those with the "right" cultural capital, dogmatically asserting that individuals' knowledge results from their own efforts and talents alone, rather from their specific social situation, their "habitus," aptly termed by Bourdieu.

The return to the meritocratic principles of the 1950s has unleashed powerful discriminatory mechanisms, which have racial, as well as class, and gender effects. This retreat is happening despite the accumulated evidence of the last thirty years' efforts to develop multidimensional selection processes for schools and jobs. Indeed, it seems clear that this retreat is happening *because* of the successes of affirmative action, ethnic studies, ESL programs, and so on. The increasing numbers of African Americans, Latinos, and Asian Americans in previously all-white professions and selective schools had the potential to permanently alter the culture of American institutions. Derrick Bell argues that affirmative action programs run into increasing resistance as the numbers of minorities in a selective institution increase toward a "tipping point," beyond which there are sufficient people of color in institutional positions to redefine institutions' missions and standards and to challenge discriminatory selection and promotion mechanisms with or without "race-conscious" policies.[29] Bell's observation may well be accurate, but he explains this resistance as a permanent and unchangeable fact of American society. Racism, he concludes, will always be with us.[30] This fatalism is unwarranted. The resistance to affirmative action is not inherent in white people, but is historically situated in the climate of fear and inequality created by globalization. The middle class's mounting anxiety over the scarcity of good jobs, in the context of the decline of social consciousness fomented by the private accumulation state, is stimulating a virulent predisposition to defend racial privileges, including the demagogic return to race-neutral meritocratic criteria.

The racial consequences of "neutral" policies are patently obvious—if we can get the data to prove it. But another part of the reassertion of white privilege in the era of globalization is the effort to stop the collection of such data. For example, the architect of California's Proposition 209, Ward Connerly, has succeeded at placing a Racial Privacy Initiative on the California ballot in March 2004. The act would bar state agencies from collecting data on the race, ethnicity, or national origins of applicants for jobs, contracts, or social services. If it passes, this ballot initiative could well render the resurgence of racial privileges invisible.[31] For another example, Attorney General John Ashcroft opposes data collection on the race of people involved in police traffic stops. This data is essential to ascertain whether racial profiling is being practiced by local, state, and national police departments.[32] If the collection of racial impact data is banned, the myth of individual selection on the basis neutral and universalistic standards can be perpetuated.

The War on Crime, Individual Responsibility, and Racism

From Emile Durkheim to Michel Foucault, sociologists have long maintained that prisons reveal important truths about the society in which they are located.[33] A look inside America's prisons is particularly revealing. Some 2.1 million people are currently incarcerated in state prisons and local jails. In a given year, over 12 million people are convicted of crimes. Some 6.3 million people are currently on parole or probation. The incarceration rate for the United States, 702 per 100,000 people, is the highest reported in the world.[34]

But this snapshot is incomplete without a look at the racial composition of the inmate population. Black men, who comprise only 6.5 percent of the U.S. population, constitute 46 percent of prisoners in the United States. The rate of incarceration for black men, 3,109 per 100,000 in 1990, is far and away the highest rate of incarceration of any population in the world.[35] Thirty-two percent of all black men aged twenty to twenty-nine are currently under some type of correctional control. Black men have eight times the chance of white men to be incarcerated at some point in their lives. Latino, Native American, and Asian American men are also disproportionately found in the nation's prisons. Latino men have four times the chance of serving time in prison as do white men. Twice as many Latino men as whites are currently in prison, on parole, or on probation. Incarceration of women has increased 7 percent per year since 1970, almost twice the rate (4.5 percent per year) for men.[36] The racial composition of women prisoners is similar to that of men.

Most Americans are quite aware that the nation's prison population is disproportionately nonwhite. Indeed, media and popular cultural portrayals tend to exaggerate people of color's criminality, and many whites tend to stereotype all young black and Latino men as criminals.[37] Majorities of middle-class suburbanites routinely support strong "anticrime" measures, including increased funding for police and prisons, longer mandatory minimum sentences for a growing list of crimes and people (youth, immigrants, and so on), and the death penalty. In some states, such as California and Texas, expenditures on the criminal justice system now outstrip spending for public higher education. The justification for these measures is direct and simple: The "good" people—the property-owning, fully employed suburbanites—need to be protected from the "bad" people—the people of color of the ghettoes and barrios, the illegal immigrants, and, in some places, the Chinese and Vietnamese gangs or the Native American thieves. The people who are sent to prison are presumed to be those who have violated the values of society and are deserving of punishment as a way to hold them accountable for the choices they have made. In this way, the war on crime is a morality play, a way of asserting the value of individual responsibility for each person's life and defending the "good" people who live responsibly according to the rules of society from the "bad" people. Supporters of the war on crime have no trouble explaining the fact that a large percentage of America's prisoners are poor (85 percent of those incarcerated are from the poorest fifth of the population) and people of color (72 percent of the prison population is nonwhite in a society where 70 percent of the population is white). Ghettoes, barrios, reservations, and Chinatowns are depicted as pathological communities, seething with drug-dealing gangs of violent criminals, spawned by broken families and misguided welfare policies.[38]

But is the war on crime really about stopping people from committing acts that are harmful to society's well-being? Many criminologists have long asserted that only some acts that are harmful to society are called crimes, and these are disproportionately the harmful acts committed by property-less people.[39] The harmful acts committed by corporations—assaults on the environment, unsafe product designs, work conditions endangering workers' health and safety, and so on—are rarely covered by criminal statute and even more rarely lead to criminal prosecution of individuals.[40] Even the criminal acts of those with property seldom lead to imprisonment. Corporate crimes go unreported because their private police forces do not report them; police are less likely to arrest affluent wrong-doers for fear of "damaging their career." Prosecutors are more likely to drop or reduce charges against wealthy defendants partly out of a concern that these people will be able to afford good lawyers and mount an aggressive defense.[41] Those who can afford private defense have a much lower rate of conviction, and wealthy individuals convicted of crimes generally receive more lenient sentences. Thus, a chain of bias makes the war on crime at best a highly selective war, in which only some harmful acts are criminalized and some of the people who commit those acts are punished.

As the snapshot of the incarcerated U.S. population shows, the war on crime does not just single out the poor, but particularly criminalizes people of color. To some extent, crime in America has always been racialized. Slave owners were protected against criminal prosecution when they inflicted serious injury on the human beings they had enslaved, but a person who was enslaved could be punished severely for any infraction.[42] Whites in California and other states could not be convicted of crimes based on the testimony of people of color during the nineteenth and early twentieth centuries.[43] Lynching, although technically illegal, was generally protected by the police and the courts and systematically used against both African Americans and Mexican Americans throughout the Jim Crow era.[44]

Despite the long history of racism by the criminal justice system, the staggering number of people of color incarcerated in America's prisons today is unprecedented. In 1930, some 75 percent of people incarcerated were white and 22 percent were African American, with a total prison population only 7 percent (!) the size of today's. The small numbers of black prisoners in 1930—less than 30,000 in the entire nation—suggests that the use of repressive force against people of color during the Jim Crow era was much less likely to involve legal procedures. Instead, repressive force was likely to be administered "extralegally" by institutions such as the Ku Klux Klan. In 1992, by contrast, 29 percent of people incarcerated were white, 51 percent were African American, and 20 percent were Hispanic, and the proportion of nonwhites is increasing.[45] Today, over a million black men and women are incarcerated in America's prisons and jails.

The proportion of inmates of Hispanic origin increased from 7.7 percent in 1980 to 14.3 percent in 1993 alone. During this period, the rate of imprisonment of Hispanics soared from 163 per 100,000 to 529 inmates per 100,000 Hispanic residents in the United States.[46] Growing incarceration rates are partially due to the rapid increase of the U.S. Latino population. But much more is involved, including the incarceration of hundreds of thousands of people for immigration law violations (see chapter 4). In cities with sizable Asian populations, such as San Jose, California, the activities of Chinese and

Vietnamese gangs have been widely publicized, and efforts by local police to create lists of suspected Asian gang members have been blocked by Asian community activists. While small in numbers and usually not specifically reported, American Indians are incarcerated at a rate 38 percent higher than the general population and have the highest rate of incarceration of any racial group in local jails.[47]

The sheer scope of the criminal justice system's reach, and the resulting quantity of imprisoned people of color, injects a new quality into race relations in America. Increasingly, being black, Latino, Asian, and Native American involves regular encounters with the police and the criminal justice system. For example, 56 percent of all African American men aged eighteen to thirty-five in Baltimore were under some form of criminal justice system supervision on any given day in 1992.[48] A fifty-year-old black man in Washington, D.C., has an 80 percent chance of having been incarcerated at some point in his life. As a result of state laws excluding felons from voting for life, some 15 percent of all black men in the United States have been permanently disenfranchised. Many people of color find that their best chance at getting access to public education or drug treatment happens when they are incarcerated.

The most important vehicle for the criminalization of African Americans and Latinos in the 1980s and 1990s was the war on drugs, which was initiated with a panic about the crack cocaine epidemic in 1986. Crack was portrayed as "the most addictive drug known to man" in *Newsweek* and a headline in the *New York Times* warned, "Crack Addiction Spreads among the Middle Class."[49] In 1988, a national war on drugs was declared. The war on drugs was highly selective: only one drug in one form, crack cocaine, was targeted, the one used by the most marginalized and impoverished and racially oppressed segments of the United States.[50] In 1989, William Bennett, the drug czar in George H. W. Bush's administration, announced the National Drug Control Strategy. "The drug crisis," the strategy declared, "is a crisis of authority. Drugs obliterate morals, values, character, our relations with each other and God." During the 1990s, a host of tough laws were passed mandating long minimum sentences for drug law violations. Some 250 pregnant crack-addicted women were subjected to criminal prosecution. Many were incarcerated and faced temporary or permanent loss of custody of their children. In one Florida study, black women were reported to health authorities for illicit drug use during pregnancy ten times more often than white women, although their rates of substance abuse were similar.[51]

Despite the hype by politicians and highly publicized but erroneous early statements by "drug experts," crack cocaine is no different a drug than powdered cocaine, which had been used by affluent white suburbanites for years, and is not uniquely dangerous among addictive substances. The major killer drugs of the United States, alcohol and tobacco, remain legal. Even the criminalization of crack is racialized: While whites comprise one-half of crack users, 90 percent of those incarcerated for crack possession or distribution are African American.[52] Furthermore, while scientists have decisively demonstrated that drug treatment is the most effective way to combat addiction, the National Drug Control Strategy virtually ignored treatment in the late 1980s and focused on the criminalization of drug use and dealing. Another concern arose during the Iran-Contra scandal that rocked the Reagan administration in 1987: that U.S. foreign policy actually supported the production and trafficking of the very drugs criminalized in the United States.[53]

Based on these observations about the arbitrary character of the war on drugs, critics have suggested that the demonization of crack is not about drug control, but is for the twin purposes of criminalizing the black and Latino communities and serving as a justification for U.S. military intervention around the world.[54] Using Los Angeles as a case study, Mike Davis shows in terrifying detail the process by which the police, empowered by the war on drugs, steadily broadened their definition of black people as criminals.[55] Operation Hammer started in 1988 by targeting the drug dealers allegedly responsible for the "crack epidemic." But within a short time, the police had widened the scope of their war on drugs to criminalize gang members, all of whom were now called drug dealers. Next, the police began to target "suspect gang members," where gang affiliation was defined as wearing gang colors (red or blue), or walking down the street with a known gang member. In a series of street sweeps in 1989 and 1990, the Los Angeles Police Department (LAPD) stopped and entered the names of 103,000 young people onto a list of suspect gang members. What makes this number even more remarkable is that there were only 130,000 African American men between sixteen and twenty-five in all of Los Angeles at that time. In 1990, the war on drugs was further broadened. The LAPD defined entire sections of south central Los Angeles as "high drug trafficking areas" and began to restrict vehicle flow in and out of the areas and conduct massive raids in them. As well, after a curfew was declared, the parents of teenagers could be held liable if their children violated the curfew. It is hardly surprising that the video of Rodney King being beaten by the LAPD struck a raw nerve in virtually every person of color in Los Angeles.[56]

Clearly, the trend of the last twenty years is to criminalize more social behaviors and to enforce criminal law more stringently in communities of color. But why now? Why was the war on drugs declared against crack cocaine in

1986? Two different explanations of this trend have been offered. The first, by Troy Duster, suggests that the motivation of the war on drugs (and on crime in general) is to keep order in ghettoes experiencing structural dislocations as the U.S. economy shifts from an industrial to a service base.[57] The new service-sector jobs, Duster observes, are more likely to be located in suburbs and require people with the cultural prerequisites to relate to middle-class customers. Employers are much more likely to hire white employees, even when given a choice to hire an equally qualified black applicant. The result has been that African Americans living in inner cities are losing access to full employment as industrial jobs vanish. In the poorest areas of ghettoes, Duster notes, some people who have been displaced and are losing hope have succumbed to the lure of crack capitalism and the possibility of making more money in a day than they could otherwise earn in a year. Crack use thus grows in proportion to the structural crisis, as people who lose hope turn to drug use to ease the pain. The war on drug's arbitrary and brutal treatment of people of color only deepens the social crisis of the ghettoes. To extend Duster's analysis, the criminalization of communities of color involves the deployment of the repressive apparatus of the state to maintain a social order in which significant portions of these communities are increasingly marginalized from access to stable jobs, social services, meaningful education, and adequate housing by the processes of globalization.

William J. Chambliss takes a different approach to explain the war on crime of the 1980s and 1990s. Following the tradition of Durkheim, Chambliss maintains that the purpose of criminal law is to create a powerful notion of morality to organize a cohesive social order.[58] That is, by defining bad behavior and bad people ("them"), law also defines good behavior and good people ("us"). The war on drugs, Chambliss argues, creates a "moral panic" as a way of deflecting public attention from systematic problems like inequality and cuts in social programs. The war on crime, by defining the public's problem as immoral individuals (the "criminals") deflects the white middle class's attention from the larger social crisis created by globalization, with its rapidly growing inequality and the retraction of public services.

As Chambliss notes, crime was not identified in public opinion polls as the top social problem of the United States until the late 1980s, culminating twenty years of conservative efforts to promote this issue. The war on crime can be seen as a political project to create social order based on individual responsibility, in which the role of government is to hold individuals accountable to the shared values of society. A war on drugs is particularly useful, as the depiction of drugs as bad also depicts a life of hard work, savings, and sobriety as good. Indeed, some historians of Prohibition have argued that the war on alcohol had a similar purpose.[59] The war on crime, by claiming that communities of color are dangerous, crime-ridden areas, also renders invisible the systematic efforts of white people to displace cuts in job possibilities and government services in communities of color. The highly exaggerated claims of criminal behavior in these communities become, in the minds of terrified whites, the cause of racial inequality.

Both points of view are helpful. Duster's analysis captures the ways in which racism has stripped some inner-city areas of access to stable jobs, decent schools, adequate health care, and affordable housing. In this way, Duster reminds us that the costs of globalization are borne disproportionately by people of color, and particularly by those ghettoized in inner-city areas that are the most vulnerable to suburban whites' efforts to displace these costs. Furthermore, Duster's analysis underscores the destabilizing effects of globalization and the political imperative of using force to maintain order in communities excluded from access to stable jobs, housing, schools, health care, and so on. Likewise, Chambliss's analysis is helpful at looking at the other side of the same coin: the mind-set of the white suburbanites who provide the political support for the war on crime. Both analyses can be understood as complementary in the context of the impact of globalization and the restructuring of the state now under way. In short, the war on crime sacrifices millions of men, women, and children of color to the effort to convince the white middle class that a "good" life is a matter of individual responsibility. The current rethinking of the war on drugs, the death penalty, and mandatory minimum sentencing laws thus opens the possibility of a broader discussion about the role of the state in society and the basic assumptions Americans make about the ordering principles of society itself.

Conclusion: Structured Racism in the Era of Globalization

The analysis presented in the previous two chapters suggests that the advent of globalization, with its increased inequality and disruption of the middle-class social order, has encouraged political elites and many middle-class whites to explore ways to reassert white privileges. The racial projects of the global era are different from those of the slave or Jim Crow epochs, however, as whites can now mobilize racial privileges without any explicit appeal to white supremacy. The new vehicles for racial privileges—localism, nationalism, privatization of welfare, selecting the most qualified, and getting tough on criminals—can operate without open racial bigotry precisely because the privileges are structured, built in, embedded, and patterned in the day-to-day workings of mass society.

The racial privileges are embedded in far more than the patterns of inter-action of one institution or another; they are structured into the reciprocal ef-fects of institutional arrangements on one another. That is, the fact that local control gives white communities higher property values means the white chil-dren of that area can attend better-funded schools. The graduates of better-funded schools have a better chance of getting credentialed for high-paying professional, technical, or managerial jobs. The higher incomes secured by these jobs, coupled with inherited wealth, enable people to buy homes in "better" communities. Structured racial inequality is produced by the recip-rocal effects of racial privileges in many different institutionalized forms. The mobilization of structured racism in the global era is a prime example of what Thurgood Marshall calls the "present effects of past discrimination." The rea-son whites can claim the suburbs, positions in selective institutions of higher education, and elite professional and managerial jobs today is that, until the 1960s, all institutions were racially segregated by law and informal practice. The vast racial inequalities of private wealth, social capital, and cultural cap-ital today are all present effects of past discrimination.

The preceding analysis also suggests that globalization is creating condi-tions that may undermine these racial projects. In chapter 4, we saw that sub-urban efforts to use localism as a way to fend off the social crisis of globaliza-tion are being undermined by the reintegration of cities and suburbs into new global cities. Similarly, anti-immigrant policies are increasingly vulnerable to challenge as the proportion of immigrants and their children in the United States continues to grow. Thus far, I have addressed the ways that globaliza-tion is creating conditions intensifying the mobilization of white privileges. But this is only half the story. Globalization is simultaneously creating con-ditions favorable to the efforts to undermine racial privileges in the United States. It is to the assessment of these factors, and their impact on social movements for racial justice in the United States, to which I now turn.

Notes

1. Anthony Giddens, *The Consequences of Modernity* (Cambridge, Mass.: Polity, 1990).

2. Bruce J. Schulman, *The Seventies: The Great Shift in American Culture, Society, and Politics* (New York: The Free Press, 2001).

3. Jill Quadagno, *The Color of Welfare: How Racism Undermined the War on Poverty* (New York: Oxford University Press, 1994).

4. Theda Skocpol, *Boomerang: Clinton's Health Security Effort and the Turn against Government in U.S. Politics* (New York: Norton, 1996).

5. Kevin Phillips, *The Boiling Point: Democrats, Republicans and the Decline of Middle Class Prosperity* (New York: Random House, 1993).

6. Andrew Hacker, *Money: Who Has How Much and Why?* (New York: Scribner, 1997); Sheldon Danziger and Peter Gottschalk, *America Unequal* (Cambridge, Mass.: Harvard University Press, 1995).

7. Melvin L. Oliver and Thomas M. Shapiro, *Black Wealth, White Wealth* (New York: Routledge, 1997).

8. Oliver and Shapiro, *Black Wealth, White Wealth*, 86, table 4.4.

9. Oliver and Shapiro, *Black Wealth, White Wealth*.

10. Dalton Conley, *Being Black, Living in the Red: Race, Wealth, and Social Policy in America* (Berkeley: University of California Press, 1999).

11. Barry Bluestone and Bennett Harrison, *The De-industrialization of America* (New York: Basic, 1982).

12. Andrew Hacker, *Two Nations: Black and White, Separate, Hostile, Unequal* (New York: Scribner's, 1992), 116.

13. For an excellent discussion of the evolution of school desegregation decisions away from individual responsibility to group rights, and then back again to individual responsibility, see Owen Fiss, "The Uncertain Path of School Desegregation Law," in *Equality and Preferential Treatment*, ed. Marshall Cohen, Thomas Nagel, and Thomas Scanlon (Princeton, N.J.: Princeton University Press, 1977), 155–191.

14. Richard J. Herrnstein and Charles Murray's, *The Bell Curve* (New York: The Free Press, 1994), constitutes just such an effort. Their book received enormous publicity despite the rapid and almost universal repudiation of the book's thesis by geneticists and social scientists. See Claude S. Fischer et al., *Inequality by Design: Cracking the Bell Curve* (Princeton, N.J.: Princeton University Press, 1996).

15. Magali Sarfatti Larson, *The Rise of Professionalism: A Sociological Analysis* (Berkeley: University of California Press, 1977).

16. Michael Dunlop Young, *The Rise of the Meritocracy* (New Brunswick, N.J.: Transaction, 1994).

17. Kingsley Davis and Wilbur Moore, "Some Principles of Stratification," *American Sociological Review* 10 (April 1945): 242–249.

18. The critique first became popular in the free speech movement at Berkeley in 1964 and became widespread in the May 1968 protests in Europe.

19. Cornel West, "The New Cultural Politics of Difference," in *Keeping Faith* (New York: Routledge, 1993), 3–32.

20. R. C. Leowintin, Steven Rose, and Leon J. Kamin, "I.Q.: The Rank Ordering of the World," in *The "Racial" Economy of Science*, ed. Sandra Harding (Bloomington: Indiana University Press, 1993).

21. Justice Thurgood Marshall, dissent in *Bakke v. U.C. Regents* 438 U.S. 482 (1978).

22. Allan Bloom, *The Closing of the American Mind* (New York: Simon and Schuster, 1988).

23. Jerome Karabel, "The Rise and Fall of Affirmative Action at the University of California," *The Journal of Blacks in Higher Education* 25 (Autumn 1999): 109–112.

24. William C. Kidder, "The Rise of the Testocracy: An Essay on the LSAT, Conventional Wisdom, and the Dismantling of Diversity," *Texas Journal of Women and the Law* 9, no. 2 (2000): 167–218.

25. J. Morgan Kousser, *Colorblind Injustice: Minority Voting Rights and the Undoing of the Second Reconstruction* (Chapel Hill: University of North Carolina Press, 1999); Lani Guinier, *The Tyranny of the Majority: Fundamental Fairness in Representative Democracy* (New York: The Free Press, 1994).

26. William Bowen and Derek Bok, *The Shape of the River: Long-Term Consequences of Considering Race in College and University Admissions* (Princeton, N.J.: Princeton University Press, 1998).

27. Conley, *Being Black*, 55–84.

28. Pierre Bourdieu, "Cultural Reproduction and Social Reproduction," in *Power and Ideology in Education*, ed. Jerome Karabel and A. H. Halsey (New York: Oxford University Press, 1977), 487–511.

29. Derrick Bell, *And We Are Not Saved* (New York: Basic, 1987), 140–161.

30. Derrick Bell, *Faces At the Bottom of the Well* (New York: Basic, 1992), makes this point explicit.

31. I was the lead plaintiff in a suit against California governor Pete Wilson over a 1998 executive order barring state agencies from keeping records on the percent of their contracts to women- and minority-owned businesses (*Barlow v. Davis Cal. Appl. 4th 1258 [1999]*). The suit was resolved when the California Legislature re-enacted the data collection provision (California Public Contract Code section 10116). See Troy Duster and Andrew Barlow, "Sociologist Sues over Data Collection," *American Sociological Association Footnotes* (January 1999): 2.

32. This is despite the findings of the New Jersey State courts that the New Jersey State Police had systematically stopped black and Latino drivers on state highways. Between 1995 and 1997, over 80 percent of all people stopped were black or Latino, although African Americans and Latinos comprise less than 20 percent of the state's population.

33. Michel Foucault, *Discipline and Punish* (New York: Pantheon, 1977); see also Jeffrey Reiman, *The Rich Get Richer and the Poor Get Prison* (New York: Macmillan, 1990).

34. The Sentencing Project, *Facts about Prisons and Prisoners* (Washington, D.C.: Sentencing Project, 2001).

35. Theodore G. Chiricos and Charles Crawford, "Race and Imprisonment: A Contextual Assessment of the Evidence," in *Ethnicity, Race and Crime: Perspectives across Time and Place*, ed. Darnell F. Hawkins (Albany: SUNY Press, 1995), 281–309.

36. Bureau of Justice Statistics, *National Prisoner Statistics* (Washington, D.C.: Department of Justice, 1998).

37. Who can forget the powerful words of Nathan McCall, who, as a graduate student at the elite University of Chicago, reports how he, a black man, would hear the

sounds of car doors being locked by frightened white drivers as he walked down the street? Nathan McCall, *Makes Me Want to Holler* (New York: Random House, 1994).

38. This image of inner-city communities of color, long associated with conservatives, has found its way into liberal politics though the writings of William Julius Wilson. See Stephen Steinberg, "The Liberal Retreat from Race," in *Race and Ethnicity in the United States: Issues and Debates*, ed. Stephen Steinberg (Malden, Mass.: Blackwell, 2000).

39. Reiman, *Rich Get Richer*; Steven R. Donziger, ed., *The Real War on Crime: The Report of the National Criminal Justice Commission* (New York: HarperPerennial, 1996).

40. Christopher D. Stone, *Where the Law Ends: The Social Control of Corporate Behavior* (New York: Harper and Row, 1975).

41. Gil Garcetti, the Los Angeles district attorney, explicitly stated this as the reason for not charging O. J. Simpson with a capital offense in his infamous 1995 murder trial.

42. Mark V. Tushnett, *The American Law of Slavery, 1810–1860: Considerations of Humanity and Interest* (Princeton, N.J.: Princeton University Press, 1981).

43. *People v. Hall*, 35 Calif. 3d 161 (1856).

44. John Hope Franklin, "History of Racial Segregation in the United States," in *The Making of Black America*, vol. 2, ed. August Meier and Elliott Rudwick (New York: Atheneum, 1977), 3–13.

45. Donziger, *Real War on Crime*, 103–104.

46. Donziger, *Real War on Crime*.

47. Lawrence A. Greenfield and Steven K. Smith, *American Indians and Crime*, NCJ 173386 (Washington, D.C.: Department of Justice, Bureau of Justice Statistics, February 1999), viii.

48. Jerome G. Miller, *Hobbling a Generation: Young African American Males in the Criminal Justice System of America's Cities* (Baltimore, Md.: National Center on Institutions and Alternatives, 1992).

49. Craig Reinarman and Harry G. Levine, "Crack in Context," in *Crack in America: Demon Drugs and Social Justice*, ed. Craig Reinarman and Harry G. Levine (Berkeley: University of California Press, 1997), 3.

50. Reinarman and Levine, "Crack in Context," 55.

51. I. J. Chasnoff, H. J. Landress, and M. E. Barrett, "The Prevalence of Illicit Drug or Alcohol Use during Pregnancy and Discrepancies in Mandatory Reporting in Pinellas County, Florida," *New England Journal of Medicine*, 26 April 1990, 1202–1206.

52. Dorothy Lockwood, Anne E. Pottieger, and James A. Inciardi, "Crack Use, Crime by Crack Users, and Ethnicity," in *Ethnicity, Race and Crime: Perspectives across Time and Place*, ed. Darnell F. Hawkins (Albany: SUNY Press, 1995), 212–234.

53. This case involved charges that the crack epidemic was the result of Central Intelligence Agency (CIA) efforts to circumvent a congressional ban on U.S. aid to the Nicaraguan contras. The CIA, it was alleged, allowed cocaine to enter the

United States to fund the secret war to overthrow the Sandinista government of Nicaragua. See Peter Dale Scott and Jonathan Marshall, *Cocaine Politics: Drugs, Armies and the C.I.A. in Central America* (Berkeley: University of California Press, 1991).

54. Ethan A. Nadelmann, *Cops across Borders: The Internationalization of U.S. Criminal Law Enforcement* (University Park: Pennsylvania State University Press, 1993).

55. Mike Davis, *City of Quartz* (London: Verso, 1990), 265–322.

56. Judith Butler, "Endangered/Endangering: Schematic Racism and White Paranoia," in *Reading Rodney King/Reading Urban Uprisings*, ed. Robert Gooding-Williams (New York: Routledge, 1993), 15–22.

57. Troy Duster, "Pattern, Purpose, and Race in the Drug War," in *Crack in America: Demon Drugs and Social Justice*, ed. Craig Reinarman and Harry G. Levine (Berkeley: University of California Press, 1997), 260–287.

58. William J. Chambliss, "Crime Control and Ethnic Minorities: Legitimizing Racial Oppression by Creating Moral Panics," in *Ethnicity, Race and Crime: Perspectives across Time and Place*, ed. Darnell F. Hawkins (Albany: SUNY Press, 1995), 235–258; Emile Durkheim, *The Rules of Sociological Method* (Glencoe, Ill.: Free Press, 1966), 138–140.

59. John J. Rumbarger, *Profits, Power and Prohibition: Alcohol Reform and the Industrializing of America, 1800–1930* (Albany: SUNY Press, 1989).

PART THREE

GLOBALIZATION AND THE SEARCH FOR RACIAL JUSTICE IN THE UNITED STATES

~

Introduction to Part III: Finding Hope in the Era of Globalization

This book has, up to this point, considered the ways in which globalization creates conditions in which whites are likely to turn to racial privileging to protect themselves from the downward pressures of inequality. The next two chapters examine the other side of the coin: The openings that globalization creates for efforts to overcome racism. The focus of these chapters is on the civil rights movement, the great effort begun in 1955 to combat racism through government action. Chapter 6 looks at the ways that globalization has created new challenges for the civil rights movement in the last twenty years. Chapter 7 seeks to identify the ways in which globalization creates spaces that may potentially provide new possibilities for undermining racial privileges and identifies the social forces with the capacity and interest to advocate for racial justice. These new conditions may well lead to the reemergence of civil rights as a central issue in American society. Before undertaking these investigations, a few preliminary observations are in order.

Part II of this book explored the ways political elites and many whites deploy racial and national privileges to buffer themselves from growing inequality and the social crisis of globalization. As we have seen, globalization has breathed new life into the system of structured racism that was constructed in the United States during the 1950s and 1960s. How, then, can globalization, the very force that is fueling racist and nationalist reaction, also be creating conditions for undermining racism? The ability to find hope in the midst of crisis must be based on the understanding that globalization, for all of its disruptive and disequalizing impact today, is actually a progressive

135

force in human history. The productive forces that make the current stage of globalization possible are fundamentally reshaping human relationships in ways that have the potential to bring humanity to a new stage of understanding and cooperation. Samir Amin puts it well, "Globalization is, for me, not a fact of modern history to be erased by an autarkic and culturalist response; but a positive fact, a progress in history. . . . But history has no end and globalization is far from being realized."[1]

The enormous human potential that lies in the scientific and technical revolution now under way cannot be dismissed solely because the new technologies are today producing global convulsions. We are living in a paradoxical era, in which world poverty and environmental crises are growing at an unprecedented rate on the one hand, and scientists are revolutionizing fields as disparate as genetics, astronomy, and cybernetics on the other. But, as previous eras of scientific and technical discovery have demonstrated, there is no turning back from these new frontiers of knowledge. The hope for the future lies in learning to use these ideas for, and not against, humanity. It is therefore incumbent on those who are opposed to the inequities of the present era to not simply oppose globalization, but to articulate a vision of globalization that is equitable and just.[2]

The progressive potential of globalization can be discomforting to those who are aware that market globalization creates poverty and excludes much of the world's populations from its benefits. But market globalization has already begun to reshape societies in ways that enhance the potential for challenging the arrangements sought by transnational capital. The global cities are already, in the words of Saskia Sassen, "contested places," where growing pluralities (and even majorities) of the population who are marginalized from the middle classes—mostly immigrants and nonimmigrant people of color—have a growing capacity to contest the terms of the social order.[3] As well, the declining significance of national borders in economic and social relationships creates new possibilities for transnational and global social cooperation to address common global problems, ranging from immigration, to labor issues, to the environment. Reflecting these structural changes, transnational and global social movements are beginning to affect the agendas of local and national politics around the world.

The potential for renegotiating the terms of globalization is quite real. The fundamental problem facing transnational capital today is that the social arrangements most profitable in the short run are socially destabilizing in the long run, and markets require social stability to be profitable. Furthermore, social stability requires strong state intervention into markets, and market globalization tends to undercut the state's autonomy. The problem for transnational corporations and political elites who serve them is that they are interested only in creating global markets, not in the social conditions that maintain social stability. Put another way, transnational capital has developed new forms of global markets, but has very little capacity to develop the political and social institutions needed to stabilize societies.[4] Because market systems depend on a stable social order, market globalization is vulnerable to challenges, in which people excluded from the benefits of globalization, who are in various ways placed outside the social order, can contest the political and economic arrangements both within nations and on a global level.

In particular, the U.S. middle-class order that was created during the 1950s and 1960s is today being threatened by the disequalizing effects of globalization and by the restructuring of the U.S. nation-state. While whites may try to utilize racial and national privileges to buffer themselves from the downward pressures associated with globalization, these efforts will fail to insulate many if not most of them in the long run. As more people find the promises of the middle-class social compact (full-time jobs with benefits, good schools, social services, and affordable housing) unattainable, we can expect to see differing forms of political and cultural destabilization. In chapter 7, I consider the idea that the unraveling of the middle-class order may not be a complete disaster after all and that its demise may open up possibilities for reorganizing society on a more humane, communal, and egalitarian basis. The Mandarin word for "crisis" has two characters: one signifies danger, the other, opportunity. One can view the crisis of the middle-class social order either way, or both ways. In Chapter 7, I explore the ways in which the crisis opens new opportunities for redistributing social resources and renegotiating the terms of globalization.

A final observation: Efforts to eradicate racism in this era undoubtedly require the mobilization of social movements capable of giving birth to fundamental social change. The weight of history and the constraints of the present era suggest that national political elites cannot be relied on to remove racism. There are simply too many ways that racism and national and religious chauvinism can be used to bolster national unity to assume that political elites will not seek to use them to maintain social order. Even worse, as part II of this book suggests, the conditions of globalization are intensifying these tendencies. Consequently, efforts to eradicate racism today can only succeed by bringing pressure "from below" (i.e., from noninstitutionalized, autonomous, community-based power).

But insurgencies, however unjust the social order they oppose, rarely succeed in toppling institutionalized power by themselves. The power mobilized by those disenfranchised from the existing social order must be sufficient to cause a significant section of political elites (i.e., people who exercise state power) to abandon a particular form of oppression and to renegotiate the terms for maintaining social order.[5] As we shall see in chapter 6, this was an important reason why the civil rights movement was successful during the period from 1956 to the mid-1970s. Grassroots Black Power was brought to bear on the federal government, compelling a major section of national elites to turn against the Jim Crow system and to include people of color in the welfare state regime.

Today, those who work for racial justice need to develop a new agenda in the context of globalization. What is needed is a new analysis of (a) the sources of autonomous power that are potentially available to challenge the existing social order and (b) the ways by which political and corporate elites might be won over to a new social contract more favorable to people of color in the United States. This analysis, as we will see in the next two chapters, leads to a questioning of the civil rights strategy and suggests that a resurgence of the civil rights movement may be just over the horizon.

Notes

1. Samir Amin, *Capitalism in the Age of Globalization* (London: Zed, 1997), 75.

2. Michael Hardt and Antonio Negri, "What the Protesters in Genoa Want," *New York Times*, 20 July 2001, A23. This vision was also articulated by 25,000 attendees at the Second World Social Forum, held in January 2002 in Brazil.

3. Saskia Sassen, *Globalization and Its Discontents* (New York: The New Press, 1998), xxxii.

4. Malcolm Waters, *Globalization* (London: Routledge, 1995).

5. Theda Skocpol, *States and Social Revolutions: A Comparative Analysis of France, Russia, and China* (New York: Cambridge University Press, 1979).

〜

CHAPTER SIX

Possible Futures of
Racial Justice in the Global Era

The crisis consists precisely in the fact that the old is dying and the new cannot be born.

—Antonio Gramsci[1]

Throughout this book, it has been argued that globalization is creating a specific type of racialized social crisis in the United States in the context of the destabilization of the middle-class social order. On the one hand, the "fear of falling" has energized many white people to engage in a variety of projects to mobilize racial and national privileges to buffer themselves from the crisis. On the other hand, it has also been suggested in earlier chapters that globalization is a stage in history, an irreversible fact of life. How, then, are people to find hope in this new epoch of human history? How will people dreaming of and working for racial justice and equity make headway in light of the new realities of globalization? This chapter inquires into the possible new openings that have arisen in the context of globalization for advancing the goal of racial justice in the United States.

We saw in part II that the capacity of investors to rapidly move capital around the world and to reorganize economic life has altered the relationship between capital and the state, on the one hand, and capital and workers, on the other. The result has been a widening gap between the rich and the poor, and the reduction of the state's capacity to regulate capital or redistribute social assets downward. As well, the growing mobility of capital and labor has blurred the meaning of national boundaries and membership in national societies. In short, the middle-class social order, hegemonic in the 1950s through the 1970s, is becoming unstable. The problematic relationship between markets and social order is the subject of Karl Polanyi's seminal work *The Great Transformation*.[2] In chapter 3, we saw how Polanyi's framework was useful to explain how market relationships undermine social stability. But there is another side to Polanyi's analysis: the efforts to reconstitute social order. Capitalists need social order for markets to be stable and profitable, but they cannot produce social stability themselves. Polanyi details the search for order in early capitalist England, which involved the interplay of different class forces seeking an acceptable modus vivendi through the development of the nation-state. As Polanyi shows, people harmed by the extension of markets could and did play a significant independent role in creating the arrangements that stabilized the new capitalist society.

Polanyi's thesis is useful for understanding the potential for marginalized people to play a role in negotiating the impact of globalization on societies today. From the most developed to the least developed societies, the globalization of markets is bringing about massive changes that are disrupting existing social orders. The fundamental problem facing transnational capital today is that the social arrangements most profitable in the short run—reduction of the nation-state's regulatory and redistributive capacities and growing inequality—are socially destabilizing in the long run. Markets require social stability to be profitable and social stability requires strong state intervention into markets.[3] The problem for transnational corporations (TNCs) and the political elites who serve them is that they are currently interested only in creating the infrastructure for global markets, not in the social conditions that maintain or create social stability. The problem goes beyond political will: Transnational capital has developed new forms of global markets, but has very little capacity to develop the political and social institutions needed to stabilize global social relationships or national societies. Because market systems require social stability, but cannot produce it, market globalization is vulnerable to challenges, in which people excluded from the benefits of globalization, who are, in various ways, placed marginal to or outside the global social order, can contest the political and economic arrangements both within nations and on a global level. The potential to challenge the current neoliberal dogma of the TNCs and their institutions is thus quite realistic.

Things cannot continue on the way they have been going indefinitely in the United States. As the middle-class order becomes more difficult to maintain, and the threat of disruptive protests become more realistic, new ideas about the best way to maintain social order will have to be developed. We have seen that the difficulties that growing portions of U.S. society experience purchasing a private home, paying for college, or affording health or retirement insurance have already had significant political consequences: the intensification of racist and nationalist projects discussed in chapters 4 and 5. The crisis of the middle class, while borne disproportionately by people of color, is also a crisis for many white people, who may find themselves unable to afford a private home, a college education, or a car. Sooner or later, the willingness of people to accept either marginalization or exclusion from the global arrangements—domestically or internationally—is bound to end. Sooner or later, with enough pressure from the discontented, some political elites in the United States might move from knee-jerk support for market globalization, with its lethal mix of neoliberalism and American global dominance (and the implicit or explicit defense of racial and national privileges that comes with this stance), to support for a different concept of social order: a model that provides for stable jobs, access to education and health services, and gives people hope for upward mobility in the global era. This conception of globalization can be termed "social globalization," the recognition of the need to find ways to regulate markets and to counter their disequalizing effects in the name of social justice.

At this time, the efforts to define and realize social globalization, to be discussed in this chapter, are still at a very early stage in development. Both in terms of their power and their ideology, the people who have an interest in social globalization are today still peripheral to American and global politics. For now, the majority of Americans (of all races) stubbornly clings to the idea of the middle class, the ideology that organizes its aspirations around the pursuit of the American dream.[4] The fabric of the middle-class order is today stretched, but it has not yet been torn. The impact of globalization is eroding the material basis for the middle class—full-time jobs with benefits, entitlement programs, and so on—but not yet the ideology of the middle class itself. As the economic and political conditions needed to maintain the middle-class social order continue to erode, American politics will continue to focus on the problem of saving the middle class (which it already does) on the one hand, and seeking new concepts of social stability that address the needs of the growing legions of the discontented on the other.

As the crises created by market globalization deepen, a number of questions will become increasingly pressing: On whose terms will social order be defined? Will social order be maintained by increasingly repressive means, to defend the status quo of increasingly concentrated private wealth and deregulated markets? Will fear and defensiveness continue to dominate American responses to globalization? Or will people being cut out of the new global arrangements become politically powerful enough to insist on a renegotiation of the social order on terms that include those now marginalized or excluded outright from the benefits of global markets? Will possibilities arise for new forms of social cooperation and regulation of transnational capital in the global era? Will we find hope, instead of fear, in the global era?

Here, I explore three political projects aimed at addressing the problems created by globalization in the United States. As we will see, the success of each of these efforts depends on making race and ethnicity of central importance. That issues of race and ethnicity loom large in the effort to define social order in the global era should be of no surprise to readers of this book by now. The crisis of globalization has been met by the intensification of racism and nationalism in the United States. Any effort to create a more equitable and just social order will have to address the problems of people of color currently marginalized from and, in some cases, excluded outright from the benefits of globalization.

One final preliminary thought: A crisis may be both a time of danger and of opportunity.[5] Globalization in its current form is producing growing hardships for tens of millions of people in the United States, but new social forces are being unleashed that allow for a rethinking of what in the past might have been considered fundamental truisms. Among these unexamined beliefs is the idea of the middle class itself. The middle-class order only became hegemonic in the historically anomalous conditions of the post–World War II era and is certainly not the only way in which a social order can be organized. We would do well to remember that the middle-class arrangement was developed on a racist basis, was used to undermine the militancy of the American labor movement (see chapter 2), and justifies the new emphasis on localism and individualism that are the hallmarks of structured racism today (see chapters 4 and 5). Perhaps, the end of the middle-class social order, with its fetishes of private property, individual status, and malls, would not be such a terrible thing.

Studies of social movements show the importance of the destabilization of power structures for the creation of effective efforts to demand social change "from below."[6] The danger that social destabilization poses to capital and the nation-state offers the possibility that corporate and national political elites, in the face of sufficient countervailing power, could decide to rein in at least the most egregious destabilizing features of globalization. The destabilization of the middle-class order thus opens up *potential* opportunities for other ideas about how to redistribute social resources domestically and to negotiate global relationships on a more equitable basis.

The crisis of the middle-class order, then, might well become a time of opportunity for grassroots politics to have a significant social impact. The erosion of the American dream may open up new ideas about the "good life," especially about the affirmative responsibilities of corporations and government to civil society. Frequently unasked questions may be posed, while new answers to the distribution of scarce social resources may be found. New ways for people to understand their relationship to one another may be explored. In particular, the crisis may open up the opportunity to advance the cause of racial justice, that is, to renegotiate the relationships of people of color and immigrants to American society in the era of globalization. With this sense of crisis as a time of danger and opportunity, we can now explore the potential for responses to the social crisis that might—or might not—produce a more just and equitable form of globalization.

Civil Rights, the Defense of
Democracy, and Racial Justice

Market globalization's main impact on the nation-states of the most developed countries (MDCs) is to pressure them to abandon the regulatory mechanisms and redistributive programs that were the hallmark of the welfare-state era. For people of color, often lacking the assets to partake in the bounty of private investments, the state is increasingly being transformed into a repressive apparatus, with growing reliance on the military, the police, and the prisons to maintain order. The reduced scope of, and even the wholesale abandonment of civil rights, is a central feature of politics in the global era. The days when government ensured people's social rights—that is, the right to a job, the right to a good education, the right to health care, the right to decent, affordable housing, and the right to retire with a decent income—are vanishing, especially in societies with relatively weak welfare states, such as the United States and Great Britain. The civil rights movement's successes at extending state power to provide people of color greater access to employment, education, housing, and welfare, as well as voting and citizenship, make civil rights laws the particular targets of those who want to limit the role of government to protecting the new "individualism" of the private-investment state.

At the extreme, the retraction of social rights and the increasing use of police and military power to maintain social order take a particularly ominous form: the direct assault on democracy as a whole. As disequalizing pressures increase and social welfare programs are abandoned, the role of government in maintaining social order is being reassessed, with more emphasis on the authoritarian use of repressive state power. Some portion of political elites and a section of the white middle class may abandon support for democratic rights altogether in favor of fascist notions of elite rule and chauvinist claims of national superiority, wrapped in racist and anti-immigrant ideology. This fascist tendency has already made its appearance in a host of European societies, ranging from Russia, Austria, and France to the Netherlands and Italy.

The retraction of democratic rights in the name of "homeland defense" has a growing appeal in the United States. During the 1990s, this political trend was still on the margins of American politics, primarily articulated by Pat Buchanan.[7] The terrorist attacks of September 11, 2001, provided the Bush administration with a pretext to open this space to a qualitatively greater extent. The Bush administration's initiatives, and Congress's responses to them, indicate a breathtaking eagerness to abandon fundamental democratic rights in the name of "homeland defense" against vaguely (and even contradictorily) defined international and domestic terrorism. In the first few months after the attack, the U.S. government took the following initiatives:

- Congress enacted, with only one dissenting vote, antiterrorism legislation (officially titled the Uniting and Strengthening America by Providing Appropriate Tools Required to Intercept and Obstruct Terrorism—USAPATRIOT—Act) permitting the attorney general to detain noncitizens (some 20 million legal residents in the United States alone) for vaguely defined "suspicion of terrorism." The act weakens Fourth Amendment search warrant protections and allows the attorney general to designate domestic groups as terrorist organizations. Separate executive orders allow the Federal Bureau of Investigation (FBI) and the Central Intelligence Agency to spy on American citizens even if there is no evidence that a crime might be committed.
- President George W. Bush created military tribunals by executive order to try people, including U.S. citizens, accused of being terrorists by the president. These tribunals, in violation of the Geneva Conventions, can conduct secret trials, with public disclosure of only the names of defendants and the outcome of the proceedings. Defendants will be judged by military officers appointed by the president—that is, the prosecuting official. Defendants will not be able to choose their own counsel, will not have the right to a jury trial, and will not be allowed to see all the evidence or to confront all the witnesses used against them. No appeal of the tribunal's judgment will be allowed, even for the death penalty. Those people apprehended may be detained indefinitely without trial or held after a trial, even if they are found innocent by a tribunal.
- The Department of Justice refused to release the names or the number of people detained since September 11 for "suspicion of terrorist activ-

ities." At the time of the gag order, the government claimed to have 1,182 people in custody. Of the 600 or so whose charges were publicly known, only one was accused of having any ties to the September 11 attacks.

- Racial profiling, which was under attack because of the exposure of widespread abuses by the New Jersey State Police and other police departments in 1999 and 2000, after September 11, 2001, is now openly advocated as necessary for national security.[8] Visa holders from vaguely defined "Muslim countries" are now singled out to be fingerprinted and tracked in the United States.

These policies, among others, are justified as the price necessary for the defense of the "homeland," and have, at least initially, widespread public support.

The assault on civil rights is more than a panicky response to September 11. It is a significant part of the restructuring of the nation-state in the global era. Politicians who propose antidemocratic policies do so primarily to maintain the middle-class order even as inequality, immigration, and new global ties are undermining it. Left with little bargaining power, the political elites who are now in power believe that their best strategy is to externalize the social crisis and blame it on terrorists, immigrants, and criminals, in short, people of color (see chapters 4 and 5). This exclusion and repression is particularly aimed at racial minorities and non-European national minorities, who are offered up as scapegoats to pacify and co-opt the white middle class, the people who in this country are considered by the elite to be the "politically relevant" members of society.[9] As the social crisis of globalization deepens, especially with the growing disruption of the middle class, one response to it is the increasingly repressive and authoritarian uses of state power to shore up the social order by defining who is in and who is outside it on a racial, national, and religious basis. The growth of nonofficial hate crimes and domestic terrorism against communities of color is another bi-product of the official policies.

Antiracist politics today has to remain focused on the state even at a time of the retraction of civil rights, if for no other reason than to repel the most serious attacks on people of color. But, even more, the nation-state will remain central to the negotiations over the future of globalization as a whole. As Brigette Young writes:

> While the authority of the state has declined within its territorial borders, the nation-state is still the institutional encasement of the national territory providing average citizens with political influence and an avenue to exercise their

democratic rights. As a result, the nation-state is still the only place and space in which the irreconcilable principles of the market and democracy can come together and citizens can achieve and share a common identity of a "national community of fate."[10]

Efforts to stop authoritarian tendencies may produce demands for socially responsible globalization. These efforts can also be expected to become more energized as the crisis of globalization deepens. Ethnic communities have long led the efforts to stop the repressive tendencies of government. Antipolice brutality protests and litigation, as well as efforts to stop racial profiling and to protect prisoners and immigrants' rights, have been consistently led by people of color. Immigrant and nonimmigrant Latino and Asian American communities have been politicized and mobilized by the necessity of responding to attacks on immigrant rights, ranging from protesting the deaths of thousands at the U.S.-Mexican border to criticizing the FBI's false spying charges against nuclear scientist Wen Ho Lee.[11] The increasing tendencies of a section of political elites to use state power to repress people of color will thus continue to motivate and energize ethnic community politics.

Efforts to defend communities of color are inextricably bound up with the defense of democracy itself. There can be no successful defense of democracy in the United States in the global era without clear opposition to the mounting attacks on communities of color. From the defense of people's right to education, to health care, to the right to vote, to defense against the suspension of constitutional protections for people accused of criminal activities, to the criminalization of immigration, it is necessary to recognize that people of color are the first and foremost to be deprived of democratic rights. The coalitions that form in defense of democracy must find a common ground in which specific antiracist issues are recognized and central. To do so would bring into existence a multiracial, multiclass prodemocracy movement of historic proportions.

Unfortunately, there is no guarantee that this will happen. To the extent that the attacks on communities of color are not forcefully rebuffed, the defense of democracy itself is weakened. The current performance of the Democratic Party is not encouraging in this regard, for example. Despite the growing importance of voters of color to the Democratic Party, and the presence of virtually the entire leadership of the labor, women's, gay and lesbian, and environmental movements in its ranks, party leaders continue to focus on the fears of the white middle class, with strong support for neoliberal globalization, criminal sanctions, and anti-immigrant policies, and only lukewarm support (at best) for affirmative action programs. For these reasons, the ongoing efforts to inject the concerns of people of color into Democratic

Party politics are far more than "interest group" politics, they are efforts to force the Democratic Party to confront the erosion of democracy itself.

The reluctance of the Democratic Party to aggressively pursue issues identified by communities of color produces a constant pressure toward independent ("third party") progressive politics. This tendency will intensify as racist assaults on people of color increase and grassroots ethnic community organizations take the lead in demanding justice. The process of building a serious, independent, progressive political party positioned to the left of the Democratic Party is, of necessity, a long-term project. Elected officials and grassroots organizations with real power will only leave the Democratic Party if they believe that an alternative vehicle is needed and has sufficient political power to defend democracy. A viable third party will only come about if grassroots political leaders succeed in building the broadest possible civil rights coalition and become convinced that political elites in the Democratic Party have no intention of renegotiating the basis for social order on terms demanded by communities of color, labor, women, gays and lesbians, and so on. If elites are willing to make significant concessions, of course, the Democratic Party might be able to redefine the "center" of American politics, as it did in the 1930s and 1960s. Consequently, while independent political action is now a requirement of antiracist politics, the need for, or possibility of, a third party is still an open historic question.

In sum, democracy is clearly in jeopardy in these early days of the global era, with no certainty for its future. If democracy is to be saved, and in the process redefined, it will require a new focus on the marginalization and repression of communities of color. If this were to happen, the effort to defend democracy could thrust the civil rights movement into the center of American politics for the first time since the early 1970s.

International Accords, Human Rights, and Racial Justice

The U.S. civil rights movement is primarily national in scope, as it inherently focuses on issues of nation-state power. In this period, for reasons explained earlier, civil rights projects will likely be primarily defensive in character. Another promising arena that is available to advance issues of racial justice in potentially less constricted ways are efforts to insert antiracist human rights issues into the growing web of international accords.

"Human" rights are conceptually distinct from civil rights. Civil rights are behaviors specifically protected by government action and are codified at the national level. Human rights are claimed to be universally recognized protections, with the expectation that all nation-states accept them. The chief importance of human rights protocols is the pressure that can be placed on governments to conform to them. For example, Amnesty International cites international legal standards on the treatment of prisoners to urge the early release of people incarcerated in overcrowded U.S. prisons.[12] The 1979 Convention on the Elimination of All Forms of Discrimination against Women strengthened the hand of U.S. feminist organizations to pressure Congress to enact the Violence against Women Act, which includes recognizing the rights of immigrant women fleeing domestic violence to seek political asylum.[13] As well, human rights protocols are valuable for local grassroots movements as a way of linking up with international allies for political and material support.[14]

International accords have gradually taken form and become institutionalized over the last century to address a host of global issues, ranging from trade and investment regulations to the regulation of war, immigration, health problems, immigration, and women's issues. The scope of these efforts has expanded as government and nongovernmental organizations (NGOs), as well as grassroots movements, define an increasing number of issues as global problems. The efforts by nation-states and international bodies of nation-states to address global issues are, however, limited by national elites' dependence on global capital. The greater bargaining power of capital over nation-states motivates those exercising state power to comply with capital's requests for the establishment of neoliberal legal and political "rights" that facilitate freedom of investment, but generally leave people's needs unacknowledged.[15] Thus, the World Bank–International Monetary Fund (IMF) structural adjustment programs require national governments to curtail social services and protection for local industries and labor as conditions to receive loans. Dependence on governmental and foundation backing also constrains the work of many NGOs.

Another constraint on the development of international accords derives from the fact that the main responsibilities for the stabilization of global arrangements rest with the constituent nation-states.[16] Global politics is still primarily international, not global, in this era. Political elites, particularly those of the most powerful nations, often do not want to compromise their sovereignty. Consequently, international accords typically proclaim only symbolic ideas or establish merely skeletal organizations rather than create the basis for well-developed global institutions. For example, a court with general jurisdiction over international crimes, which is a fundamental institution of global government, was not established until 2002. Often, despite lofty goals, very little money or specific policies have been put in place to make human rights in particular a social reality on a global basis. The UN fund for women in developing countries, for example, had an annual budget of $11.6 million in the mid-1990s.[17]

The development of international institutions and rules is also limited and even undermined by the United States' subversion of international agreements in pursuit of its national interests. Global capital's reliance on the American "superpower" for coordination and rule making in the new era gives the United States the ability to subvert nascent global arrangements that might undermine American national sovereignty. The following are some recent examples of the imposition of U.S. national interests on global issues:

- The United States revoked in May 2002 its signature of the treaty creating the first International Criminal Court, citing the need to protect Americans' national sovereignty from "politicized prosecutions."
- The United States unilaterally withdrew from the Anti-Ballistic Missile Treaty in December 2001, citing national security needs. This pact had provided the main architecture of global strategic arms agreements since 1972.
- The United States refused to sign the Kyoto Accords on the regulation of fossil fuel emissions in 2000, while all other participant nations signed it.
- The United States refused to abide by the North American Free Trade Agreement (NAFTA) to allow Mexican truckers into U.S. markets in September 2001.
- The United States refused to accord people it captured in Afghanistan prisoner-of-war status, a position seen as a clear violation of the Geneva Conventions by even its staunchest allies.
- The United States threatened to pull out of the General Agreement on Trades and Tariffs in 1996 when Canada, Mexico, and Venezuela threatened to sue the United States over its boycott of Cuba.

Despite these serious limitations, pressures to develop and implement international accords, and human rights accords in particular, will continue to grow. Market globalization is rapidly creating and accelerating a host of social problems that can no longer be solved by any one nation. These problems range from environmental issues (global warming, ozone depletion, destruction of the rain forests, the loss of potable water, and so on) to regional wars, to immigration issues, to labor issues, to health issues, such as the AIDS epidemic. It is increasingly evident that these problems will have to be addressed globally, not only at an international or national level.[18]

This contradiction between the growing need to address global problems and nation-states' curtailed capacity to deal with these problems has created a space for transnational networks of people concerned with global problems, that is, grassroots global movements. While global agreements are still largely a matter of international politics, and are dominated by the MDCs' national interests, the manifestations of these problems are of growing concern to people all over the world and are spawning the development of grassroots organizations and movements in every country. A large majority of these grassroots organizations, especially those located in less developed countries, address problems of people who are marginalized from the "new world order." Consequently, many grassroots movements focused on global problems address problems of racism in their work. While globalization "from above," that is, from national elites or TNCs, tends to downplay the problems caused by market globalization, the space created by international accords provides grassroots organizations and movements with the opportunity to demand that marginal peoples' needs be taken into account.

Despite the power of national and transnational elites to limit international accords, protocols addressing problems of racism and national chauvinism as global human rights issues have long been an element of international understandings.[19] Official statements of global opposition to racism, colonialism, and xenophobia appeared early in the development of the modern framework of international cooperation, such as in the 1948 Universal Declaration of Human Rights.[20] But grassroots movements have been much more consistent than formal international accords in identifying global problems of racism. Opposition to the Vietnam War was linked explicitly to racism in the United States by Martin Luther King Jr., Malcolm X, the Black Panthers, and the Chicano Moratorium, among others.[21] International solidarity with the South African antiapartheid movement in the late 1970s and 1980s, mostly by grassroots movements, further crystallized opposition to racism as a global issue. Efforts to address immigration issues on a multilateral basis have also grown during the past twenty years.[22] The UN Conference on Racism, Xenophobia, and Related Problems, held, appropriately enough, in Durban, South Africa, in 2001, marked an important stage in the development of human rights by providing an international setting to develop a global antiracist agenda for the first time. The conference, comprised of official delegations from UN member nations as well as a parallel conference for NGOs, was modeled after the highly successful UN Conferences on the Status of Women. While the United States and Israel withdrew their official delegations from the conference, allegedly over a proposed resolution to condemn Israel's occupation of the West Bank (the large majority of U.S. NGOs did not withdraw), the remaining delegates produced two documents summing up global problems of racism and the responsibilities of nation-states to address them.[23] The final documents produced by the conference set the stage for further global efforts to address racism and anti-immigrant xenophobia as human rights issues.

The extent to which there is growing attention to problems of racism in international agreements is a reflection of a fundamental reality of the post-colonial era: The large majority of peoples and nations of the world, who have directly experienced racism and national oppression through colonialism, slavery, and postcolonial racist regimes for centuries, are gaining enough autonomous power to place problems of racism on the international agenda. Even in the earliest days of postcolonialism, the newly freed nations throughout Africa and Asia were able to influence the debate over the Jim Crow system in the United States. One of the reasons the U.S. government shifted its position on segregation and actively sought to overturn the legal support for Jim Crow in the late 1940s and 1950s was in response to pressure brought on by newly independent African and Latin American nations.[24] The vehicle of human rights accords today presents people historically oppressed by colonialism, slavery, and neocolonialism with the opportunity to raise issues about their marginalization from the new global arrangements.

A process of interplay between grassroots organizations, NGOs, and nation-states has gradually emerged around global issues. This capacity was evident as early as the Earth Summit in Rio de Janeiro in 1992, when NGOs compelled the attending governmental representatives to reach agreements controlling greenhouse gases.[25] Since then, global protests have accelerated in scope and frequency against World Bank and IMF restructuring policies; the movement to outlaw landmines; the protests against Nike, Jessica McClintock, and Kathy Lee Gifford's sweatshop practices; and numerous other global problems.[26] The protests in Seattle at the Ministerial Conference of the World Trade Organization (WTO) in 1999 marked another stage in the development of global grassroots political power, as a coalition of labor, environmental, and women's organizations virtually shut down the meeting, while President Bill Clinton implored the delegates to make the WTO's secret arbitration process more "transparent" to the public. Since Seattle, every major meeting of the WTO and the IMF has been met with large and militant protests, in Melbourne, Prague, Quebec, Genoa, and New York City. Regular global meetings of NGOs, such as the World Social Forum, bring together tens of thousands of grassroots activists to develop alternatives to the current models of globalization and to strategize about the most effective ways to advance their agendas.

Efforts to regulate globalization through international accords are thus historically contingent: Their success depends on the mobilization of world pressure against neoliberal international accords and the containment of the United States' arrogant abrogation to itself of global power. As with the defense of democracy, there are no guarantees of success. But globalization increasingly creates opportunities for the formation of global agreements and institutions to address global problems, and these opportunities will continue to grow. Most importantly, the formation of global rules and institutions can be important sites of mobilization for the nations and peoples with a long memory of colonialism and postcolonial racism. These are favorable conditions to compel international accords to become increasingly focused on issues of racial justice.

A key issue for the United States—indeed, given the United States' global domination, for the entire world—will be whether antiracist human rights protocols will be linked to domestic politics that require the United States to conform to global standards. Given the resistance to these standards by the U.S. government, this task will require ongoing and concerted effort by grassroots movements. The Seattle protest that signaled a coming of age of the U.S. efforts to address globalization, however, was marked by a low level of participation by people of color.[27] Conversely, participation by women of color in the third UN Conference on the Status of Women was important for the reorientation of many U.S. women's movement organizations to prioritize issues of concern to women of color. The arena of human rights offers important possibilities for people in the United States and around the world to challenge market globalization and American nationalism. The capacity to develop the power to do so will depend on the extent to which human rights issues are taken up by national and local organizations as a way of framing their work.[28]

In sum, the process of expanding international accords to address the rights of people oppressed by racism and national chauvinism is central to efforts to make globalization socially responsible. The denial of these issues is possible only to the extent that international accords are made by the political and economic elites of the MDCs. Without the participation and leadership of people of color, international accords and human rights protocols will not be able to address the problems of globalization.

Working-Class Solidarity and Antiracist Politics

Another potential challenge to neoliberal market globalization may come from transnational networks of labor unions and working-class political parties. It stands to reason that the growing globalization of capital would foster internationalist and antiracist activities by American workers. Workers' defense against the growing bargaining power of capital can be accomplished only through international solidarity between labor unions that are still primarily organized on a national basis. This is especially so given the burgeoning international division of labor and global marketing strategies typifying TNCs. Working-class solidarity also requires efforts to organize immigrant and other unorganized workers of color within the United States, for these are the workers who are experiencing the dislocations and downward pressures of globalization the most. As well, the reduction in state regulatory functions encourages unions to adopt militant organizing and strike tactics, ones that seek to skirt the legal apparatus constructed to mediate labor-management relations after World War II.[29]

Some efforts to develop the capacity to address these global labor issues are under way within the U.S. labor movement. John Sweeny, the president of the American Federation of Labor and Congress of Industrial Organizations (AFL-CIO), is a longtime advocate of international solidarity and of efforts to organize immigrant workers in the low-wage service sector into unions. Since his election in 1995, the AFL-CIO executive office has for the first time officially prioritized and funded activities toward these ends. As Tamara Kay shows, one effect of NAFTA is that it created a context that has encouraged some U.S. unions to develop closer international ties with their Canadian and Mexican counterparts.[30] As well, some of the biggest union organizing drives in the last fifty years have targeted drywall workers, nursing home workers, and janitors, almost all of whom are immigrants or U.S.-born people of color.[31] The historic Seattle protest against the WTO in 1999 was also instigated in significant part by labor unions.

Despite these efforts, however, the post–World War II trend toward the declining proportion and number of American workers organized into labor unions continues. Unions' share of the workforce dropped from a high of 37 percent in 1946 to less than 14 percent today, with only 9.5 percent in the private sector.[32] Despite the AFL-CIO executive office's calls, most of the largest unions in the United States have shown little interest in expanding their membership or in international cooperation. Two of the biggest setbacks to global trade in recent years—the U.S. refusal to allow Mexican international truckers equal access to U.S. markets and the U.S. decision to impose high tariffs on foreign steel, both in 2001—were policies aggressively spearheaded by the Teamsters Union and the United Steel Workers, respectively. The continuing resistance of most of organized labor to the new global realities should surprise no one familiar with the labor movement's history.

From the prosegregation American Federation of Labor and American Socialist Party of the early twentieth century, to the antiaffirmative action efforts led by AFL-CIO president Al Shanker in the 1970s and 1980s, to the AFL-CIO's Buy American campaign in the 1980s and 1990s, the U.S. labor movement has by and large clung to defending the standard of living of the existing unionized workers in the United States.[33] The weak connections between the immigrant rights movement and the labor movement are problematic for both movements.

The logic of defending the existing membership ineluctably leads many unions to defend the racial and national privileges of their members. As Kim Voss and Rachel Sherman show, the inertia behind unions' prioritizing "service" to their existing membership is quite powerful at the level of the union local, as the entire organization of union activities and leadership is predicated on this assumption. The potential for a revitalized American labor movement, Voss and Sherman suggest, requires a fundamental change in orientation: unions must shift from providing services to their members toward becoming organizers of the unorganized. This reorientation requires a substantial shift in unions' priorities and resources, as the priority is given to organizers who can link the unions to broad networks of unorganized workers outside the workplace and to linking up with social movements that share the same strategic interests. Globalization is creating fertile new conditions for this revitalization, both by increasing the importance of international solidarity in the face of TNCs' practices and by increasing the numbers of immigrant workers within the United States.

But globalization, with capital's greater bargaining power over workers, is also creating more fear and defensiveness on the part of many unionized American workers. As long as unions remain focused on defending their existing membership, especially on the basis of racial and national exclusiveness, the power and numbers of unionized workers will continue to dwindle. The question is: What will compel the American labor movement to break out of its defense of an increasingly narrow section of the working population? Voss and Sherman argue that change will occur in a fragmented way, as locals that have experienced a disastrous political crisis, such as a failed strike, seek a new orientation, turn to the leadership of organizers with a long history of movement building, and accede to pressure for change from the international union leadership.

Perhaps incremental and sporadic change is all that can be currently hoped for from the labor movement itself, as Voss and Sherman suggest. But history also shows that there are periods when an upsurge in protests from communities of color can lead to efforts to revitalize the labor movement, in what Sidney G. Tarrow describes as "cycles of protest."[34] If history is any predictor of the future, the attempt to organize workers of color may happen out-side the existing labor movement and be driven by ethnic community poli-tics. In their remarkable account of the rise and fall of the League of Revo-lutionary Black Workers, Dan Georgakas and Marvin Surkin demonstrate that the efforts to organize black and Arabic workers in the automobile in-dustry were initiated not by the United Auto Workers, but by a grassroots federation of black workers, the Detroit Revolutionary Union Movement, that arose during the Detroit uprisings of 1967 and 1968.[35] While some 2.5 million black workers were organized in AFL-CIO unions, the unions' racism meant that the black workers had little choice but to engage in independent action apart from existing labor organizations. The rise of the League of Rev-olutionary Black Workers, a product of black insurrections and anti–Vietnam War activism as well as labor militancy, demonstrates the capacity of ethnic politics to transform itself into working class consciousness. However, the in-stability of this early effort is notable as well: without the institutional sup-port of the unions, the radical black labor movement of the 1970s was un-able to survive more than a few years.

It is notable that the most successful union organizing drives of the last decade have taken place in the most global of American states—California—and in sectors with high concentrations of Latino and Asian immigrant workers. As Miriam J. Wells notes, Latino and Latina immigrants in the ho-tel industry in San Francisco are often eager to participate in unions because of their experiences with labor unions and labor parties (let alone revolu-tions) in Latin America.[36] Ethnic community ties are the key to at least some of the organizing drives' successes. Concerning the drywall workers' strike in Los Angeles, Ruth Milkman and Kent Wong observe "the fact that at least a few hundred men from the tiny Mexican village of El Maguey worked in the drywall trade, and were bound together by close kin and friendship ties, was by all accounts an important source of the solidarity that emerged in the or-ganizing campaign."[37] Latinos from many nationalities are able to overcome their divisions and work closely together in the Hotel and Restaurant Em-ployees organizing drive, a measure of how their common racial and class sit-uation in the United States provides a basis for unity. Many of the successful organizing drives incorporate leadership from outside the labor movement, especially from church and grassroots community organizations.

The dynamics of globalization will continue to create conditions favorable for the development of a transnational and antiracist labor movement to con-front global capital. Such a movement will probably arise from both within the existing labor movement and outside it, from ethnic communities. As Milkman and Wong note, "[T]he success of the drywall campaign depended on the unusual combination of bottom-up organizing by workers themselves on the basis of preexisting immigrant social networks, on the one hand, and the financial and legal support provided by the labor movement on the other."[38] If the labor movement is to be revitalized, this "unusual combination" will have to become the rule. It is likely that the continuing marginalization of people of color within the U.S. labor movement, and the continuing reliance of organized labor on nationalist buffers to protect its members from globalization, will compel working-class politics to arise, as they did in the 1960s, from ethnic community organizations. The test will be whether there will be sufficient new vitality in the labor movement to be able to relate to and support the working-class aspirations that arise in ethnic communities.

Ethnic Politics and Globalization

Globalization is creating more than the opportunity for renegotiation of the social order; it is producing conditions that are invigorating both transnational networks of activists and ethnic community resistance that may play a decisive part in that process. It has been argued throughout this book that the stubborn reality of market globalization is that all people are not being organized into the market system—let alone into a transnational "modern" social order. Even those who are being organized into global markets often enter them on racialized and increasingly unequal terms. Globalization's tendency to marginalize or exclude people of color has given new life to ethnic community formation and resistance.

From the neoliberal perspective, the growing ethnic consciousness of the global era is depicted as a reactionary withdrawal in the face of modernization. Ethnic groups are seen as those who are resisting the restructuring of society necessary to enable people to participate in the global economy.[39] From the other end of the political spectrum, some Marxists also decry ethnicity as mere "identity politics," a devolution of consciousness that marks a turning away from working-class politics. Francis Fox Piven and Richard A. Cloward argue:

> [T]he fatal flaw of identity politics is easily recognized. Class politics, at least in principal, promotes vertical cleavages, mobilizing people around axes which broadly correspond to hierarchies of power, and which promote challenges to these hierarchies. By contrast, identity politics fosters lateral cleavages which are unlikely to reflect fundamental conflicts over social power and resources and, indeed, may seal popular allegiance to the ruling classes that exploit them.[40]

"The thickening of identity politics," Todd Gitlin writes from the left, "is inseparable from a fragmentation of commonality politics."[41] Similar criticisms of ethnic "balkanization" have been proclaimed by Arthur M. Schlesinger Jr. from the "center" and Dinesh D'Souza from the right.[42] The rightest, neoliberal, and Marxist critics of ethnicity all miss the central point: Ethnicity is born of necessity, created by people who are otherwise left out of the social contract with little or no voice in the restructuring of society.

Certainly, as Piven and Cloward suggest, it is possible for ethnic cleavages to undermine working-class unity. But working-class unity—such as it ever was in the United States—has been on the decline for many years. The rising emphasis on ethnicity in this era is not a cause of the declining influence of working-class movements, but one of the results of this decline. The disorganization of white workers in the United States is a legacy of the creation of the middle-class social order in the 1950s and the assault on organized labor ever since then.[43] The prominence of ethnicity thus results in part from the weakness of working-class forms of resistance to market globalization. But ethnic communities are not backward or deformed. They are comprised of dense social networks that enable people to take autonomous action. Ethnic communities are consequently, at times, the best organized sites of resistance to both racial *and* class problems associated with market globalization. Rather than dogmatically rejecting ethnicity as a reactionary impulse, it is more useful to recognize the progressive potential within it.

As Robin D. G. Kelley observes, critics of ethnicity miss one of the most crucial elements of ethnic politics: People who are struggling for liberation from one form of oppression do not necessarily, or even usually, do so to the exclusion of other issues.[44] Instead, as Kelley observes, people who are oppressed typically develop an expansive agenda that seeks to build alliances with all people struggling for social equality. Black feminism, for example, has generally been concerned with both redefining black unity on a nonsexist basis and linking the struggle for black unity with the struggle for human emancipation from economic inequality, racism, sexism, and homophobia. Kelley quotes black feminist Anna Julia Cooper, who in 1893 wrote:

> We take our stand on the solidarity of humanity, the oneness of life, and the unnaturalness and injustice of all special favoritisms, whether of sex, race, country, or condition. . . . The colored woman feels that woman's cause is one and universal; and that . . . not till race, color, sex, and condition are seen as accidents, and not the substance of life; not till the universal title of humanity to life, liberty, and the pursuit of happiness is conceded to be inalienable to all; not till then is woman's lesson taught and woman's cause won—not the white

woman's nor the black woman's, not the red woman's but the cause of every man and every woman who has writhed silently under a mighty wrong.[45]

This duality, the articulation in this case for the particular interests of black women and the recognition that these issues are a component of a universal interest of all humanity, is the very essence of the dialectic of ethnic solidarity itself.[46]

The growing inequality and racism that are hallmarks of market globalization in the United States, then, provide a context in which people can, and often do, seek to build ethnic solidarity *and* to find ways to build bridges across the ethnic divides. American history is full of examples of ethnic community politics that take on a broader democratic or working-class coalition form. From the abolitionists, to the Niagara movement, to the Sleeping Car Porters' Union, to the civil rights movement, black community-based activists have participated in and anchored a wide variety of multiracial coalitions.[47] Mexican, Japanese, and Filipino workers formed multinational unions in the early California labor movement.[48] Black feminists have long sought to unite with all women and with black men.[49]

Too frequently, these political or economic impulses fail to produce stable multiethnic, multiracial coalitions around societywide (or global) issues. Unfortunately, the principal reason for this instability is the enmity of established organizations toward the issues and leadership of ethnic communities. The ongoing problems of racism and national chauvinism have been well documented for the labor, women's, peace, environmental, and gay and lesbian movements.[50] But history also reveals successful periods of multiracial coalition building, most notably the abolitionists in the 1850s and 1860s, the labor movement in the 1930s, and the civil rights movement from the 1960s to the present.

The prospects for ethnic community unity and empowerment have been hotly debated for decades. At the dawn of the global era, in 1977, William Julius Wilson proclaimed that race was of declining significance in the shaping of people's opportunities in the United States.[51] One of Wilson's arguments was that the growing economic gap between middle-class and poor African Americans was undermining their racial-ethnic unity. John Mollenkopf argues that the growing numbers of black immigrants (Haitian, West Indian, African, and so on) who do not share African American ethnicity have fragmented black unity.[52] Mexican Americans and Chinese Americans also face challenges to ethnic unity, both in the form of greater class divisions and the growing national origins of Latino and Asian immigrants, conditions brought on by the globalization of markets.

But the racialized and nationalist responses to globalization in the United States, combined with growing immigration from the postcolonial countries, simultaneously raise racial consciousness and ethnic unity. Faced with assaults on jobs, social services, education, housing, citizenship, and so on from the private sector and the public sector alike, people of color of all classes and nationalities have to find new ways to survive and resist. One of the most important resources available for both survival and resistance is ethnic community itself. The process of being marginalized, coupled with historic cultural, familial, and institutional ties, provides people with a powerful basis to come together to address their common problems. The resulting ethnic communities— both located in geographic space (ghettoes, barrios, Chinatowns, reservations, and so on) and as political and cultural constructs (the black community, the Asian community, and so on)—provide their members with sets of social networks, cultural identities of inclusiveness and belonging, and chances of access to political power and economic resources that the dominant group would not voluntarily concede.[53] The new manifestations of ethnicity in the United States, like those around the world, are quite fluid, as people grope with the new conditions of globalized society in search of community and the means to effectively respond to new political and economic challenges.

The dynamic ways in which people use the experiences of racial and national oppression to construct ethnicity in the United States have been explored in a number of studies. Yen Le Espiritu describes the ways in which Asian immigrants overcome the fragmentation and isolation that small numbers of people from many different Asian nationalities experience in the United States.[54] As Espiritu shows, people from a vast array of different nationalities and class locations use their common racial experience as Asians in America to construct what she terms "panethnic" blocs to accomplish common goals, such as increasing access to social services and education, protection of civil rights, and political power. Similarly, M. Annette Jaimes examines the ways in which the many diverse indigenous peoples of North America have used their common racial status as "Indians" to unite across tribal lines to achieve common goals.[55] Mary S. Pardo shows how Mexican American women find common ground despite significant national, cultural, and class differences among recent immigrants and first- or second-generation U.S. citizens.[56]

Globalization is altering the conditions in which ethnic unity is developed in the United States. Certainly, as Wilson maintains, class divisions are becoming increasingly evident within ethnic groups as part of the growing inequality between rich and poor in American society as a whole. Certainly, increasing immigration is creating new national divisions within and tensions between racial groups. It is reasonable to expect that as class and national divisions grow, different interests should fracture ethnic solidarity. But this is not primarily what is happening. Instead, ethnic unity continues to be reproduced in the face of growing immigration and economic inequality due to the pressures of racism and nationalism, a fact revealed in ethnic voting patterns and support for community-specific social services, civil rights, and immigrant rights. African Americans, for example, became increasingly well organized as a voting bloc throughout the 1980s and 1990s and played a vital role in the 2000 elections.[57] As well, middle-class people of color continue to actively maintain ties to the working-class and poor base of their communities. For example, a survey of all medical doctors who graduated medical school in the last twenty years found that African American physicians were remarkably likely to enter practices where they provided services to underserved black populations.[58] Pardo similarly finds that middle-class, suburban Mexican Americans regularly return to East Los Angeles to renew their ties to La Raza.[59] The resurgence of Native American ethnicity marks an important renaissance of many traditional societies.

A singular feature of the global era is that common antiracist interests operate to unite ethnic solidarity even as class and national divisions undermine it.[60] The persistence of ethnicity, and the innovative forms that ethnic groups have adapted in changing circumstances, stand as testimony to people's need for collective identities and vehicles for the defense of, and advance of, their interests. We can expect a continuation of progressive resistance to globalization to find expression through ethnic formations.

Conclusion: The Possible Futures
of Antiracist Politics in the Global Era

What will it take to create socially responsible globalization? Given the growing leverage of capital over the state in the era of unfettered market globalization and efforts by the United States to substitute its own national power for global governance, attempts to hold capital accountable to people's social needs will require massive grassroots responses to the growing crises of market globalization. Movements for socially responsible globalization will initially arise around many different issues, in many different places. Creating a global movement capable of constraining the destructive effects of market globalization will require these movements to link up around a common vision of socially responsible globalization. This vision will have to advocate for a social order that is democratic, inclusive, and open, rather than authoritarian, exclusive, and built on fear. To achieve social justice, transnational capital will have to submit to governmental regulation and to the redistribution of resources from the top downward. A movement for socially responsible globalization will have to wield significant political power to overcome the powerful resistance of transnational capital to social arrangements that will constrain profitability.

In the previous sections, I explored the potential for a civil rights movement, a human rights movement, and a labor movement to develop in the United States in the context of globalization. What is clear from this analysis is that the successful defense of democracy, equity, and world peace in the global era will require all movements for social justice to come to terms with the growing importance of racism and ethnic communities, both in the United States and around the world. If they fail to do so, they will ignore the worst problems of market globalization and will therefore be disarmed as the assaults on racially and nationally oppressed peoples become increasingly powerful.[61] But the previous analysis also suggests that each of these movements faces significant barriers to accomplishing this reorientation.

What will it take to reorient the American labor movement to the new global realities? What will compel the U.S. government to acknowledge the human rights of people marginalized by globalization? And what will motivate people to defend democracy in the face of mounting nationalist and fascist tendencies? The previous analysis suggests that the likeliest impetus for movements for socially responsible globalization will not come from within existing institutions, but from the self-organization and political power of ethnic communities. Social movements, as they succeed, tend to become institutionalized in ways that undercut their militancy. The impetus for change is unlikely to come from within established movements themselves. Rather, movement revitalization is likely to require external stimulus. The people most directly affected by the crisis of globalization—the direct targets of repressive state power, the people pushed down the hardest by the disequalizing trends of globalization—are initially the people with the greatest capacity to challenge the self-serving dogma of market globalization. The growth of ethnic communities' political capacity will present democratic, transnational, and working-class movements with new energy and ideas. The revitalization of working-class politics and the civil rights and human rights movements in the global era require placing ethnic communities' leadership at the center of those movements' agendas. Ethnic politics, while capable of sparking movement revitalization, also depends on movement success, for without the resurgence of movements for peace, justice, and equity, ethnic communities will continue to be marginalized and oppressed.

Efforts to achieve socially responsible globalization will require transnational social movements to develop a new orientation, one that is simultaneously global, national, and local. Transnational social movements will have to simultaneously be rooted in local ethnic communities, work for the defense of national democracy, and seek to create new global forms to advance social justice. In the global era, as Peter Waterman puts it, "the external invests the internal, the local redefines the global."[62] The development of transnational social movements and the development of local ethnic resistance to globalization are interdependent: Transnational networks will gain influence to the extent that they tap into the energy of ethnic community resistance, and ethnic community resistance will break out of its isolation and become stabilized by the organization of transnational networks. Only such a dialectic between the global and the local will produce sufficient power to compel national political elites, especially in the United States, to face up to the need to rein in unregulated global capital.

The interplay between these levels of political work offers important new possibilities in these early decades of the global era. Grassroots community leaders, especially in ethnic communities, are becoming increasingly skilled in mediating between these levels.[63] This legacy goes back at least as far as the efforts by Martin Luther King Jr. in the 1960s to link the civil rights movement to the Non-Aligned Movement and by Malcolm X to connect his work to the Organization for African Unity.[64] At this time, it may appear that such linkages are not particularly influential. But if the middle-class social order becomes destabilized, as this analysis suggests, possibilities for social movements to have a significant effect on the future of globalization will continue to present themselves. Whether or not these possibilities are acted on is a matter for history to decide.

Notes

1. Antonio Gramsci, *Selections from the Prison Notebooks* (New York: International, 1971), 276.

2. Karl Polanyi, *The Great Transformation* (Boston: Beacon, 1944).

3. Peter Evans, "The Eclipse of the State?: Reflections on Statelessness in an Era of Globalization," *World Politics* 50 (October 1997): 62–87.

4. Jennifer L. Hochschild, *Facing up to the American Dream* (Princeton, N.J.: Princeton University Press, 1995).

5. The Mandarin word for "crisis" consists of two characters: danger and opportunity.

6. Doug McAdam, *Political Process and the Development of Black Insurgency, 1930–1970* (Chicago: University of Chicago Press, 1982); Charles Tilly, *From Mobilization to Revolution* (Reading, Mass.: Addison-Wesley, 1978).

7. Buchanan, who is a right-wing activist, has selectively defended Adolf Hitler's policies and blames immigration, affirmative action, English as Second Language programs, and free trade for the woes of the white middle class. Buchanan's main television spot in his 2000 presidential campaign depicted a white man choking to death because he couldn't reach a dispatcher who spoke English when he dialed 911. His message found limited support, mostly among the poorer section of the white middle class.

8. Nicholas A. Kristof, "Liberal Reality Check," *New York Times*, 31 May 2002, A25.

9. Max Weber, *Economy and Society*, vol. 2 (Berkeley: University of California Press, 1977), 667.

10. Brigette Young, "Globalization and Gender: A European Perspective," in *Gender, Globalization and Democratization*, ed. Rita Mae Kelly et al. (New York: Rowman & Littlefield, 2001), 44.

11. Mervin D. Field and Mark DiCamillo, "Big Drop in Support for Prop. 187," Field Poll 1734 (San Francisco: Field Institute, 1994).

12. Amnesty International, *Annual Report* (Washington, D.C.: Amnesty International, 2002).

13. A. Winslow, ed., *Women, Politics, and the United Nations* (Westport, Conn.: Greenwood, 1995).

14. The ways in which human rights protocols reframe local struggles is explored by Margaret E. Keck and Kathryn Sikkink, *Activists beyond Borders: Advocacy Networks in International Politics* (Ithaca, N.Y.: Cornell University Press, 1998), especially chapter 4.

15. Joseph E. Stiglitz, *Globalization and Its Discontents* (New York: Norton, 2002).

16. Malcolm Waters, *Globalization* (London: Routledge, 1995), chapter 5.

17. Jan Aart Scholte, *Globalization: A Critical Introduction* (New York: St. Martin's, 2000), 254.

18. Young, "Globalization and Gender," 45.

19. Eduardo Bonilla-Silva, "'This Is a White Country': The Racial Ideology of the Western Nations of the World-System," *Sociological Inquiry* 70, no. 2 (Spring 2000): 188–214; Charles Mills, *Blackness Visible* (Ithaca, N.Y.: Cornell University Press, 1998).

20. Carol Devine et al., *Human Rights: The Essential Reference* (Phoenix, Ariz.: Oryx, 1999).

21. James H. Cone, *Malcolm and Martin and America* (Maryknoll, N.Y.: Orbis, 1991).

22. Saskia Sassen, *Guests and Aliens* (New York: The New Press, 1999).

23. These documents can be accessed at the UN website www.un.org (last accessed January 21, 2003).

24. For a discussion of the national security arguments used by the United States in amicus curiae briefs before the U.S. Supreme Court in antidiscrimination lawsuits in the late 1940s and 1950s, see Richard Kluger, *Simple Justice: The History of* Brown v. *Board of Education and Black America's Struggle for Equality* (New York: Knopf, 1976), especially 253.

25. "The Non-governmental Order," *The Economist*, 11–17 December 1999.

26. Randy Shaw, *Reclaiming America: Nike, Clean Air, and the New National Activism* (Berkeley: University of California Press, 1999).

27. Elizabeth Martinez, "Where Was the Color in Seattle," *ColorLines* 3, no. 1 (Spring 2000).

28. Peter Evans, "Fighting Marginalization with Transnational Networks: Counter-hegemonic Globalization," *Contemporary Sociology* 29, no. 1 (January 2000).

29. Dan Clawson and Mary Ann Clawson, "What Has Happened to the US Labor Movement?: Union Decline and Renewal," *Annual Review of Sociology* 25 (1999): 95–119.

30. Tamara Kay, "Labor Relations in a Post-NAFTA Era" (paper presented at the Berkeley Journal of Sociology Conference on Globalization and Racism, Berkeley, California, April 2002).

31. Ruth Milkman, ed., *Organizing Immigrants: The Challenge for Unions in Contemporary California* (Ithaca, N.Y.: ILR Press, 2000).

32. Kim Voss and Rachel Sherman, "Breaking the Iron Law of Oligarchy: Union Revitalization in the American Labor Movement," *American Journal of Sociology* 106, no. 2 (September 2000): 313.

33. Herbert Hill, "Race and Labor," *Journal of Intergroup Relations* 10, no. 1 (Spring 1982).

34. Sidney G. Tarrow, *Power in Movement: Social Movements and Contentious Politics* (Cambridge: Cambridge University Press, 1998).

35. Dan Georgakas and Marvin Surkin, *Detroit: I Do Mind Dying* (Boston: South End, 1998).

36. Miriam J. Wells, "Immigration and Unionization in the San Francisco Hotel Industry," in *Organizing Immigrants: The Challenge for Unions in Contemporary California*, ed. Ruth Milkman (Ithaca, N.Y.: ILR Press, 2000), 119–121.

37. Ruth Milkman and Kent Wong, "Organizing the Wicked City: The 1992 Southern California Drywall Strike," in *Organizing Immigrants: The Challenge for Unions in Contemporary California*, ed. Ruth Milkman (Ithaca, N.Y.: ILR Press, 2000), 181.

38. Milkman and Wong, "Organizing the Wicked City," 195.

39. B. C. Smith, "Modernization and Political Change," in *Understanding Third World Politics* (Bloomington: Indiana University Press, 1996), 61–87.

40. Francis Fox Piven and Richard A. Cloward, *The Breaking of the American Social Contract* (New York: The New Press, 1997), 44.

41. Todd Gitlin, "The Rise of 'Identity Politics,'" *Dissent* 49 (Spring 1993): 172–177; see also Todd Gitlin, *Twilight of Our Common Dreams: Why America Is Wracked by Culture Wars* (New York: Metropolitan, 1995).

42. Arthur M. Schlesinger Jr., *The Disuniting of America* (New York: Norton, 1992); Dinesh D'Souza, *The End of Racism* (New York: The Free Press, 1995).

43. Mike Davis, *Prisoners of the American Dream* (London: Verso, 1986).

44. Robin D. G. Kelley, "Identity Politics and Class Struggle," in *Race and Ethnicity in the United States: Issues and Debates*, ed. Stephen Steinberg (Malden, Mass.: Blackwell, 2000), 328–335.

45. Anna Julia Cooper, quoted in Kelley, "Identity Politics and Class Struggle," 332.

46. Institute for the Study of Social Change, *Diversity Task Force Report* (Berkeley: University of California, 1992).

47. Robert L. Allen, *The Reluctant Reformers* (Washington, D.C.: Howard University Press, 1974); see also the discussion over the black-Jewish coalitions of the early to mid-nineteenth century in Jack Salzman, ed., *Bridges and Boundaries: African Americans and American Jews* (New York: George Braziller, 1992).

48. Tomás Almaguer, *Racial Fault Lines* (Berkeley: University of California Press, 1994), 183–204.

49. Angela Davis, *Women, Race and Class* (New York: Random House, 1981); Toni Morrison, ed., *Race-ing Justice, En-gendering Power* (New York: Pantheon, 1992); Anita Faye Hill and Emma Coleman Jordan, eds., *Race, Gender, and Power in America* (New York: Oxford University Press, 1995).

50. For a general overview, see Allen, *Reluctant Reformers*; on the labor movement, see Hill, "Race and Labor"; and on the women's movement, Davis, *Women, Race and Class*.

51. William Julius Wilson, *The Declining Significance of Race: Blacks and Changing American Institutions* (Chicago: University of Chicago Press, 1978).

52. John Mollenkopf, "The Decay of Reform," *Dissent* (Fall 1987): 495.

53. Carol B. Stack, *All Our Kin* (New York: Basic, 1997) and Michel Duneier, *Slim's Table* (Chicago: University of Chicago Press, 1992) explore the formation and reproduction of gendered social networks by people in ethnic communities.

54. Yen Le Espiritu, *Asian American Panethnicity* (Philadelphia: Temple University Press, 1992).

55. M. Annette Jaimes, "American Racism: The Impact on American Indian Identity and Survival," in *Race*, ed. Steven Gregory and Roger Sanjek (New Brunswick, N.J.: Rutgers University Press, 1994), 41–61.

56. Mary S. Pardo, *Mexican American Women Activists: Identity and Resistance in Two Los Angeles Communities* (Philadelphia: Temple University Press, 1998).

57. Marjorie Connely, "Who Voted: A Portrait of American Politics, 1976–2000," *New York Times*, 12 November 2000, 4–5.

58. Robert Steinbrook, "Diversity in Medicine," *New England Journal of Medicine* 334, no. 20 (May 1996).

59. Pardo, *Mexican American Women Activists*, 87–90.

60. Of course, this is not new to the global era. Both slavery and Jim Crow segregation had similar effects on people of color. But the dynamics of racism, and therefore the dynamics of ethnic formation, are different in this era.

61. It would do well to remember the words of Bishop Martin Niemöller, the Lutheran minister who founded the Pastors' Emergency League to Resist Hitlerism during the Nazis' rise to power in Germany: "First they came for the Communists, but I was not a Communist so I did not speak out. Then they came for the Socialists and the Trade Unionists, but I was neither, so I did not speak out. Then they came for the Jews, but I was not a Jew so I did not speak out. And when they came for me, there was no one left to speak out for me." See the American-Israeli Cooperative Enterprise, www.jewishvirtuallibrary.org/jsource/Holocaust/Niemoller_quote.html (accessed January 21, 2003). Niemöller spent eight years confined in Nazi concentration camps.

62. Peter Waterman, *Globalization, Social Movements and the New Internationalisms* (Washington, D.C.: Mansell, 1998), 203.

63. Jeremy Brecher, Tim Costello, and Brendan Smith, *Globalization from Below: The Power of Solidarity* (Cambridge, Mass.: South End, 2000).

64. Malcolm X was assassinated the night of the planned founding of the Organization for African American Unity, an NGO to be part of the Organization for African Unity.

CHAPTER SEVEN

Globalization and the Revitalization
of the Civil Rights Movement

The previous chapter examined the potential openings for social movements for equity, justice, and democracy in the global era. As we saw in chapter 6, globalization is not only creating new conditions for the mobilization of white privileges, but it is also reshaping the possibilities for opposition to racism. The purpose of this chapter is to examine the challenges globalization has created for one social movement and what might be done, given the reality of globalization, to revitalize its capacity. This chapter focuses on the civil rights movement because it is, even today, the most sustained and successful effort to confront racism in modern American history. As well, if the analysis in chapter 6 is correct, conditions demanding the revitalization of a broad civil rights movement are emerging today.

The successes of the civil rights strategy in the past were due to its focus on the uses of state power against racism and for racial equity and justice. This strategy was to a degree successful because it recognized that the power of the state is increasingly important for the organization and stabilization of capitalist societies, both at the national and the global levels. But the civil rights strategy also reveals the limitations of reliance on state power in the global era. Globalization is undercutting some of the civil rights movement's central assumptions about state power and highlighting the need for a shift in priorities from litigation, legislation, and policy advocacy toward grass-roots organizing and community empowerment strategies. At the same time, the past achievements of the civil rights movement, especially in the electoral arena, may become increasingly important in advocating for a more just social order in the face of the destabilizing forces of globalization.

The civil rights movement is undoubtedly experiencing grave difficulties. The lawyers, students, politicians, and community activists who have mobilized for government protection from discrimination for people of color and immigrants have found themselves increasingly on the defensive over the past two decades. Civil rights activists' efforts now mostly go into preventing anticivil rights legislation from passing. The federal courts, and the U.S. Supreme Court in particular, once so receptive to the civil rights movement's agenda, have become so hostile that civil rights attorneys now often try to keep cases away from them. The assault on the civil rights movement has become so intense that those who are trying to destroy it now claim to be a "new" civil rights movement. The opponents of affirmative action, for example, called their California ballot initiative the "California Civil Rights Initiative" and formed the American Civil Rights Institute to advance their cause. Opponents of civil rights are also trying to obliterate the history of the civil rights movement. During the campaign for Proposition 209 in California, proponents of the abolition of affirmative action attempted to use Martin Luther King Jr.'s words to justify their position.[1] Stephan Thernstrom and Abigail Thernstrom argue, with complete disregard for the words and deeds of the civil rights leaders of the 1960s, that opposition to affirmative action is consistent with the "original" philosophy of the civil rights movement.[2] After a generation of defensive battles, many people who want to work to end racism, particularly youth, now question the civil rights movement's relevance. Many antiracist activists agree with constitutional law scholar Derrick Bell that the civil rights movement failed to end racism and instead perpetuated people of color's subordination to white power in a myriad of ways.[3] Many young people now think of the civil rights movement as a part of the past, of little relevance to their lives today.

For all these reasons, an analysis of the impact of globalization on the civil rights movement is needed. Such an analysis enables us to more clearly assess the weaknesses and strengths of the civil rights strategy for ending racism in the context of new economic and political conditions. This analysis highlights the problems facing the civil rights movement today by showing that the assumptions about economic expansion and the expanding role of the welfare state that were true when the civil rights movement arose are no longer valid. But, as we have already explored in chapter 6, the civil rights movement might become increasingly important in the United States in the very near future as the defense of democracy becomes an all-important task. A critical assessment of the civil rights movement's strengths and weaknesses is thus essential to prepare the ground for what is likely to become its greatest test since the 1970s.

The Civil Rights Movement and the Middle-Class Social Order, 1955–1975

The concept of civil rights, explains Max Weber, refers to the formal promise that government will protect specific behaviors against discrimination.[4] The adequacy of the civil rights strategy—the use of state power to undermine racial privileges and oppression—has as much to do with the capacity of the state to meet the demands placed on it as it does with the movement's grassroots power. The civil rights movement is only one particular phase of the antiracist struggle for freedom, justice, and equality, one that arose in a specific historical context. Throughout the 500-year-long history of the European colonization of Africa and the Americas, and the creation of the United States, a wide range of strategies to combat racism were attempted, ranging from slave rebellions and abolitionism, to trade unionism, to political empowerment, to different forms of cultural, political, and economic separatism. Like other antiracist movements, the power of the civil rights movement of the 1950s and 1960s was rooted in the black community, a power that was highly visible during the insurgencies against both the Jim Crow system of legal racial segregation in the South and the system of structured racism in the North from the 1950s to the 1970s.[5] But the civil rights movement of that era was more than a black insurgency; it was a complex, multiracial, multiclass coalition aimed at mobilizing state power at a time when the mass middle-class social order was stable and growing.[6]

The early civil rights movement was in some ways a creature of the middle-class social order. As discussed in chapter 2, national political and corporate elites seized the opportunities presented by American global dominance in the 1940s and 1950s to create a new political and economic arrangement: the middle-class social order. The mass middle class, constructed by both expanding nation-state action and private labor-management agreements, constituted a new basis for social stability predicated on the ownership of a private home, a job that paid a "family wage," and access to a college education. National political elites were vulnerable to the black insurgency against the Jim Crow system during the 1950s and 1960s for reasons rooted in the logic of this new middle-class social order. First, support for racial equality under the law presented national elites with numerous opportunities to expand federal (welfare state) power over the states by creating a national concept of civil rights.[7] Second, the black insurgency against racism compelled national elites to make good on their avowed commitment to the ideology of a mass middle-class social order based on merit and equal opportunity for all.[8] And third, the civil rights movement's exposure of the Jim

Crow system posed an increasingly serious liability for U.S. strategic interests in the establishment of its global influence, particularly in the newly liberated colonies of Africa and the Caribbean.

Martin Luther King Jr. well understood the relationship between the black community insurgency and the middle-class social order of the 1950s and 1960s. In 1967, he wrote, "The American racial revolution has been a revolution to 'get in' rather than to overthrow. We want a share in the American economy, the housing market, the educational system and the social opportunities."[9] There was nothing about the middle-class order of the 1950s or the expanding role of the federal government, however, that automatically guaranteed the eradication of legal segregation, let alone racial equality. It was altogether feasible for the new middle-class order to be erected on a racially segregated basis (as it was in apartheid South Africa, for example). The power of the white South in the 1950s was formidable, entrenched in the leadership of both houses of Congress and the Democratic and Republican Parties.[10] The McCarthy-era witch-hunts deterred a progressive challenge to the emerging middle-class order. The profound impact of the black insurgency on national, political, and corporate elites and on the U.S. economy, politics, and culture required enormous courage, persistence, and a clarity of vision of the possibilities in that period. Nevertheless, it was the fact that national elites were compelled to support its demands that turned the black insurgency into a force that transformed the U.S. legal and political systems.

The expanding influence of the civil rights movement was bound up with the growth of the welfare state in the 1950s through the mid-1970s. Civil rights demonstrations were coordinated with lawsuits and executive or legislative lobbying to pressure political elites to take action. As victories were won, grassroots organizing was further invigorated. As the dialectic between movement mobilization and state action produced tangible results, the civil rights movement gradually expanded its political influence and agenda and took on a more multiracial and multiclass character.[11] But this coalition was short lived. In the years 1964–1968, an unprecedented series of over 110 urban insurrections took place in virtually every city with a significant black (and, in places, Latino) population. These massive urban insurrections unleashed a wide range of political movements, including revolutionary black and Chicano nationalisms and a militant black labor movement.[12] The fact that these insurrections took place during the Vietnam War also critically focused attention on the United States' global dominance, captured by the Black Panther's antidraft slogan "No Vietnamese ever called me nigger" and by the Chicano Moratorium rally in Los Angeles in 1968. The civil rights movement, by this time well positioned with national political elites and supported by a large section of white liberals, was compelled to develop a new political agenda in response to these events.

The urban insurrections and antiwar protests of the 1960s provided the impetus for the development of a new form of civil rights politics, one that escaped quickly from the bounds of the struggle for the integration of people of color into the middle-class social order.[13] Before 1966, the main focus of the civil rights movement was the creation of legal equality, that is, the abolition of Jim Crow segregation laws. In 1966, most of the civil rights movement's leaders put forward the proposition that people of color could only achieve equal opportunity if they had equal access to decent schools, adequate housing, and good jobs. To ensure this, civil rights activists demanded that the national government enable and fund programs to actively redistribute social and economic resources from whites to people of color, a set of "affirmative action" programs. Such affirmative action required white liberals to take a major step beyond their support for integration. Affirmative action meant that whites would have to be willing to surrender racial privileges, such as advantages in getting jobs, education, housing, political power, and so on. As soon as the new agenda was articulated, most whites abandoned the civil rights coalition.[14]

Propelled by the power of black, and (in 1968 and 1969) Chicano, Puerto Rican, and American Indian insurrections, the civil rights movement developed a broader and more ambitious political agenda, one that raised issues far beyond the "affirmative" responsibility of government to remedy the effects of past discrimination. In 1966, the civil rights movement's foremost advocate of integration, Martin Luther King Jr., reached the conclusion that racism was inextricably linked with poverty and militarism. Unless the government addressed the economic causes of widespread poverty and stopped spending one-third of its budget on the military and waging war on people of color overseas, he reasoned, it would be impossible for government to take the meaningful steps necessary to eliminate racial disparities and barriers. King threw down the challenge:

T]here is a need for a radical restructuring of the architecture of American society. For its very survival's sake, America must re-examine old presuppositions and release itself from many things that for centuries have been held sacred. For the evils of racism, poverty and militarism to die, a new set of values must be born. Our economy must become more people-centered than property- and profit-centered. Our government must depend more on its moral power than on its military power. Let us, therefore, not think of our movement as one that seeks to integrate the Negro into all the existing values of American society.

Let us be those creative dissenters who will call our beloved nation to a higher destiny, to a new plateau of compassion, to a more noble expression of humaneness.[15]

The civil rights movement thus underwent a remarkable transformation in 1966, turning its attention away from "getting in" to the middle class toward redressing the unequal distribution of resources in American society and the relationship of the United States to the rest of the world.

The problem facing the civil rights movement was that its new agenda far outstripped the political, economic, and cultural arrangements of the middle-class social order, as well as people of color's power to alter the social order. After 1966, many civil rights advocates understood the enormity of this challenge, the "radical restructuring of American society" that would be necessary to end racism. The demand to equalize opportunities for people of color entailed broad and fundamental social change: The movement's agenda called for basic alterations in the role of government and the workings of the economy to effect a redistribution of wealth, power, and social services like health care, welfare, and education. The movement sought a redefinition of the basic culture of the nation, to root out assumptions of white racial superiority from literature, cinema, the theater, sports, and schools. The movement also called for a redefinition of the definitions of merit that determined who was "qualified" for access to selective educational and employment opportunities. And the movement was thoroughly international in its vision, calling for a new U.S. foreign policy that eschewed militarism and imperialism. The idea of racial justice now was rooted in a concept of social justice, both domestically and globally.

The more sober and serious activists quickly realized that the civil rights movement did not have the power to successfully accomplish its goals by itself. King wrote in 1967, "We must frankly acknowledge that in past years our creativity and imagination were not employed in learning how to develop power."[16] In the mid-1960s, the attention of many civil rights activists turned to the development of political power. As the civil rights activists took up this task, they began to support the development of ethnic community solidarity as a vehicle for autonomous power. Indeed, in the mid-1960s activists began to grasp the relationship between separation and integration as a creative dialectic rather than as opposite ideas. King, reflecting on the Student Non-violent Coordinating Committee's slogan "Black Power," put it this way, "We want to be integrated, but we don't want to be integrated out of power. We want to be integrated into power."[17] Elsewhere, King argued "there are times when we must see separation as a temporary way-station to a truly integrated society."[18] King and other civil rights leaders warned against separatism as a strategic goal, insisting that autonomous political power exercised by people of color had to be linked in coalition with whites if it was to produce meaningful changes in American society. But, from 1966 onward, the main energy of grassroots organizing was focused on developing black, Chicano, Puerto Rican, and American Indian power movements and exploring the possibilities for working-class antiracist politics, not building coalitions with white national elites.

The achievements of the 1955–1975 civil rights movement were historically significant. The movement's success at eliminating the system of Jim Crow laws in 1964 and 1965 was a fundamental prerequisite for any effort to equalize opportunity for housing, employment, education, or any other scarce social resource. The civil rights movement also had a major effect on the development of the welfare state, compelling national political elites, still enjoying the resources available in the waning days of American global hegemony, to respond to urban insurrections and civil rights activism by channeling significant state resources toward addressing racial inequalities, including the problems of the neglected inner-city poor.[19] The civil rights movement was also successful in its demands for the creation and enforcement of equal employment opportunity laws.[20] Another area in which the civil rights movement had a direct impact was on school desegregation efforts.[21]

All told, the civil rights movement succeeded in directing significant economic and social benefits of the middle-class social order to people of color. Buoyed by newly won access to higher education and public-sector jobs in particular, the black middle class doubled in size between 1960 and 1980 to 36 percent of all blacks.[22] Of course, not all black, Latino, Asian American, and Native American progress in the 1960s and 1970s was the result of welfare state programs.[23] For example, the decline in black poverty rates (from over 70 percent in 1940 to 40 percent in 1960, from nearly seven times that of whites in 1940 to three times that of whites in 1990) had something to do with African Americans leaving the rural South and entering the urban industrial labor markets.[24] But whites stubbornly resisted the desegregation of urban labor and housing markets, even during the longest economic expansion in U.S. history.[25] The civil rights movement was instrumental in redistributing employment, educational, and housing opportunities toward people of color, opportunities to participate in the middle-class social order of that era.

Perhaps even more significantly for the long run, civil rights movement activists got valuable experience learning how to win and exercise institutional power during this period. For example, civil rights activists were not content to simply administer federal War on Poverty funds, but often used

public programs as sites of community organizing. Jill Quadagno com-
pellingly chronicles this struggle for power. Citing the Community Action
Program, for example, Quadagno writes, "Community action originated as a
[federal] program to consolidate social services and improve service provision. In transferring resources directly from the federal government to the
poor, it rapidly became an agent in the struggle for political rights. . . . [T]he
civil rights movement absorbed community action programs, using them to
redistribute political power from local machines to black organizations and
black leaders."[26]

Other communities of color initiated similar efforts. Carlos Muñoz Jr.
notes that many founders of the Chicano movement had been spurred to activism by their involvement in community-based War on Poverty programs.[27] Similarly, the founders of the American Indian Movement had initially hoped to organize urban Native Americans to demand access to federal
poverty funds.[28] During the 1970s, the first wave of black civil rights activists
became mayors of large cities and members of Congress and state legislatures.
This process of political empowerment also occurred in the Latino and Asian
American communities, although later and slower to develop in large part
due to racialized citizenship laws and anti-immigrant policies. A different
process of empowerment, the struggle for treaty recognition, was initiated by
Native Americans.[29]

The power of communities of color was not only expressed through the
political process. Cultural self-determination became an increasingly promi-
nent theme in the period after the Watts rebellion in 1965. The influence of
African American intellectuals, ranging from Dick Gregory, to James Bald-
win, to Imamu Amiri Baraka, to the Last Poets, sparked a Black Consciousness movement that changed American culture. The American Indian
Movement, the Asian consciousness movement, and the Chicano liberation
movement all took cultural forms, crystallized by the Third World Strike at
San Francisco State University in 1968. By the mid-1970s, black studies,
Chicano studies, and a few Native American and Asian American studies
programs were founded at leading universities. Many of the faculty who
founded these departments were themselves community activists.[30]

In sum, the civil rights movement, from its inception until the mid-1960s,
was in many ways responding to the new opportunities for racial justice in
the middle-class social order. Sustained economic growth and national elites'
concomitant effort to develop a mass middle-class social order and a welfare
state to bolster it provided the civil rights movement with the opportunities
to succeed. But the civil rights movement was far more than an effort to "get
in" to the middle class: Its vision and energy was rooted in people of color's

aspirations for freedom and justice, a vision that was global, a vision that always challenged and quickly outstripped the support of national elites and most middle-class whites.

The dynamics of globalization began to reshape the possibilities for the restructuring of American society almost as soon as the demand for restructuring had been made. The new economic and political conditions of globalization—ever-widening inequality, elimination of entitlement programs, and growing immigration—posed fundamental challenges to the civil rights movement. Without a summation of what they had accomplished, and without clarity about the new conditions in which they operated, civil rights activists often became disoriented and dispirited. But as we will see, the civil rights actions of the 1980s and 1990s lay important groundwork by developing new capacities that may someday be of historic significance.

The Civil Rights Movement
in the Era of Globalization

As globalization ended the expansion of full-time jobs with benefits and the welfare state began to contract in the mid-1970s, the civil rights movement entered a new phase of its efforts to achieve a democratic, nonracial society. In this new period, many of the assumptions of the previous era were no longer valid. National elites no longer had the capacity to expand the welfare state to control social and political conflicts. Many whites became more defensive of their racial privileges as their access to good jobs and benefits were threatened. The new political and economic conditions of globalization challenged civil rights activists to find a new way to advance demands for racial justice, one that no longer relied as much on national elites or white liberals to open the doors to the middle class.

The urban fiscal crises of the mid-1970s were both an early manifestation of globalization and a signal of the civil rights movement's future troubles. The extensive closure of urban core businesses, especially in manufacturing, left many people of color (who had been blocked from moving to the suburbs) without access to full-time jobs that could serve as entry-level positions in expanding economic sectors, which were now located in white suburbs. This economic "restructuring" deprived inner-city African Americans, Latinos, Asian Americans, and Native Americans of access to the single most important factor that had lifted generations of European immigrants and their children out of poverty: entry-level jobs in expanding economic sectors.[31] The erosion of urban tax bases as businesses and high-income, mostly white, workers fled the cities also left city governments unable to meet the increasing demands of urban residents.[32] Cuts in public spending on education, subsidized low-income housing, health care, and food subsidies further crippled poor urban communities in the 1980s.

The civil rights movement's challenge in the face of these trends was to find new ways to compel government to take action, for only the commitment of the nation-state to equal opportunity and justice could stem the growing tide of jobs and capital leaving the central cities—and their ghettoized residents—behind. But the new conditions meant that national political elites were no longer as capable of, or interested in, redistributing resources to people of color. The conditions of growing political intransigence and hostility toward people of color provided a prod for the civil rights movement to develop a new approach to power: a greater focus on developing the autonomous political mobilization of communities of color to compel national elites to take action.

During the late 1970s and 1980s, black political empowerment became increasingly important as a way to influence the uses of state power to promote racial justice. But, as growing numbers of black elected officials took office in the mid-1970s, it appeared to many grassroots activists that African Americans had gained political office in cities too late to help many poor urban residents. Manning Marable observes of the black electoral victories of the 1970s and 1980s:

> Most of the cities they managed—Newark, Hartford, Chicago, Detroit, Cleveland—suffered from an exodus of industry and a declining tax base. . . . Increasingly, black mayors were placed in a quasi-neocolonial posture: they depended upon black votes to guarantee their success at the polls, but once elected, they often implemented public policies that contradicted their constituency's material interests. They had assumed "electoral responsibility," yet they had no power to resolve the crisis created by capital.[33]

There was another unintended consequence of black political empowerment: Due to the civil rights movement's successes, as many as half of the black middle class, often blocked from private-sector jobs by discrimination, was employed in the public sector during the 1970s.[34] The reliance on public-sector employment left the black middle class vulnerable to layoffs when hundreds of thousands of government jobs were eliminated in the late 1970s and 1980s. The wave of cutbacks in public-sector jobs, continued with the 1990s' military base closures, severely and disproportionately hurt the black middle class.

Finally, as King was all too aware at the end of his life, the civil rights movement had never succeeded in forging a lasting coalition with whites. Even as the civil rights movement was expanding its vision and political capacity in the 1960s and early 1970s, white reaction against the civil rights movement's efforts had begun. But, in that era, even in the face of growing white hostility, the civil rights movement had successfully maintained an alliance with political elites to develop programs that addressed minorities' barriers to employment, education, and social services. Richard Nixon, for example, had built his Silent Majority political base for the 1968 presidential election by appealing to white reaction against the civil rights movement. But once in office, Nixon supported the development of the most aggressive affirmative action programs in U.S. history.[35] The job growth and concomitant expansion of welfare state programs during the era of the expanding middle class made it possible for political elites and many nonelite whites (however reluctantly) to accept redistributive programs because white people were not at that time being asked give up jobs, education, housing, or social services to achieve racial equity. They needed only to make room at the table as the economic and social pie expanded. Put another way, during the 1960s and 1970s, gains for people of color were acceptable because it was also a period of gains for whites.

The new conditions imposed on the United States by globalization rapidly eroded national elites' and nonelite whites' willingness to support expensive and redistributive social programs. Growing numbers of white suburbanites abandoned the Democratic Party and put Republican presidents in office from 1981 to 1992. By 1992, twelve years of Republican appointments left the federal courts dominated by judges who were hostile to the basic tenets of civil rights law of the previous era. Opponents of affirmative action and expansive interpretations of voting rights were installed in the Equal Employment Opportunity Commission and the Department of Justice Civil Rights Division. During the late 1980s and 1990s, most of the legal precedent that had opened doors to people of color in education, employment, and political power was struck down or reframed beyond recognition.[36]

But even in the hostile climate of the 1980s, the civil rights movement's political power continued to grow. Despite his enormous popularity among whites, President Ronald Reagan was singularly unsuccessful in dismantling some of the key components of the civil rights agenda, particularly affirmative action programs, school desegregation efforts, and the expanded use of the Voting Rights Act to redraw congressional and local districts.[37] Even though the Supreme Court retracted much of the legal basis for affirmative action in a series of 1989 decisions, Congress in 1991 passed a Civil Rights Act that restored much of the law the Court's decisions had undermined. During the so-called Reagan Revolution, Jesse Jackson mounted two impressive campaigns for the presidency and for a time became a central figure in the Democratic Party and American politics. The Free South Africa Movement became a significant force in American politics. In 1992, the largest number of African Americans and Latinos ever elected to Congress took their seats, including six African Americans from majority black districts in the South that had not elected a black representative since Reconstruction.[38] The Congressional Black Caucus became one of the main power centers of the period. In the 1980s and early 1990s, the civil rights movement might have been increasingly on the defensive, but it was also increasingly powerful.

By the mid-1990s, however, the continuing erosion of the welfare state and the rise of the private accumulation state, as well as growing inequality and attacks on civil rights—especially of people of color—had taken its toll on the civil rights movement's political influence. The Republican seizure of control of both houses of Congress in 1994, in particular, empowered a massive assault on civil rights, including the elimination of the welfare system, assaults on immigrants' rights, and harsh mandatory sentences for a long list of crimes (see chapter 5). In the face of defeat after defeat, civil rights activists' reliance on elected officials, judges, and administrative regulations to achieve some measure of equal opportunity and justice made less sense.

The problem was further complicated by the position in which many civil rights activists found themselves. A generation of activists had made the decision to "go in" to American institutions as lawyers, professors, health care workers, social workers, and managers. By the 1980s and 1990s, many activists had succeeded in getting themselves into positions in which they exercised some institutional power. But, as Bell warns, the relatively small numbers of such activists meant that they were often unable to challenge the fundamental ways in which resources were distributed and power exercised in their institutions.[39] In the increasingly hostile climate of globalization, many of these activists have been frustrated by their inability to transform the mission and processes of their institutions. Indeed, by the end of the 1990s, rebuffed by courts for over a decade and unable to mount effective electoral campaigns to reverse the government's direction, even the most stalwart civil rights activists were reconsidering their strategy.

The irony of the 1980s and 1990s was that civil rights activists won more elections and people of color voted in unprecedented numbers, but the civil rights movement had less capacity to compel government action against racism. As the politics of the global era emerged, civil rights activists increasingly expended what power they had simply to defend gains of the past, rather than to address the growing racial problems of the present. The civil rights movement had reached a crossroads. How were people opposed to racial privileging supposed to achieve equality and justice at a time when selective universities were slashing minority admissions, when cuts in government programs were adversely affecting minority communities and the black middle class in particular, when courts were reversing thirty years' worth of civil rights rulings, and when the criminal justice system was being unleashed on communities of color?

The civil rights movement's vision of a just society remains today, in the most general terms, similar to that of 1966. The eradication of racism will take a "radical restructuring of society" in which the state plays a key role in redistributing resources and curtailing market forces' destructive capacity. The eradication of white privilege and the creation of a society without racism will require, as the movement articulated it in 1966, the end of militarism and poverty. In the global era, this vision—one of world peace and socially responsible governmental regulation of capital to mitigate inequality— remains compelling. The problem is not the civil rights movement's vision of social justice; it is its lack of sufficient power to compel the "radical restructuring" that its vision mandates. In the conditions created by globalization— the racialization of growing inequality and the emergence of the private accumulation state—how are people going to be able to effectively mobilize around demands for racial equity and justice?

The Relationship between Community Power and State Power in the Era of Globalization

The preceding analysis suggests that the civil rights movement has to eschew dependence on state power at a time when government is decreasingly likely to take action to create a just society. The need for state action, however, has never been greater: Only a revitalized nation-state can curtail the growing inequality and greater divisiveness between whites and people of color, U.S. citizens and immigrants caused by market globalization. These trends are tearing at the fabric of the dominant, middle-class social order. The need for state intervention into the growing social crisis of globalization in the United States is becoming increasingly urgent: to develop a new basis for social stability in the face of the disequalizing effects of market globalization. Efforts to regulate global capital and to redistribute assets will necessitate expanding the role of transnational state power and, to some extent, subordinating all nation-states under global institutions. In many ways, these are the ideas about the "radical restructuring of the architecture of American society" en-visioned by King over thirty-five years ago.

The challenge for civil rights activists in the era of globalization is to en-hance their capacity to insist on this "radical restructuring," even as the shift from the welfare state to the private accumulation state is today undermin-ing that capacity. The potential opportunities for such a radical restructuring of the state rests in a combination of three factors: the growing instability of the middle-class social order, the growing size and potential political influ-ence of ethnic communities, and the growing momentum toward the devel-opment of transnational accords. As we saw in chapter 6, there are today po-tential opportunities for the development of new movements aimed at compelling state action for socially responsible globalization, movements based on working-class interests, human rights, and civil rights. In that chap-ter, it was argued that all movements in the global era will have to centrally focus on the demands and capacities of ethnic communities if they are to make headway in challenging market globalization. In this chapter, I exam-ine the ways that civil rights activists can today take advantage of the po-tentials for change in this period.

The greatest achievement of the civil rights movement over the past twenty years is its activists' institutional positioning. As discussed earlier, civil rights activists have succeeded in embedding themselves in institutional positions where they exercise some influence on state power, either as policy makers or elected officials, and direct the resources of private institutions to-ward communities of color. Today, many thousands of individuals who iden-tify with the civil rights movement work in institutions where they have a degree of institutional decision-making power. From elected officials to pro-fessors to lawyers, the status and power of people committed to racial justice is impressive.[40] As well, thousands of nonprofit organizations continue to op-erate within and advocate for ethnic communities, providing effective fo-rums for people's needs. The problem, however, is that these civil rights ac-tivists rarely have much independent power within their institutions or access to significant community-based, grassroots power and that the community-based programs rarely have much influence over government programs. As a result, the power of the civil rights activists is primarily shaped and con-strained by the institutions in which they are located. Most civil rights move-ment activists, having devoted the last twenty or thirty years to getting into positions of institutional authority, have lost the capacity to mobilize power autonomous from state power, that is, power rooted in communities of color, or movements of workers, women, or sexual minorities. The inability of many civil rights activists to mobilize such autonomous power is becoming a more significant liability as the capacity of the state to address the needs of people of color continues to decline—indeed, as the state becomes increasingly repressive in its relationship to ethnic communities.

The major exception to this observation is in the field of electoral politics. By definition, electoral politics involves the direct organizing of people within their communities. As such, electoral politics is both directed at institutional power and is a form of grassroots organizing, especially in ethnic communities, where social networks distinct from governmental institutions are found.[41] Politicians representing ethnic communities thus have a dual role: on the one hand, to effect governmental policies and programs to help their community, and on the other hand, to empower their community to exercise autonomous power. The contradiction between these two tasks is of great importance to the civil rights movement. Governmental programs often have the effect—and the intent—of preventing the autonomous exercise of power by marginalized people by limiting the political options for elected and unelected officials. The question, then, is: Under what conditions can civil rights activists influence state power while continuing to increase the autonomous political capacity of communities of color?

As we saw earlier, the civil rights movement's success in the 1960s was due to its ability to link grassroots movement power to state power in a highly creative and effective way in the context of the development of the middle-class social order. In the global era, reestablishing the relationship between state power and community power will take a reorientation of civil rights advocates who are now in positions of institutional power. Essentially, the conditions created by globalization now require advocates for communities of color to place primary emphasis on grassroots organizing rather than on the exercise of state power. It may appear to civil rights advocates that this reorientation is asking that they give up what power they have to fight the crucial defensive battles of this era. To the contrary, this proposal recognizes the potential for changing the role of the state in society in this era, a potential due to the growing social significance of ethnic communities and the loss of social stability in the global era.

As communities of color are increasingly cut out of the social order by racist and nationalist responses to market globalization, ethnic solidarity will be more important as a necessity of survival in the face of growing underemployment, cuts in state services, and increasing state violence and repression. The dynamics of globalization will also continue to increase the size of ethnic communities by encouraging the immigration of people from less developed countries into the United States. Despite efforts to restrict citizenship, the political capacity of ethnic communities will continue to grow, and probably grow rapidly, in the decades to come, as immigrants' children exercise their right to vote and to dissent from repressive policies. Meanwhile, more of the population that currently identifies as middle class, both whites and people of color, will find it difficult to sustain the basic elements of the American dream: home ownership, an income sufficient for discretionary spending, and access to a college education. State power will be used for increasingly repressive projects, undermining fundamental democratic principals in the process. And international problems will escalate, especially as American power and neoliberal dogma undermine the development of transnational means to regulate market globalization. This combination of growing ethnic power, declining middle-class stability, and escalating social problems opens up important new opportunities for social change.

It was suggested in chapter 6 that these conditions are potentially supportive of the revitalization of working-class and transnational movements. But the likeliest focus for ethnic politics in the immediate period will continue to be on civil rights, for this is where the links of ethnic community grassroots power and advocates for racial justice in institutional positions are best organized and where the assaults on people of color are most visible. As ethnic power is organized to advocate directly for the needs of people of color through electoral politics and protests of government actions, the potential for the revitalization of working-class movements, as well as efforts to support international peace and stability, will increase.

What can civil rights advocates accomplish, given their institutional positioning and, typically, their distance from community power today? The simple answer: Civil rights advocates need to return to community organizing, but in a new form, as activists in institutional positions. To do this will require a radical new vision of working inside social institutions.[42] Rather than just "doing the job," activists will have to reinvent their positions and their relationships to the institutions in which they are located. To do this will require civil rights advocates to undergo a fundamental reorientation, away from using institutional positions to provide services for constituents or clients toward learning how to use institutional positions for the purpose of community organizing and empowerment. The institutionalization of social movements can be regarded as both a success and a problem.[43] Institutionalization brings with it stability and access to power, prestige, visibility, and economic resources. But institutionalization also compels activists to "play by the rules" and to be "realistic" about the possibility for change. The institutionalization of social movement organizations and leaders, then, can potentially co-opt social movements and greatly restrict the activists' range of options.

But this need not be the case. Instead, it is possible for leaders of social movement organizations, or activists in institutional positions, to use their resources for the purpose of community empowerment. As Kim Voss and Rachel Sherman show for the labor movement, such a reorientation is difficult to accomplish, as it requires a major shift in resource allocation and a change in the organizational culture and structure itself.[44] It also requires a change in the concept of leadership, away from that of a dispenser of resources and gate-keeper of power toward a model of leadership based on assisting people to identify their grievances, to get organized, and to enable them to act on those grievances. For example, instead of just being school teachers, activist teachers can make their school a site of community organizing, focusing on bringing together parents, students, and community leaders to make demands on the school system as a core component of their jobs. Instead of being just public health doctors providing health care for patients, medical personnel can learn how to turn their hospital or health agency into a community center, where they organize and empower community members to demand better health care. Instead of being just elected officials trying to make deals that deliver services and resources to the community, elected officials can learn to focus on community organizing as central to all of their work, and not just during elections. Instead of providing legal services to clients, civil rights attorneys can learn to organize community meetings around specific issues and empower people to address the problem themselves.[45]

In making this transformation, civil rights advocates will be able to draw on their existing institutional capacities, which many have retained despite increasingly hostile conditions. But even more importantly, advocates in institutional positions might learn to draw on the political capacity of communities of color. To do so, they must be willing to sacrifice short-term gains (or even efforts to minimize losses) in the interests of long-term community empowerment. Rather than taking the position of professionals providing services to subordinate clients, advocates must learn how to become community activists and empower communities to make direct demands on public and private institutions. Professional activists are going to have to set aside the institutional imperatives—winning a lawsuit, seeking to provide much needed services to people with bottomless needs, and so on—in favor of efforts to organize people and to empower them to set the agenda and to create the grassroots leaders and organizations to carry them out. This orientation goes against the grain of institutions' own logic and may lead them to issue formal or informal sanctions against those who advocate it. Advocates are going to have to learn how to be simultaneously "insiders" and "outsiders," using the institutional resources to which they have access not to further the institution's mission (or their own careers), but to organize and empower marginalized communities. At times, this may even require advocates to not use skills they have developed for institutional purposes, and may compel them to remember "nonprofessional" skills, such as how to organize a community meeting or how to do media work. Despite the risks inherent in this reorientation, the power that can be mobilized "from below" may become much more politically significant in the coming years, thereby increasing the capacity of advocates in institutional positions to make demands on their institutions or the state as a whole, and thus to participate in an effective way in the efforts to make globalization socially responsible.

The civil rights movement is a favorable setting for this reorientation to take place. Those activists in institutional positions are clearly frustrated by their growing inability to win substantive reforms for people of color, a frustration that can be an impetus to try out new ideas. People of color need no convincing that civil rights are important, be it to curtail police violence, to defend affirmative action in education or employment contexts, or to advance the rights of immigrants and refugees. And, the large majority of civil rights activists still have strong ties to ethnic communities. Unleashing the capacity of ethnic communities requires making the connection between the institutional activists and communities of color.

As we saw in chapter 6, ethnic community politics will not be limited to one arena, such as civil rights. Ethnic community politics is all-sided, reflecting the complex class, gender, sexual orientation, and racial and international issues that are the impetus for the development of ethnicity in the first place. The revitalization of the civil rights movement, then, has immediate implications for the revival of all movements for socially responsible globalization.

Case Study: The Campaign to Stop Proposition 209 in California, 1994–1996

The strengths and weaknesses of the civil rights movement were in full view during the campaign to stop the passage of Proposition 209, the 1996 California ballot initiative to end public-sector affirmative action programs. As discussed in chapter 5, Proposition 209 did not use direct racist claims to attack affirmative action; instead, it used language suggesting that affirmative action was inconsistent with the fundamental idea of merit, that is, the idea that everyone should be treated equally. Proposition 209 supporters charged that the civil rights movement had abandoned its principles after the passage of the 1964 Civil Rights Act by supporting "preferential treatment" for people of color and that they, the supporters of Proposition 209, were the "true" civil rights activists.[46] For this reason, they named their ballot initiative the California Civil Rights Initiative.

The task facing supporters of affirmative action was daunting because they had to convince the majority of the California electorate that (a) racism is still a major fact of life in California and (b) affirmative action programs are essential to create equal opportunity. Initial polls in 1994 suggested that Proposition 209 had over 70 percent support among likely voters and that its passage was all but inevitable. When California governor Pete Wilson decided to back the initiative, Proposition 209's passage seemed ensured. Despite these odds, a group of civil rights activists—comprised mostly of attorneys working for nonprofit public interest law firms, but also including some union organizers, women's advocates, and a few grassroots community organizers—decided to oppose the proposition. The group that initiated the campaign to prevent the passage of Proposition 209 began with an impressive track record of victories in the courts and successful lobbying of the California legislature. By working together consistently for decades and developing institutional positioning (mostly in nonprofit organizations and unions), the leaders of the anti-209 coalition began with access to some funding and some political clout.

Mounting an effective electoral campaign in the most populous state (35 million people) was going to require expertise in polling and message development. And, to pull off a campaign that had to use television and radio ads to reach all the voters in a large, spread-out state, millions of dollars would have to be raised. None of the core activists had the experience to pull off such a task. To make matters worse, many Democratic Party leaders, especially President Bill Clinton, considered the effort to oppose Proposition 209 too risky and warned potential donors, elected officials, and candidates to avoid making affirmative action into a "wedge issue" that would drive white voters away from Democratic candidates for office.[47]

Despite the long odds, the campaign against Proposition 209 picked up momentum and supporters. Efforts to build a stable coalition between feminist organizations, civil rights organizations, and labor unions did not succeed. Neither did efforts to develop a sustained grassroots campaign—although one organization, Californians for Justice, did outstanding grassroots organizing through voter registration and "get out the vote" drives in the Bay Area counties and Los Angeles. But the two coalitions that emerged to oppose Proposition 209 did have sufficient historic standing to have access to resources (mostly through labor unions and feminist organizations) and were able to mount effective media campaigns, both through "free" media (articles, editorials, and op-ed pieces) and paid advertising. As a result, by the last stage of the election in October 1996, polls showed that Proposition 209's passage was by no means guaranteed.

Despite the good fight, Proposition 209 passed with 54 percent of the vote. The campaign against Proposition 209 ran into two significant problems rooted in the history of the civil rights movement. The first stemmed from activists' lack of expertise in running a statewide electoral campaign. The activists in the No on 209 Campaign decided that the complexity of the campaign required leadership by a professional campaign director and pollsters. Professional political consultants were hired to take responsibility for polling, message development, and paid advertising. These professionals were long-term Democratic Party workers, who earned their living and made their reputations by running electoral campaigns, mostly for candidates running for national offices. As the decisive last stage of the campaign neared, however, the professional campaign staff repeatedly delayed developing a campaign message. Without a unifying message, campaign materials remained unfocused and uninformed by polling results. Finally, the campaign's television ad was developed with little input from the campaign steering committee, and, when it was aired, activists saw to their horror that the wrong message was used.[48] The lack of a clear message certainly contributed to Proposition 209's passage.

Why were highly skilled pollsters, media advisers, and political consultants unable to develop a message or an effective television ad? The problem was not a lack of skill, but a lack of commitment to defeat Proposition 209. Political consultants' long-term career interests require that they appease powerful interests in their political party. The No on 209 Campaign was run largely outside the Democratic Party and was perceived as a threat by powerful Democrats, including the president, who adamantly refused to utter the words "vote no on 209" at any time during the campaign. The professional consultants therefore had a conflict of interest with the civil rights activists, a conflict resulting in the failures that sabotaged the campaign.

The other problem in the No on 209 Campaign was its decision not to prioritize a grassroots campaign. The choice facing the campaign leadership was between taking all steps to try to win the campaign or to focus on long-term base-building efforts. In a state the size and complexity of California, media-driven campaigns are essential to reach all potential voters. Media campaigns for ballot initiatives cost between $2 and $8 million, although the record for a California ballot proposition is over $20 million. The campaign leadership decided that its priority was to defeat Proposition 209, which meant that priority had to be given to raising the money to run a media campaign. Grass-roots organizing was left up to constituent organizations. The failure to develop a statewide grassroots organization meant that, once the campaign was over, people who had been active in the effort to defend affirmative action had virtually no way to continue to work together and nowhere to sum up the experiences of the 209 campaign.

The combination of these two problems suggests that civil rights movement activists may have to take a longer-term view of each campaign they wage in the present conditions of globalization. The problem for the No on 209 Campaign was that it relied too heavily on political elites with a vested interest in state power and did too little to organize and mobilize community-based power. While trying to defeat Proposition 209 made sense in the short run, this decision made long-term base building virtually impossible. A grassroots base building strategy would concentrate on organizing communities of color and progressive whites so that the next time (and there will surely be a next time) an effort to roll back civil rights appears, activists will be organized, educated, skilled, and ready to take on the challenges of stopping it more effectively. The problem for the activists in the No on 209 Campaign was they that lacked the power and the experience necessary to accomplish both defeating Proposition 209 and base building simultaneously.

It may well be, however, that future campaigns to defend civil rights will be capable of managing both electoral tasks because of the lessons learned in the 209 campaign. The effort to defeat the ban on racial classifications in California, for example, is being led by the same activists who worked to stop Proposition 209. They bring to this effort the skills and lessons gleaned from the No on 209 Campaign. Also, the growing number of Latino and Asian voters, as well as the redistricting of California after the 2000 census, is altering the political landscape, increasing the likelihood of a successful effort to block a racist ballot initiative. Finally, the racial polarization that resulted from strong Republican support for every anti-immigrant and anticivil rights ballot initiative of the last two decades has begun to worry top Republicans, including President George W. Bush, who is warning California Republicans to stay away from the racial classification initiative. In short, all of the elements of globalization are at work in California, both increasing the propensity toward anti-immigrant and racist measures and the capacity of people who would oppose them.

Conclusion: Finding Hope in a Time of Fear

The beginning of a new era in world history is always a time of fear and of hope. New ideas and new social relationships are being glimpsed, but they are superimposed on top of old ideas and old social patterns, producing an effect Saskia Sassen aptly refers to as "decentering." Globalization is developing through the extension of markets and capital investments, and is creating extraordinary contradictions everywhere. As we have seen, globalization is simultaneously undermining the significance of space and territory and enhancing the importance of localism as a way of fending off social crisis. Globalization is simultaneously creating the possibilities for a greater sphere of cooperation between peoples and encouraging efforts to wall people off from its benefits. Globalization is simultaneously undermining people's traditions and enhancing ethnic solidarity. In the most general sense, globalization offers up a dazzling vision of all humanity living together in a global village, while simultaneously ripping apart social orders and spreading social crisis everywhere. In many ways, people today are torn between worlds, uncertain of the past, the future, and even the present.

It is not surprising, then, that racism and nationalism are on the rise today. When people are afraid, they fall back on known ways to buffer themselves, to fend off what they perceive as a threat. This fear is supported by the material benefits that can accrue from the defense of their racial or national privileges. The challenge in this era is to give people hope in the face of the uncertainties and dangers of the present, to demonstrate to them that the crisis of globalization can best be addressed by going outward into the world, not inward into the old forms of privilege and oppression.

Coming to grips with the challenges and possibilities for racial and social justice in the era of globalization is a daunting business, indeed. Just at the time when civil rights activists have gotten themselves entrenched in legislatures, courts, classrooms, and professional and managerial positions in private enterprise, the dynamics of racism and the potential spaces for antiracist politics are changing again. The evidence that change is upon us is mostly bad news: increasing assaults on racial and national minorities, the wholesale abandonment of democratic principles, growing insecurity, and rapidly escalating inequality. The only way for people committed to racial and social justice to not become paralyzed in the face of these negative changes is to see the potential for social justice that lies nascent in globalization at this moment.

We can be certain of some enduring truths: People everywhere will continue to yearn for freedom and justice, and, consequently, systems of oppression will not stand without challenge for very long. I have argued that the potential challenges to the crisis of globalization comes from two sources: first, the continuous if episodic upsurges in popular resistance in the face of growing crises in the global era and second, economic and political elites' need for, and interest in, social stability. But most of all, hope comes from a longer-term view of the present situation. Globalization itself will continue to steadily undermine the racist and "localizing" practices discussed in this book. No matter what the U.S. government does, the capacity of any nation-state to deal with the crisis on its own is declining. No matter how white suburbanites try to wall off the effects of globalization, local communities are being rapidly absorbed into global cities. No draconian restrictions on immigration will stop the process of the erosion of national boundaries, especially between the United States and Mexico.

All of these efforts to forestall the impact of globalization are at best short-term fixes. Increasingly, the world is inexorably being bound together. The only question is on whose terms.

Notes

1. Unfortunately for them, King was an explicit and forthright advocate of affirmative action policies, and so the Proposition 209 campaign had to back away from wrapping itself in the mantle of his authority.

2. Stephan Thernstrom and Abigail Thernstrom, *America in Black and White* (New York: Simon and Schuster, 1997) 149–180.

3. Derrick Bell, *And We Are Not Saved* (New York: Basic, 1987).

4. Max Weber, *Economy and Society*, vol. 1 (Berkeley: University of California Press, 1978), 311–319.

5. The centrality of the black insurgency has been well analyzed by Doug McAdam, *Political Process and the Development of Black Insurgency, 1930–1970* (Chicago: University of Chicago Press, 1982); Aldon D. Morris, *The Origins of the Civil Rights Movement: Black Communities Organizing for Change* (New York: The Free Press, 1984).

6. Andrew L. Barlow, "The Student Movements of the 1960s and the Politics of Race," *The Journal of Ethnic Studies* 19 (Fall 1991): 3–22.

7. Jill Quadagno, *The Color of Welfare: How Racism Undermined the War on Poverty* (New York: Oxford University Press, 1994); Robert A. Caro, *The Years of Lyndon Johnson: Master of the Senate* (New York: Knopf, 2002), especially 938–1007.

8. This was the logic of the landmark school desegregation decision *Brown v. Board of Education of Topeka*. See Richard Kluger, *Simple Justice: The History of Brown v. Board of Education and Black America's Struggle for Equality* (New York: Knopf, 1976).

9. Martin Luther King Jr., *Where Do We Go from Here: Chaos or Community?* (Boston: Beacon, 1968), 130.

10. Caro, *Years of Lyndon Johnson*.

11. This process is explored in McAdam, *Political Process*, and in Jack M. Bloom, *Race, Class and the Civil Rights Movement* (Bloomington: Indiana University Press, 1987).

12. Clarence Lusane, *African Americans at the Crossroads: The Restructuring of the Black Leadership and the 1992 Elections* (Boston: South End, 1994); Dan Georgakas and Marvin Surkin, *Detroit: I Do Mind Dying* (Boston: South End, 1998).

13. T. H. Marshall, "Citizenship and Social Class," in *States and Societies*, ed. David Held et al. (Oxford: Martin Robertson, 1983).

14. King, *Where Do We Go from Here?* 90.

15. King, *Where Do We Go from Here?* 133.

16. King, *Where Do We Go from Here?* 137.

17. James H. Cone, *Malcolm and Martin and America* (Maryknoll, N.Y.: Orbis, 1991), 229.

18. Martin Luther King Jr., address at the 1968 annual convention of the Rabbinical Assembly, cited in Cone, *Malcolm and Martin and America*, 234.

19. Quadagno, *Color of Welfare*.

20. Herbert Hill, "Black Workers, Organized Labor, and Title VII of the 1964 Civil Rights Act," in *Race in America*, ed. Herbert Hill and James E. Jones (Madison: University of Wisconsin Press, 1993).

21. Gary Orfield, "School Desegregation after Two Generations," in *Race in America*, ed. Herbert Hill and James E. Jones (Madison: University of Wisconsin Press, 1993), 234–262.

22. Orlando Patterson, *The Ordeal of Integration: Progress and Resentment in America's "Racial" Crisis* (Washington, D.C.: Civitas/Counterpoint, 1998), 24–25.

23. This point is well made by Thernstrom and Thernstrom, *America in Black and White*.

24. Reginald Farley and Walter R. Allen, *The Color Line and the Quality of Life in America* (New York: Oxford University Press, 1989), 280.

25. Stephen Steinberg, "Occupational Apartheid and the Origins of Affirmative Action," in *Race and Ethnicity in the United States: Issues and Debates*, ed. Stephen Steinberg (Malden, Mass.: Blackwell, 2000), 64–73.

26. Quadagno, *Color of Welfare*, 11.

27. Carlos Muñoz Jr., *Youth, Identity, Power* (London: Verso, 1989), 56.

28. Vine Deloria Jr. and Clifford M. Lytle, *American Indians, American Justice* (Austin: University of Texas Press, 1983).

29. Alvin M. Josephy Jr., Joanne Nagel, and Troy Johnson, *Red Power: The American Indians' Fight for Freedom*, 2nd ed. (Lincoln: University of Nebraska Press, 1999).

30. This is well explored by Muñoz, *Youth, Identity, Power*, 127–170.

31. William Julius Wilson, *The Declining Significance of Race: Blacks and Changing American Institutions* (Chicago: University of Chicago Press, 1978); Joel Perlmann and Roger Waldinger, "Are the Children of Today's Immigrants Making It?" *The Public Interest* 132 (Summer 1998): 73–96.

32. Roger E. Alcaly and David Mermelstein, *The Fiscal Crisis of American Cities: Essays on the Political Economy of Urban America with Special Reference to New York* (New York: Vintage, 1977); see also James O'Connor, *The Fiscal Crisis of the State*, 2nd ed. (New Brunswick, N.J.: Transaction, 2002).

33. Manning Marable, *Race, Reform and Rebellion*, 2nd ed. (Jackson: University Press of Mississippi, 1991), 123.

34. Steinberg, "Occupational Apartheid."

35. Some analysts have attributed Nixon's support for affirmative action to his desire to split white labor from communities of color and thus to weaken Democratic Party unity. While this was certainly part of the equation, the more significant point is that at that time, support for affirmative action was politically necessary. See John David Skrentny, *The Ironies of Affirmative Action: Politics, Culture, and Justice in America* (Chicago: University of Chicago Press, 1996).

36. Bell, *And We Are Not Saved*; Quadagno, *Color of Welfare*.

37. Lani Guinier, *The Tyranny of the Majority: Fundamental Fairness in Representative Democracy* (New York: The Free Press, 1994).

38. Manning Marable, *Black American Politics* (London: Verso, 1985); Lusane, *African Americans at the Crossroads*, 130–132.

39. Bell, *And We Are Not Saved*, 142–143.

40. While no definitive census of civil rights activists has been taken, James Max Fendrich's longitudinal study of activists in Florida finds a remarkable stability in their worldview, with a direct effect on their career decisions. See James Max Fendrich, *Ideal Citizens: The Legacy of the Civil Rights Movement* (Albany: SUNY Press, 1993).

41. The distinction between the 1964 Civil Rights Act and the 1965 Voting Rights Act is that the former put the power to remedy discrimination in the hands of judges, while the latter directly empowered people of color. Malcolm X actively campaigned for the passage of the Voting Rights Act, the only piece of civil rights legislation he supported. See Malcolm X, "The Ballot or the Bullet," in *Malcolm X Speaks: Selected Speeches and Statements*, ed. George Breitman (New York: Merit, 1965), 23–44. Mary S. Pardo, *Mexican American Women Activists: Identity and Resistance in Two Los Angeles Communities* (Philadelphia: Temple University Press, 1998), provides a useful comparison of electoral politics in an inner-city barrio and a mixed-race suburb.

42. Many of these ideas appeared at the moment that the first wave of civil rights activists became institutional actors, especially in law. See Robert Lefcourt, *Law against the People: Essays to Demystify Law, Order, and the Courts* (New York: Random House, 1971).

43. The critique of institutionalization has been most forcefully made by Francis Fox Piven and Richard A. Cloward, *Poor Peoples Movements* (New York: Pantheon, 1977).

44. Kim Voss and Rachel Sherman, "Breaking the Iron Law of Oligarchy: Union Revitalization in the American Labor Movement," *American Journal of Sociology* 106, no. 2 (September 2000).

45. Some activists are today developing this orientation. This is the conception of legal work practiced at La Raza Centro Legal in San Francisco and Centro Legal de la Raza in Oakland, California.

46. Thernstrom and Thernstrom, *America in Black and White*.

47. Nicholas Lemann, *The Big Test: The Secret History of the American Meritocracy* (New York: Farrar, Strauss and Giroux, 1999), 324.

48. The television ad, costing over $1.8 million, implied that anyone who voted for 209 was the equivalent of David Duke, the former Ku Klux Klan head. The ad is widely believed to have polarized undecided voters away from opposition to 209 at the end of the campaign.

~

Selected Bibliography

Abraham, Henry J. *Freedom and the Court: Civil Rights and Liberties in the United States*. 3rd ed. New York: Oxford University Press, 1977.

Alba, Richard D. *Ethnic Identity: The Transformation of White America*. New Haven, Conn.: Yale University Press, 1990.

Albrow, Martin. *The Global Age*. Stanford, Calif.: Stanford University Press, 1997.

Alcaly, Roger E., and David Mermelstein. *The Fiscal Crisis of American Cities: Essays on the Political Economy of Urban America with Special Reference to New York*. New York: Vintage, 1977.

Allen, Robert L. *The Reluctant Reformers*. Washington, D.C.: Howard University Press, 1974.

Almaguer, Tomás. *Racial Fault Lines*. Berkeley: University of California Press, 1994.

Amin, Samir. *Capitalism in the Age of Globalization*. London: Zed, 1997.

Andreas, Peter. *Border Games: Policing the U.S.-Mexican Divide*. Ithaca, N.Y.: Cornell University Press, 2000.

Andreas, Peter, and Timothy Snyder, eds. *The Wall around the West: State Borders and Immigration Controls in North America and Europe*. Lanham, Md.: Rowman and Littlefield, 2000.

Anelauskas, Valdas. *Discovering America As It Is*. Atlanta, Ga.: Clarity, 1999.

Balibar, Étienne, and Immanuel Wallerstein. *Race, Nation, Class: Ambiguous Identities*. London: Verso, 1991.

Barlow, Andrew L. "The Student Movements of the 1960s and the Politics of Race." *The Journal of Ethnic Studies* 19 (Fall 1991): 3–22.

Bell, Derrick. *And We Are Not Saved*. New York: Basic, 1987.

———. *Faces At the Bottom of the Well*. New York: Basic, 1992.

Benjamin, Lois. *The Black Elite*. Chicago: Nelson-Hall, 1991.

Berg, Ivar E.. *Education and Jobs: The Great Training Robbery*. New York: Praeger, 1970.

Bloom, Jack M. *Race, Class and the Civil Rights Movement*. Bloomington: Indiana University Press, 1987.

Bluestone, Barry, and Bennett Harrison. *The De-industrialization of America*. New York: Basic, 1982.

Bobo, Lawrence. "Group Conflict, Prejudice, and the Paradox of Contemporary Racial Attitudes." In *Eliminating Racism: Profiles in Controversy*, ed. Phyllis A. Katz and Dalmas A. Taylor. New York: Plenum, 1988.

Bonacich, Edna. "Inequality in America: The Failure of the American System for People of Color." *Sociological Spectrum* 9 (1989): 77–99.

Bonilla-Silva, Eduardo. "Rethinking Racism." *American Sociological Review* 62 (1997): 465–479.

———. "'This Is a White Country': The Racial Ideology of the Western Nations of the World-System." *Sociological Inquiry* 70, no. 2 (Spring 2000): 188–214.

———. *White Supremacy and Racism in the Post–Civil Rights Era*. Boulder, Colo.: L. Rienner, 2001.

Bourdieu, Pierre. "Cultural Reproduction and Social Reproduction." In *Power and Ideology in Education*, ed. Jerome Karabel and A. H. Halsey. New York: Oxford University Press, 1977.

Bowen, William G. and Derek Bok. *The Shape of the River: Long-Term Consequences of Considering Race in College and University Admissions*. Princeton, N.J.: Princeton University Press, 1998.

Bradshaw, York W., and Michael Wallace. *Global Inequalities*. Thousand Oaks, Calif.: Pine Forge, 1996.

Braverman, Harry. *Labor and Monopoly Capital*. New York: Monthly Review, 1975.

Brecher, Jeremy, Tim Costello, and Brendan Smith. *Globalization from Below: The Power of Solidarity*. Cambridge, Mass.: South End, 2000.

Breines, Wini. *Young, White and Miserable: Growing up Female in the Fifties*. Boston: Beacon, 1992.

Brodkin, Karen. *How Jews Became White Folks and What That Says about Race in America*. New Brunswick, N.J.: Rutgers University Press, 1998.

Carmichael, Stokely, and Charles V. Hamilton. *Black Power: The Politics of Liberation in America*. New York: Random House, 1967.

Caro, Robert A. *Lyndon Johnson: Master of the Senate*. New York: Knopf , 2002.

———. *The Power Broker: Robert Moses and the Fall of New York*. New York: Vintage, 1975.

Castells, Manuel. "Information, Technology and Global Capitalism." In *Global Capitalism*, ed. Will Hutton and Anthony Giddens. New York: The New Press, 2000.

———. *The Rise of the Network Society*. Malden, Mass.: Blackwell, 1996.

Castillo, Ana. *The Massacre of the Dreamers*. New York: Penguin, 1994.

Chase-Dunn, Christopher. *Global Formation: Structures of the World-Economy*. Cambridge, Mass.: Blackwell, 1989.

Chávez, Lydia. *The Color Bind: California's Battle to End Affirmative Action*. Berkeley: University of California Press, 1998.

Clawson, Dan, and Mary Ann Clawson. "What Has Happened to the US Labor Movement?: Union Decline and Renewal." *Annual Review of Sociology* 25 (1999): 95–119.

Coetzee, J. M. *Disgrace*. New York: Viking, 1999.

Collins, Randall. *The Credential Society*. New York: Academic, 1979.

Cone, James H. *Malcolm and Martin and America*. Maryknoll, N.Y.: Orbis, 1991.

———. *Speaking the Truth: Ecumenism, Liberation and Black Theology*. Grand Rapids, Mich.: Eerdmans, 1986.

Conley, Dalton. *Being Black, Living in the Red: Race, Wealth, and Social Policy in America*. Berkeley: University of California Press, 1999.

Danziger, Sheldon, and Peter Gottschalk. *America Unequal*. Cambridge, Mass.: Harvard University Press, 1995.

Davis, Angela. *Women, Race and Class*. New York: Random House, 1981.

Davis, Mike. *City of Quartz*. New York: Verso, 1990.

———. *Magical Urbanism*. London: Verso, 2000.

———. *Prisoners of the American Dream*. London: Verso, 1986.

DeLaet, Debra L. *U.S. Immigration Policy in an Age of Rights*. Westport, Conn.: Praeger, 2000.

Deloria, Vine, Jr., and Clifford M. Lytle. *American Indians, American Justice*. Austin: University of Texas Press, 1983.

Denton, Nancy A., and Douglas S. Massey. *American Apartheid: Segregation and the Making of the Underclass*. Cambridge, Mass.: Harvard University Press, 1993.

Devine, Carol, et al. *Human Rights: The Essential Reference*. Phoenix, Ariz.: Oryx, 1999.

Diamond, Jared. *Guns, Germs, and Steel*. New York: Norton, 1999.

Donziger, Steven R., ed. *The Real War on Crime: The Report of the National Criminal Justice Commission*. New York: HarperPerennial, 1996.

Drake, W. Avon, and R. D. Holsworth. *Affirmative Action and the Stalled Quest for Black Progress*. Urbana: University of Illinois Press, 1996.

Du Bois, W. E. B. *Black Reconstruction in America*. New York: Atheneum, 1975.

———. *The Souls of Black Folk*. New York: Signet Classics, 1969.

Duster, Troy. *The Back Door to Eugenics*. New York: Routledge, 1990.

Duster, Troy, and Andrew Barlow. "Sociologist Sues over Data Collection." *American Sociological Association Footnotes* (January 1999): 2.

Espiritu, Yen Le. *Asian American Panethnicity*. Philadelphia: Temple University Press, 1992.

Evans, Peter. "The Eclipse of the State?: Reflections on Stateness in an Era of Globalization." *World Politics* 50 (October 1997): 62–87.

———. "Fighting Marginalization with Transnational Networks: Counter-hegemonic Globalization." *Contemporary Sociology* 29, no. 1 (January 2000).

Farley, Reginald. "Black-White Residential Segregation: The Views of Myrdal in the 1940s and Trends of the 1980s." In *An American Dilemma Revisited: Race*

Relations in a Changing World, ed. Obie Clayton Jr. New York: Russell Sage Foundation, 1996.

Farley, Reginald, and Walter R. Allen. *The Color Line and the Quality of Life in America*. New York: Oxford University Press, 1989.

Farley, Reginald, Howard Schuman, Suzanne Bianchi, Diane Colasanto, and Shirley Hatchett. "'Chocolate Cities, Vanilla Suburbs': Will the Trend toward Racially Segregated Communities Continue?" *Social Science Research* 7 (1978).

Feagin, Joe R., and Hernán Vera. *White Racism: The Basics*. New York: Routledge, 1994.

Fendrich, James Max. *Ideal Citizens: The Legacy of the Civil Rights Movement*. Albany: SUNY Press, 1993.

Fenton, Steve. *Ethnicity: Racism, Class and Culture*. Lanham, Md.: Rowman and Littlefield, 1999.

Ferrante, Joan, and Prince Brown Jr. *The Social Construction of Race and Ethnicity in the United States*. 2nd ed. Upper Saddle River, N.J.: Prentice-Hall, 2001.

Fischer, Claude S., et al. *Inequality by Design: Cracking the Bell Curve*. Princeton, N.J.: Princeton University Press, 1996.

Fiss, Owen. "The Uncertain Path of School Desegregation Law." In *Equality and Preferential Treatment*, ed. Marshall Cohen, Thomas Nagel, and Thomas Scanlon. Princeton, N.J.: Princeton University Press, 1977.

Foucault, Michel. *Discipline and Punish*. New York: Pantheon, 1977.

Franklin, John Hope. "History of Racial Segregation in the United States." In *The Making of Black America*. Vol. 2. Ed. August Meier and Elliott Rudwick. New York: Atheneum, 1977.

Franklin, Raymond S. *Shadows of Race and Class*. Minneapolis: University of Minnesota Press, 1991.

Georgakas, Dan, and Marvin Surkin. *Detroit: I Do Mind Dying*. Boston: South End, 1998.

Giddens, Anthony. *The Consequences of Modernity*. Cambridge, U.K.: Polity, 1990.

Gilpin, Richard. *The Political Economy of International Relations*. Princeton, N.J.: Princeton University Press, 1987.

Gitlin, Todd. *Twilight of Our Common Dreams: Why America Is Wracked by Culture Wars*. New York: Metropolitan, 1995.

Gramsci, Antonio. *Selections from the Prison Notebooks*. New York: International, 1971.

Guinier, Lani. *The Tyranny of the Majority: Fundamental Fairness in Representative Democracy*. New York: The Free Press, 1994.

Habermas, Jürgen. *The Structural Transformation of the Public Sphere: An Inquiry into a Category of Bourgeois Society*. Cambridge: MIT Press, 1989.

Hacker, Andrew. *Money: Who Has How Much and Why?* New York: Scribner, 1997.

———. *Two Nations: Black and White, Separate, Hostile, Unequal*. New York: Scribner's, 1992.

Halberstam, David. *The Fifties*. New York: Villard, 1993.

Harding, Sandra, ed. *The "Racial" Economy of Science*. Bloomington: Indiana University Press, 1993.

Hardt, Michael, and Antonio Negri. *Empire*. Cambridge, Mass.: Harvard University Press, 2000.

Harris, Nigel. *The New Untouchables: Immigration and the New World Order*. London: Penguin, 1995.

Harvey, David. *The Condition of Post-Modernity*. London: Blackwell, 1989.

Hawkins, Darnell F. ed. *Ethnicity, Race and Crime: Perspectives across Time and Place*. Albany: SUNY Press, 1995.

Hill, Anita Faye, and Emma Coleman Jordan, eds. *Race, Gender, and Power in America*. New York: Oxford University Press, 1995.

Hill, Herbert. "Black Workers, Organized Labor, and Title VII of the 1964 Civil Rights Act." In *Race in America*, ed. Herbert Hill and James E. Jones. Madison: University of Wisconsin Press, 1993.

———. "Race and Labor." *Journal of Intergroup Relations* 10, no. 1 (Spring 1982).

Hintzen, Percy C. *West Indian in the West: Self-Representations in an Immigrant Community*. New York: New York University Press, 2001.

Hochschild, Jennifer L. *Facing up to the American Dream*. Princeton, N.J.: Princeton University Press, 1995.

Hoogvelt, Ankie. *Globalization and the Postcolonial World: The New Political Economy of Development*. 2nd ed. Baltimore, Md.: Johns Hopkins University Press, 2001.

Hutton, Will, and Anthony Giddens, eds. *Global Capitalism*. New York: The New Press, 2000.

Jackson, Kenneth T. *Crabgrass Frontier: The Suburbanization of the United States*. New York: Oxford University Press, 1985.

Jacobson, Matthew Frye. *Whiteness of a Different Color: European Immigrants and the Alchemy of Race*. Cambridge, Mass.: Harvard University Press, 1998.

Jaimes, M. Annette. "American Racism: The Impact on American Indian Identity and Survival." In *Race*, ed. Steven Gregory and Roger Sanjek. New Brunswick, N.J.: Rutgers University Press, 1994.

Jenkins, Richard. *Rethinking Ethnicity*. London: Sage, 1997.

Josephy, Alvin M., Jr., Joanne Nagel, and Troy Johnson. *Red Power: The American Indians' Fight for Freedom*. 2nd ed. Lincoln: University of Nebraska Press, 1999.

Karabel, Jerome. "The Rise and Fall of Affirmative Action at the University of California." *The Journal of Blacks in Higher Education* 25 (Autumn 1999): 109–112.

Karabel, Jerome, and A. H. Halsey, eds. *Power and Ideology in Education*. New York: Oxford University Press, 1977.

Kay, Tamara. "Labor Relations in a Post-NAFTA Era." Paper presented at the Berkeley Journal of Sociology Conference on Globalization and Racism, Berkeley, California, April 2002.

Keck, Margaret E., and Kathryn Sikkink. *Activists beyond Borders: Advocacy Networks in International Politics*. Ithaca, N.Y.: Cornell University Press, 1998.

Kelley, Robin D. G. "Identity Politics and Class Struggle." In *Race and Ethnicity in the United States: Issues and Debates*, ed. Stephen Steinberg. Malden, Mass.: Blackwell, 2000.

Kerbo, Harold R. *Social Stratification and Inequality*. 4th ed. New York: McGraw-Hill, 2000.

Kidder, William C. "The Rise of the Testocracy: An Essay on the LSAT, Conventional Wisdom, and the Dismantling of Diversity." *Texas Journal of Women and the Law* 9, no. 2 (2000): 167–218.

King, Deborah. "Multiple Jeopardy, Multiple Consciousness: The Context of a Black Feminist." *Signs: Journal of Women in Culture and Society* 14, no. 1 (Autumn 1988): 42–72.

King, Martin Luther, Jr. *Where Do We Go from Here: Chaos or Community?* Boston: Beacon, 1968.

Kirp, David L., John P. Dwyer, and Larry A. Rosenthal. *Our Town: Race, Housing, and the Soul of Suburbia*. New Brunswick, N.J.: Rutgers University Press, 1995.

Kluger, Richard. *Simple Justice: The History of Brown v. Board of Education and Black America's Struggle for Equality*. New York: Knopf, 1976.

Kousser, J. Morgan. *Colorblind Injustice: Minority Voting Rights and the Undoing of the Second Reconstruction*. Chapel Hill: University of North Carolina Press, 1999.

Krieger, Joel. *Reagan, Thatcher and the Politics of Decline*. New York: Oxford University Press, 1986.

Larson, Magali Sarfatti. *The Rise of Professionalism: A Sociological Analysis*. Berkeley: University of California Press, 1977.

Lefcourt, Robert. *Law against the People: Essays to Demystify Law, Order, and the Courts*. New York: Random House, 1971.

Lemann, Nicholas. *The Big Test: The Secret History of the American Meritocracy*. New York: Farrar, Strauss and Giroux, 1999.

———. *The Promised Land*. New York: Knopf, 1991.

Levy, Frank. *Dollars and Dreams: The Changing American Income Distribution*. New York: Norton, 1988.

Lindblom, Charles E. *The Market System*. New Haven, Conn.: Yale University Press, 2001.

Lowe, Lisa. *Immigrant Acts*. Durham, N.C.: Duke University Press, 1996.

Lusane, Clarence. *African Americans at the Crossroads: The Restructuring of the Black Leadership and the 1992 Elections*. Boston: South End, 1994.

Malcolm X. "The Ballot or the Bullet." In *Malcolm X Speaks: Selected Speeches and Statements*, ed. George Breitman. New York: Merit, 1965.

Marable, Manning. *How Capitalism Underdeveloped Black America*. Boston: South End, 1983.

———. *Race, Reform and Rebellion*. 2nd ed. Jackson: University Press of Mississippi, 1991.

Marshall, T. H. "Citizenship and Social Class." In *States and Societies*, ed. David Held et al. Oxford: Martin Robertson, 1983.

Massey, Douglas S., and Nancy A. Denton. *American Apartheid: Segregation and the Making of the Underclass*. Cambridge, Mass.: Harvard University Press, 1993.

Matusow, Allen J. *The Unraveling of America: A History of Liberalism in the 1960s*. New York: Harper and Row, 1984.

McAdam, Doug. *Political Process and the Development of Black Insurgency, 1930–1970*. Chicago: University of Chicago Press, 1982.

McCall, Nathan. *Makes Me Want to Holler*. New York: Random House, 1994.

Milkman, Ruth, ed. *Organizing Immigrants: The Challenge for Unions in Contemporary California*. Ithaca, N.Y.: ILR Press, 2000.

Miller, Jerome G. *Hobbling a Generation: Young African American Males in the Criminal Justice System of America's Cities*. Baltimore, Md.: National Center on Institutions and Alternatives, 1992.

Mills, Charles. *Blackness Visible*. Ithaca, N.Y.: Cornell University Press, 1998.

Mohan, Giles, Ed Brown, Bob Milward, and Alfred B. Zack-Williams, eds. *Structural Adjustment Theory, Practice and Impacts*. London: Routledge, 2000.

Moore, Joan, and James Diego Vigil. "Barrios in Transition." In *In the Barrios: Latinos and the Underclass Debate*, ed. Joan Moore and Raquel Pinderhughes. New York: Russell Sage Foundation, 1993.

Morgan, Edmund S. *American Slavery, American Freedom: The Ordeal of Colonial Virginia*. New York: Norton, 1975.

Morrison, Toni, ed. *Race-ing Justice, En-gendering Power*. New York: Pantheon, 1992.

Mumford, Lewis. *The City in History: Its Origins, Its Transformations, Its Prospects*. New York: Harcourt, Brace and World, 1961.

Muñoz, Carlos, Jr. *Youth, Identity, Power*. London: Verso, 1989.

Nadelmann, Ethan A.. *Cops across Borders: The Internationalization of U.S. Criminal Law Enforcement*. University Park: Pennsylvania State University Press, 1993.

Newman, Katherine S. *Falling from Grace: Downward Mobility in the Age of Affluence*. Berkeley: University of California Press, 1988.

Noble, David F. *America by Design*. New York: Knopf, 1977.

O'Connor, James. *The Fiscal Crisis of the State*. 2nd ed. New Brunswick, N.J.: Transaction, 2002.

Oliver, Melvin L., James H. Johnson Jr., and Walter C. Farrell Jr. "Anatomy of a Rebellion: A Political-Economic Analysis." In *Reading Rodney King/Reading Urban Uprising*, ed. Robert Gooding-Williams. New York: Routledge, 1993.

Oliver, Melvin L., and Thomas M. Shapiro. *Black Wealth, White Wealth*. New York: Routledge, 1997.

Omi, Michael, and Howard Winant. *Racial Formation in the United States*. New York: Routledge, 1986.

Ong, Paul, ed. *The Impacts of Affirmative Action*. Walnut Creek, Calif.: AltaMira, 1999.

Orfield, Gary. "Ghettoization and Its Alternatives." In *The New Urban Reality*, ed. Paul E. Peterson. Washington, D.C.: Brookings, 1985.

Pardo, Mary S. *Mexican American Women Activists: Identity and Resistance in Two Los Angeles Communities*. Philadelphia: Temple University Press, 1998.

Patterson, Orlando. *The Ordeal of Integration: Progress and Resentment in America's "Racial" Crisis*. Washington, D.C.: Civitas/Counterpoint, 1998.

Phillips, Kevin. *The Boiling Point: Democrats, Republicans and the Decline of Middle Class Prosperity*. New York: Random House, 1993.

———. *The Politics of Rich and Poor*. New York: Random House, 1990.

Piven, Francis Fox, and Richard A. Cloward. *The Breaking of the American Social Contract*. New York: The New Press, 1997.

———. *Poor Peoples Movements*. New York: Pantheon, 1977.

Polanyi, Karl. *The Great Transformation*. Boston: Beacon, 1944.

Putnam, Robert D. *Bowling Alone: The Collapse and Revival of American Community*. New York: Simon and Schuster, 2000.

Quadagno, Jill. *The Color of Welfare: How Racism Undermined the War on Poverty*. New York: Oxford University Press, 1994.

———. "Creating a Capital Investment Welfare State: The New American Exceptionalism." *American Sociological Review* 64, no. 1 (February 1999): 1–11.

Reiman, Jeffrey H. *The Rich Get Richer and the Poor Get Prison*. New York: Macmillan, 1990.

Reinarman, Craig, and Harry G. Levine, eds. *Crack in America: Demon Drugs and Social Justice*. Berkeley: University of California Press, 1997.

Riesman, David. *The Lonely Crowd*. New Haven, Conn.: Yale University Press, 1950.

Ritzer, George. *The McDonaldization of Society*. Thousand Oaks, Calif.: Pine Forge, 2000.

Roediger, David R. *Wages of Whiteness*. London: Verso, 1991.

Rumbarger, John J. *Profits, Power and Prohibition: Alcohol Reform and the Industrializing of America, 1800–1930*. Albany: SUNY Press, 1989.

Salzman, Jack, ed. *Bridges and Boundaries: African Americans and American Jews*. New York: George Braziller, 1992.

Sanchez, George J. *Becoming Mexican American: Ethnicity, Culture, and Identity in Chicano Los Angeles*. New York: Oxford University Press, 1993.

Sassen, Saskia. *Globalization and Its Discontents*. New York: The New Press, 1998.

———. *Guests and Aliens*. New York: The New Press, 1999.

———. *The Mobility of Capital and Labor: A Study in International Investment and Labor Flow*. Cambridge: Cambridge University Press, 1988.

Sawhill, Isabel V., R. Kent Weaver, Ron Haskins, and Andrea Kane, eds. *Welfare Reform and Beyond: The Future of the Safety Net*. Washington, D.C.: Brookings Institute, 2002.

Schaeffer, Robert K. *Understanding Globalization*. Lanham, Md.: Rowman and Littlefield, 1997.

Schelling, Vivian. "Globalisation, Ethnic Identity and Popular Culture in Latin America." In *Globalisation and the Third World*, ed. Ray Kiely and Phil Marfleet. London: Routledge, 1998.

Schlesinger, Arthur M., Jr. *The Disuniting of America*. New York: Norton, 1992.

Scholte, Jan Aart. *Globalization: A Critical Introduction*. New York: St. Martin's, 2000.

Schulman, Bruce J. *The Seventies: The Great Shift in American Culture, Society, and Politics*. New York: The Free Press, 2001.

Scott, Peter Dale, and Jonathan Marshall. *Cocaine Politics: Drugs, Armies and the C.I.A. in Central America*. Berkeley: University of California Press, 1991.

Shaw, Randy. *Reclaiming America: Nike, Clean Air, and the New National Activism*. Berkeley: University of California Press, 1999.

Sklar, Holly. *Chaos or Community?: Seeking Solutions, Not Scapegoats for Bad Economics*. Boston: South End, 1995.

Skocpol, Theda. *Boomerang: Clinton's Health Security Effort and the Turn against Government in U.S. Politics*. New York: Norton, 1996.

Skrentny, John David. *The Ironies of Affirmative Action: Politics, Culture, and Justice in America*. Chicago: University of Chicago Press, 1996.

Small, Stephen. *Racialized Barriers: The Black Experience in the United States and England in the 1980s*. London: Routledge, 1996.

Smith, B. C. *Understanding Third World Politics*. Bloomington: Indiana University Press, 1996.

Smith, Robert C. *Racism in the Post–Civil Rights Society*. Albany: SUNY Press, 1995.

Steinberg, Stephen. *The Ethnic Myth: Race, Ethnicity and Class in America*. 3rd ed. Boston: Beacon, 2001.

———, ed. *Race and Ethnicity in the United States: Issues and Debates*. Malden, Mass.: Blackwell, 2000.

Stiglitz, Joseph. *Globalization and Its Discontents*. New York: Norton, 2002.

Tarrow, Sidney G. *Power in Movement: Social Movements and Contentious Politics*. Cambridge: Cambridge University Press, 1998.

Thernstrom, Stephan, and Abigail Thernstrom. *America in Black and White*. New York: Simon and Schuster, 1997.

Tilly, Charles. *From Mobilization to Revolution*. Reading, Mass.: Addison-Wesley, 1978.

Tushnett, Mark. *The American Law of Slavery, 1810–1860: Considerations of Humanity and Interest*. Princeton, N.J.: Princeton University Press, 1981.

Voss, Kim, and Rachel Sherman. "Breaking the Iron Law of Oligarchy: Union Revitalization in the American Labor Movement." *American Journal of Sociology* 106, no. 2 (September 2000).

Wacquant, Loic. "Ghetto, Banlieue, Favela: Tools for Rethinking Urban Marginality." In *Os Condenados da Cidade*. Rio de Janeiro: Revan, 2001.

Waldinger, Roger. *Still the Promised City?: African Americans and New Immigrants in Postindustrial New York*. Cambridge, Mass.: Harvard University Press, 1996.

Waterman, Peter. *Globalization, Social Movements and the New Internationalisms*. Washington, D.C.: Mansell, 1998.

Waters, Malcolm. *Globalization*. London: Routledge, 1995.

Weir, Margaret. "The American Middle Class and the Politics of Education." In *Social Contracts under Stress*, ed. Oliver Zunz, Leonard Schoppa, and Nobuhiro Hiwatari. New York: Russell Sage Foundation, 2002.

Williams, Eric. *Capitalism and Slavery*. New York: Putnam's, 1980.

Williams, Juan. *Thurgood Marshall: American Revolutionary*. New York: Times, 1998.

Wilson, William Julius. *The Truly Disadvantaged: The Inner City, the Underclass and Public Policy*. Chicago: University of Chicago Press, 1987.

Winant, Howard. "The Theoretical Status of the Concept of Race." In *Theories of Race and Racism*, ed. Les Back and John Solomos. London: Routledge, 2000.

———. *The World Is a Ghetto*. New York: Basic, 2001.

Young, Brigette. "Globalization and Gender: A European Perspective." In *Gender, Globalization and Democratization*, ed. Rita Mae Kelly, Jane H. Bayes, Mary S. Hawkesworth, and Brigette Young. New York: Rowman and Littlefield, 2001.

Young, Michael Dunlop. *The Rise of the Meritocracy*. New Brunswick, N.J.: Transaction, 1994.

Zinn, Howard. *Post-War America, 1945–1971*. Indianapolis, Ind.: Bobbs-Merrill, 1973.

Zweigenhaft, Richard L., and G. William Domhoff. *Diversity in the Power Elite*. New Haven, Conn.: Yale University Press, 1998.

Index

~

About the Author

Andrew Barlow teaches sociology at the University of California at Berkeley and at Diablo Valley College. His articles have appeared in sociology and law journals and in numerous newspapers. A longtime activist in peace and justice movements, Barlow has in recent years served on the Steering Committee of the No on 209 Campaign, was the lead plaintiff in a landmark lawsuit against the Governor of California's executive order barring racial data collection, and worked on the campaign opposing a California ballot initiative seeking to bar racial data. He is a member of the Board of Directors of La Raza Centro Legal. He lives with his wife and son in Oakland, California.